Praise for *On Grand Strategy*

"The best education in grand strategy available in a single volume . . . A long walk with a single, delightful mind . . . *On Grand Strategy* is a book that should be read by every American leader or would-be leader."   —John Nagl, *The Wall Street Journal*

"A remarkably erudite volume . . . [that] renders nuanced verdicts on an eclectic cohort of thinkers, writers, monarchs, and conquerors . . . Gaddis has indisputably earned the right to plow different fields of historical inquiry, which he does in *On Grand Strategy* with self-evident glee and peripatetic curiosity."   —*The Washington Post*

"Lively . . . Gaddis concludes with an invaluable warning that true morality embraces neither messianic interventionism nor the quest for utopianism. . . . Instead, ethical leadership pursues the art of the possible for the greater (not the greatest) good. . . . *On Grand Strategy* is many things—a thoughtful validation of the liberal arts, an argument for literature over social science, an engaging reflection on university education and some timely advice to Americans that lasting victory comes from winning what you can rather than all that you want."   —*The New York Times Book Review*

"[An] eminently readable book by a master historian . . . It is a brilliant book—learned, seductively written, deep."   —*The New Criterion*

"Thought-provoking . . . The approach is highly idiosyncratic and the structure loose; it has something of the feel of a personal manifesto or intellectual memoir."   —*The Weekly Standard*

"An extraordinary treatise on the need to teach the principles of sound strategy to today's leaders . . . The book . . . is a rich one. It makes sense of our world, but is also capable of beautifully crafted pithy historical judgments. . . . It is a book that cares about liberty, choice, and a moral compass, that warns against the hubris of an angry Bonaparte on the turn in a Russian winter, against leaders who do not listen or learn. A training manual for our troubled times."   —*The Times* (London)

"A lively, erudite study of the past in service of the future."
                                                   —*Kirkus Reviews*

PENGUIN BOOKS

ON GRAND STRATEGY

John Lewis Gaddis is the Robert A. Lovett Professor of History at Yale University, and was the founding director of the Brady-Johnson Program in Grand Strategy. His previous books include *The United States and the Origins of the Cold War*; *Strategies of Containment*; *The Long Peace*; *We Now Know*; *The Landscape of History*; *Surprise, Security, and the American Experience*; and *The Cold War: A New History*. Professor Gaddis teaches courses on Cold War history, grand strategy, biography, and historical methodology. He has won two undergraduate teaching awards at Yale and was a 2005 recipient of the National Humanities Medal. His *George F. Kennan: An American Life* won the 2012 Pulitzer Prize in Biography.

ALSO BY JOHN LEWIS GADDIS

George F. Kennan: An American Life

The Cold War: A New History

Surprise, Security, and the American Experience

The Landscape of History: How Historians Map the Past

We Now Know: Rethinking Cold War History

The United States and the End of the Cold War:
Implications, Reconsiderations, Provocations

The Long Peace: Inquiries into the History of the Cold War

Strategies of Containment: A Critical Appraisal
of American National Security Policy During the Cold War

Russia, the Soviet Union and the United States:
An Interpretive History

The United States and the Origins of the Cold War, 1941–1947

ON GRAND STRATEGY

JOHN LEWIS GADDIS

PENGUIN BOOKS

PENGUIN BOOKS
An imprint of Penguin Random House LLC
penguinrandomhouse.com

First published in the United States of America by Penguin Press,
an imprint of Penguin Random House LLC, 2018
Published in Penguin Books 2019

ISBN 9781594203510 (hardcover)
ISBN 9780143132516 (paperback)
ISBN 9780525557296 (ebook)

Printed in the United States of America
1   3   5   7   9   10   8   6   4   2

DESIGNED BY MEIGHAN CAVANAUGH

While the author has made every effort to provide accurate telephone numbers,
Internet addresses, and other contact information at the time of publication,
neither the publisher nor the author assumes any responsibility for errors or
for changes that occur after publication. Further, the publisher does not
have any control over and does not assume any responsibility
for author or third-party websites or their content.

For

NICHOLAS F. BRADY, '52

CHARLES B. JOHNSON, '54

and

HENRY "SAM" CHAUNCEY, JR., '57

GRAND STRATEGISTS

CONTENTS

——·——

PREFACE

The title, I know, risks raising eyebrows. But my Yale History Department colleague Timothy Snyder has preceded me (*On Tyranny*), as has, more distantly, Seneca (*On the Shortness of Life*). I'm most worried, though, about admirers of Carl von Clausewitz, being one myself. His posthumously published *On War* (1832) set the standard for all subsequent writing on that subject and its necessary corollary, grand strategy. My justification for yet another such book is concision—*not* one of Clausewitz's strengths: *On Grand Strategy* covers more years than *On War*, but at less than half the length.

It grows out of two experiences with grand strategy, separated by a quarter century. The first was teaching "Strategy and Policy" at the United States Naval War College from 1975 to 1977, under circumstances described at the end of chapter two. The second has been co-teaching Yale University's "Studies in Grand Strategy" seminar every year from 2002 to the present. Both courses have always relied more on classical texts and historical case studies than on theory. The single-semester Newport seminars, however, are chiefly for midcareer military officers. The two-semester Yale course recruits undergraduate, graduate, and professional school students, as well as, each year, an active-duty Army and Marine Corps lieutenant colonel.[1]

Both courses are collaboratively taught: normally one civilian and one military instructor for each seminar section at Newport, and, at Yale, varying combinations. My colleagues Charles Hill, Paul Kennedy, and I began as a *troika*, attending all classes, arguing with one another in front of the students, and individually advising them (not always consistently) outside of class. Remarkably, we're still neighbors and close friends.

The 2006 establishment of the Brady-Johnson Program in Grand Strategy allowed us to add practitioners: they've included David Brooks, Walter Russell Mead, John Negroponte, Peggy Noonan, Victoria Nuland, Paul Solman, Jake Sullivan, and Evan Wolfson. The course has also attracted other Yale faculty: Scott Boorman (Sociology), Elizabeth Bradley (formerly School of Public Health, director of the Brady-Johnson program in 2016–17, now president of Vassar College), Beverly Gage (History and, from 2017, Brady-Johnson program director), Bryan Garsten (Political Science and Humanities), Nuno Monteiro (Political Science), Kristina Talbert-Slagle (Epidemiology and Public Health), and Adam Tooze (formerly History, now at Columbia University).

Together these colleagues have taught me a lot, another reason I feel obliged now to try to say what I've learned. I've done so in a way that's informal, impressionistic, and wholly idiosyncratic: my teachers bear no responsibility other than for setting me off on paths they couldn't control. Because I seek patterns across time, space, and scale,[2] I've felt free to suspend such constraints for comparative, even conversational purposes: St. Augustine and Machiavelli will occasionally talk with one another, as will Clausewitz and Tolstoy. Who is, in turn, the *imaginer* I've found most helpful; others include Virgil, Shakespeare, and F. Scott Fitzgerald. Finally, I've returned often to the ideas of Sir Isaiah Berlin,[3] whom I got to know slightly while visiting the University of Oxford in 1992–93. I hope he'd be pleased to be considered a grand strategist. I know he'd be amused.

My agent, Andrew Wylie, and my editor, Scott Moyers, had greater confidence in this book than I did when I began writing it. Working with them again has been a pleasure, as it has been to benefit once more from the efficiency of the entire Penguin team: Ann Godoff, Christopher Richards, Mia Council, Matthew Boyd, Bruce Giffords, Deborah Weiss Geline, and Juliana Kiyan.

I owe special thanks to the Yale undergraduates in my fall 2017 "Foxes and Hedgehogs" seminar, who've tough-mindedly test-driven every chapter of this book: Morgan Aguiar-Lucander, Patrick Binder, Robert Brinkmann, Alessandro Buratti, Diego Fernandez-Pages, Robert Henderson, Scott Hicks, Jack Hilder, Henry Iseman, India June, Declan Kunkel, Ben Mallet, Alexander Petrillo, Marshall Rankin, Nicholas Religa, Grant Richardson, Carter Scott, Sara Seymour, David Shimer, and Jared Smith. I've also had the help of accomplished undergraduate research assistants: Cooper D'Agostino, Matthew Lloyd-Thomas, David McCullough III, Campbell Schnebly-Swanson, and Nathaniel Zelinsky.

Yale presidents Richard Levin and Peter Salovey have strongly supported our teaching of grand strategy from the beginning—as has Ted Wittenstein, their special assistant and one of our early students. Associate directors in International Security Studies and the Brady-Johnson program have kept us on course: Will Hitchcock,

Ted Bromund, the late Minh Luong, Jeffrey Mankoff, Ryan Irwin, Amanda Behm, Jeremy Friedman, Christopher Miller, Evan Wilson, and Ian Johnson; as have the staff we share at 31 Hillhouse: Liz Vastakis, Kathleen Galo, Mike Skonieczny, and Igor Biryukov. My wife, Toni Dorfman, teacher, scholar, mentor, actor, playwright, director of plays and baroque operas, manuscript critic and copy editor, gourmet chef, nightly therapist, and the love of my life, now, for twenty years (!), keeps me together in every way.

The dedication celebrates the two great benefactors of our program, along with one wise facilitator: their vision, generosity, and unvarying good advice—not least that we "teach common sense"—have been our anchor, our compass, and the vessel itself in which we sail.

JLG
New Haven, Connecticut
Fall 2017

CHAPTER ONE

CROSSING THE HELLESPONT

The date is 480 B.C.E. The place is Abydos, the town on the Asian side of the Hellespont where it narrows to just over a mile in width. The scene is worthy of Hollywood in its heyday. Xerxes, Persia's King of Kings, ascends a throne on a promontory from which he can see armies assembled, the historian Herodotus tells us, of over a million and a half men. Had the number been only a tenth of that, as is more likely, it would still have approximated the size of Eisenhower's forces on D-day in 1944. The Hellespont has no bridge now, but Xerxes had two then: one rested on 360 boats lashed together, the other on 314, both curved to accommodate winds and currents. For after an earlier bridge had broken apart in a storm, the furious king beheaded the builders and ordered the waters themselves whipped and branded. Somewhere on the bottom there presumably lie, to this day, the iron fetters he had thrown in for good measure.

On that day, though, the waters are calm and Xerxes is content—until he bursts into tears. His adviser and uncle Artabanus asks why. "Here are all these thousands," the king replies, "and not one of them will be alive a hundred years from now." Artabanus consoles his master by reminding him of all the calamities that can make life intolerable and death a relief. Xerxes acknowledges this, but demands: "Tell me the very truth." Would Artabanus have favored the task at hand—a second Persian invasion of Greece in just over a decade—had they not both had the same frightening dream? Now it's Artabanus who shudders: "I am still full, nay overfull, of fear."

Xerxes' dream had come twice after Artabanus dissuaded him from avenging the Greeks' humiliation of Darius, Xerxes' father, at Marathon ten years earlier. As if in anticipation of *Hamlet*—still two millennia into the future—an apparition, regal in aspect, paternal in attitude, had issued an ultimatum: "[I]f you do not launch your war at once, . . . just as a short while raised you to be great and mighty, so with speed again shall you be humble." Artabanus at first scoffed at the dream's significance, whereupon Xerxes made him trade clothes and sleep in the royal bed. The specter reappeared, so terrifying Artabanus that he woke up screaming, instantly urging the new invasion. Xerxes then gave the orders, the great force gathered at Sardis, sacrificed a thousand heifers at the ruins of Troy, arrived at the Hellespont, found the bridges ready, and was preparing to cross them when the king allowed his uncle one last chance to voice whatever reservations he might yet have.

Artabanus, despite his nightmare, can't resist. The enemies ahead, he warns, will not just be Greeks, formidable fighters though they are: they'll also include the land and the sea. The march around the Aegean will traverse territories incapable of feeding so large an army. There won't be enough harbors to shelter ships if storms arise.

Exhaustion, even starvation, could set in before fighting a single battle. The prudent leader "dreads and reflects on everything that can happen to him but is bold when he is in the thick of action." Xerxes listens patiently, but objects that "if you were to take account of everything . . . , you would never do anything. It is better to have a brave heart and endure one half of the terrors we dread than to [calculate] all of the terrors and suffer nothing at all. . . . Big things are won by big dangers."

That settles it. Xerxes sends Artabanus back to rule the existing empire, while turning his own attention to doubling its extent. He prays to the sun for the strength to conquer not just Greece, but all of Europe. He has myrtle branches strewn before the bridges. He orders his priests to burn incense. And he rewards the Hellespont by pouring into it a libation, followed by the golden cup that contained it, followed by the golden bowl in which it was mixed, followed as well by a sword. This clears the way for the crossing, which takes seven days and nights to complete. As Xerxes himself reaches the European shore, an awed bystander is heard asking why Zeus has disguised himself as the Persian monarch, bringing along "all the people of the world?" Could the god not have destroyed Greece on his own?[1]

I.

Two thousand four hundred and nineteen years later, an Oxford don took a break from tutorials to go to a party. Thirty at the time, Isaiah Berlin had been born in Riga, brought up in St. Petersburg, and, after witnessing the Bolshevik Revolution at the age of eight, emigrated with his family to England. There he thrived, mastering the new language through a thicket of accents that never left him, triumphing in his Oxford examinations, and becoming the first Jew ever elected to an All Souls College fellowship. By 1939 he was teaching philosophy at New College (established in 1379), developing an aversion to logical positivism (nothing means anything without reproducible verification), and hugely enjoying life.

A glittering conversationalist with a sponge-like thirst for ideas, Berlin relished opportunities to show himself off and to soak things up. At this party—the exact date isn't known—he ran into Julian Edward George Asquith, the 2nd Earl of Oxford and Asquith, then finishing a classics degree at Balliol. Lord Oxford had come across an intriguing line from the ancient Greek poet Archilochus of Paros. It was, as Berlin remembered it: "The fox knows many things, but the hedgehog knows one big thing."[2]

The passage survives only as a fragment, so its context has long been lost. But the Renaissance scholar Erasmus played around with it,[3] and Berlin couldn't help doing the same. Might it become a scheme for classifying great writers? If so, Plato, Dante, Dostoevsky, Nietzsche, and Proust would all have been hedgehogs. Aristotle, Shakespeare, Goethe, Pushkin, and Joyce were obviously foxes. So was Berlin, who distrusted most big things—like logical positivism—but felt fully at ease with smaller ones.[4] Diverted by World War II, Berlin didn't return to his quadrupeds until 1951, when he used them to frame an essay he was preparing on Tolstoy's philosophy of history. It appeared two years later as a short book, *The Hedgehog and the Fox*.

Hedgehogs, Berlin explained, "relate everything to a single central vision" through which "all that they say and do has significance." Foxes, in contrast, "pursue many ends, often unrelated and even contradictory, connected, if at all, only in some *de facto* way." The distinction was simple but not frivolous: it offered "a point of view from which to look and compare, a starting point for genuine investigation." It might even reflect "one of the deepest differences which divide writers and thinkers, and, it may be, human beings in general."

Having fired off that flare, however, Berlin failed to illuminate much with it beyond Tolstoy. The great man had wanted to be a hedgehog, Berlin claimed: *War and Peace* was supposed to reveal the laws by which history worked. But Tolstoy was too honest to neglect the peculiarities of personality and the contingencies of circumstance that defy such generalizations. So he filled his masterpiece with some of the most fox-like writing in all literature, mesmerizing his readers, who happily skipped the hedgehog-like history ruminations scattered throughout the text. Torn by contradictions, Tolstoy approached death, Berlin concluded, "a desperate old man, beyond human aid, wandering self-blinded [like Oedipus] at Colonus."[5]

Biographically, this was too simple. Tolstoy did die in an obscure Russian railway station, in 1910 and at the age of eighty-two, after abandoning his home and family. It's unlikely that he did so, though, regretting loose ends left decades earlier in *War and Peace*.[6] Nor is it clear that Berlin evoked Oedipus for any deeper purpose than to end his essay with a dramatic flourish. Perhaps *too* dramatic, for it suggested irreconcilable differences between foxes and hedgehogs. You had to be one or the other, Berlin seemed to be saying. You couldn't be both and be happy. Or effective. Or even whole.

Berlin was therefore surprised—but puckishly pleased—when his creatures went viral, long before there was an Internet to help them along. References began proliferating in print. Cartoons appeared, requiring no explanation.[7] And in university classrooms, professors began asking their students: "*Was* X [who could be any historical or literary figure] a fox or a hedgehog?" Students began asking their professors: "*Is* it better [at this or any other moment] to be a hedgehog or a fox?" Both began asking themselves: "*Where*, within this polarity, should *I* seek to be?" And then: "*Can* I stay there?" And finally: "*Who*, in the end, am I?"

By way of an Oxford party, an Archilochus fragment, and Tolstoy's epic, Berlin had stumbled upon two of the very best ways to become intellectually indelible. The first is to be Delphic, a trick known to oracles throughout time. The second is to be Aesopian: turn your ideas into animals, and they'll achieve immortality.

II.

Herodotus, who lived from the 480s to the 420s B.C.E., may have known Archilochus (ca. 680–645) on foxes and hedgehogs. He cites the poet in another context, and so could have seen the poem—if still extant—in which they first appeared.[8] Even if he didn't, it's hard to read Herodotus' account of Artabanus and Xerxes at the Hellespont without sensing, in the adviser, an uneasy fox, and, in the monarch, an unapologetic hedgehog.

Artabanus stresses prices to be paid—in energy expended, in supplies stretched, in communications compromised, in morale weakened, in everything else that can go wrong—when seeking to move any large force across any body of land or water. Success requires taking on too much. Does Xerxes not see that "the god strikes with lightning" only those who attempt big things, while the little ones "do not itch the god to action"? Dismantle the bridges, disband the armies, and send everybody back home, Artabanus urges, where the worst that can await them will be more bad dreams.

Xerxes, who weeps for the dead a hundred years hence, has a larger and longer view. If death is the price of life, why not pay the lesser prices that make lives memorable? Why be a forgettable King of Kings? Having tamed the Hellespont he can hardly stop. The bridges have to lead somewhere. Great militaries carry all they need to ensure that what can go wrong won't, or that if it does, it won't matter. "It is the god that leads us on, and so, when we of ourselves set about our many enterprises, we prosper."[9]

Artabanus respects environments, knowing that landscapes can help or hinder an army, that fleets never fully control the seas on which they sail, that weather is beyond any mortal's capacity to predict. Commanders must distinguish where they can act from what they must accept, trusting only in such craft as circumstances allow. Xerxes, in contrast, *reshapes* environments. He turns water into (more or less) solid ground by bridging the Hellespont. He makes solid ground liquid by cutting a canal across the Athos peninsula—out of "mere arrogance," Herodotus tells us—so his ships won't have to sail around it.[10] The king doesn't worry about what he'll have to accept because he'll flatten whatever gets in the way. And he trusts only the divine hand that's entrusted him with such power.

The shortsighted Artabanus sees so much on the immediate horizon that complexity itself is the enemy. The farsighted Xerxes sees only a distant horizon on which ambitions are opportunities: simplicity is the searchlight that shows the way. Artabanus keeps changing his mind. His twists and turns are meant, like those of Odysseus, to get him home. Xerxes, in crossing the Hellespont, becomes Achilles. He'll have no home, other than in the tales the future will tell of the deeds he has done.[11]

This fox and this hedgehog, therefore, find no common ground.

With his warnings unheeded, Artabanus heads east from Abydos and out of Herodotus, who makes no further mention of him. Xerxes moves west, taking his armies, his navy, and his historian with him,[12] as well as all subsequent chroniclers of the Persian invasion. The Hellespont, a boundary between continents, now also separates the two ways of thinking that Archilochus anticipated, that Berlin would make famous—and that a late twentieth-century feat of social science would still more sharply define.

III.

In an effort to determine the roots of accuracy and inaccuracy in forecasting, the American political psychologist Philip E. Tetlock and his assistants collected 27,451 predictions on world politics between 1988 and 2003 from 284 "experts" in universities, governments, think tanks, foundations, international institutions, and the media. Replete with tables, graphs, and equations, Tetlock's 2005 book, *Expert Political Judgment,* reports the findings of this most rigorous study ever done on why some people get the future right and others don't.

"*Who* experts were—professional background, status, and so on—made scarcely an iota of difference," Tetlock concludes. "Nor did *what* experts thought—whether they were liberals or conservatives, realists or institutionalists, optimists or pessimists." But "*[h]ow* experts thought—their style of reasoning—did matter." The critical variable turned out to be self-identification as "foxes" or "hedgehogs" when shown Berlin's definitions of those terms. The results were unequivocal: foxes were far more proficient predictors than hedgehogs, whose record approximated that of a dart-throwing (and presumably computer-simulated) chimpanzee.

Startled by this outcome, Tetlock sought what distinguished his foxes from his hedgehogs. The foxes relied, for their predictions, on an intuitive "stitching together [of] diverse sources of information," not on deductions derived from "grand schemes." They doubted "that the cloudlike subject of politics" could ever be "the object of a clocklike science." The best of them "shared a self-deprecating style of thinking" that "elevate[d] no thought above criticism." But they tended to be too discursive—too inclined to qualify their claims— to hold an audience. Talk show hosts rarely invited them back. Policy makers found themselves too busy to listen.

Tetlock's hedgehogs, in contrast, shunned self-deprecation and brushed aside criticism. Aggressively deploying big explanations, they displayed a "bristly impatience with those who 'do not get it.'" When the intellectual holes they dug got too deep, they'd simply dig deeper. They became "prisoners of their preconceptions," trapped in cycles of self-congratulation. These played well as sound bites, but bore little relationship to what subsequently occurred.

All of which suggested, to Tetlock, "a theory of good judgment": that "self-critical thinkers are better at figuring out the contradictory dynamics of evolving situations, more circumspect about their forecasting prowess, more accurate in recalling mistakes, less prone to rationalize those mistakes, more likely to update their beliefs in a timely fashion, and—as a cumulative result of these advantages— better positioned to affix realistic probabilities in the next round of events."[13] In short, foxes do it better.

IV.

The test of a good theory lies in its ability to explain the past, for only if it does can we trust what it may tell us about the future. Tetlock's past, however, was the decade and a half in which he ran his experiment. Herodotus offers an opportunity to apply Tetlock's findings—admittedly without his careful controls—to an age far removed from our own. They hold up, across this distance, surprisingly well.

After crossing the Hellespont, Xerxes advanced, confident that the size of his forces and the opulence of his entourage would make resistance futile: "[E]ven if all the Greeks, and moreover all the men who live in the western countries, were assembled together, they would not be able to fight me." The king's plan seemed to be working as he proceeded through Thrace, Macedonia, and Thessaly, but his progress, necessarily, was very slow.

His army was so large that it drank rivers and lakes dry before all of its units could get to the other side. Lions (still flourishing in the region) developed a taste for the camels carrying his supplies. And Xerxes was exhausting the capacity of even cooperative Greeks to meet his culinary requirements: one gave thanks that the king ate only once a day, for if his city had been asked to provide breakfast on the scale of the dinner Xerxes demanded, its inhabitants must either have fled or been "ground to dust, worse than any people on earth had ever been."[14]

Nor could Xerxes flatten all topography. The Persians, to enter Attica, would have to march through the narrow pass at Thermopylae, and it was there that Leonidas' Spartans—a far inferior force hastily recruited—delayed the invaders for several days. Neither

Leonidas nor his elite "300" survived, but their refusal to surrender showed that Xerxes could no longer rely on intimidation alone to get what he wanted. Meanwhile, late-summer storms in the Aegean were battering his fleet, while the Athenians, following the orders of their admiral-general Themistocles, were evacuating their city. This left Xerxes with Napoleon's dilemma at Moscow in 1812: what do you do when you've captured your objective, only to find it abandoned and bad weather on the way?

The King of Kings fell back, characteristically, upon still more intimidation. He burned the Acropolis, and then mounted another throne atop another promontory overlooking another body of water from which to witness what remained of his navy complete his triumph. Surely smoke rising from their holiest temple would demoralize the Athenian citizen-rowers. But the bay was Salamis, the triremes were trained, and the Delphic oracle had promised safety behind "wooden walls," presumably the kind that floated. So, as Xerxes watched, the Greeks sent his fleet to the bottom and slaughtered the survivors—who, in any event, hadn't been taught how to swim. The king had no choice now but to accept, much too belatedly, his uncle's advice to return home.[15]

Themistocles hastened the king's departure by spreading the rumor that the Hellespont bridges would be the Athenians' next target. Terrified, Xerxes hastened to get back across, leaving his demoralized armies to fend for themselves. The Greeks then defeated them at Plataea, but left further retribution, imaginatively, to a playwright. Aeschylus' *The Persians,* first performed eight years after Salamis, depicts the bedraggled Xerxes limping into his own capital to the lamentations of all who'd earlier acclaimed him—and to this warning, from the chastened ghost of Darius: "[N]ever, being mortal, ought we cast our thoughts too high."[16]

Herodotus drew on Aeschylus for his *History*.[17] Could he have also for his account of the dreams—evoking Darius' spirit if not his ghost—that drove Xerxes to the Hellespont in the first place? There's no way to know for sure: spirits are shadowy things. But it's fun to imagine this particular shadow, whoever he represented, using his supernatural powers to zoom forward in time to absorb, and then take back to the now disconsolate King of Kings, Professor Tetlock's warning about how often foxes are right and hedgehogs are chumps.

V.

Xerxes' invasion of Greece was an early but spectacular example of hedgehog-like behavior. Being King of Kings was a very big thing: if Xerxes could gather the greatest military force ever while turning water into land at the Hellespont and land into water on the Athos peninsula, then what couldn't he do? Why not, after conquering Greece, all of Europe? Why not, he even asked himself at one point, "a Persian empire that has the same limit as Zeus's sky?"[18]

But Xerxes failed, as is the habit of hedgehogs, to establish a proper relationship between his ends and his means. Because ends exist only in the imagination, they can be infinite: a throne on the moon, perhaps, with a great view. Means, though, are stubbornly finite: they're boots on the ground, ships in the sea, and the bodies required to fill them. Ends and means have to connect if anything is to happen. They're never, however, interchangeable.

The only constraints Xerxes imposed on capabilities were his own aspirations. He hoped for the best, assuming that it would be the worst. He lived only in the present, cutting himself off from the past, where experience resided, and from the future, where the unforeseen lurked.[19] Had Xerxes grasped these distinctions, he'd have seen that his armies and fleets could never have transported all that it would take just to invade Greece. Unless the king could induce those he was invading to supply his invasion (not easy), his own men (although probably not himself) would soon begin to get hungry (or thirsty, or tired). Resistance by a few, as at Thermopylae, would shake the confidence of many. And winter would be coming on.

There would have been risks too, though, in following the foxlike Artabanus. He could have warned Xerxes of the depleted rivers, hungry lions, sudden squalls, resentful locals, fierce fighters, cryptic oracles, avid rowers, and sinking nonswimmers awaiting him across the Hellespont: because their causes were knowable, their consequences were predictable. But only individually, for not even the canniest seer can specify *cumulative* effects. Little things add up in unpredictably big ways—and yet, leaders can't let uncertainties paralyze them. They must appear to know what they're doing, even when they don't.

Xerxes carried this principle to a ferocious extreme. When Pythius the Lydian provided all the troops and treasure the king had requested for the invasion save only the service of his eldest son, Xerxes found a way to show, unforgettably, his resolve: he had the young man bisected, and then ordered his armies to march between the bloody halves.[20] That left no doubt as to Xerxes' determination, but this literal red line locked him in. He couldn't have rethought his plans now, even if he'd wanted to.

The tragedy of Xerxes and Artabanus is that each lacked the other's proficiency. The king, like Tetlock's hedgehogs, commanded the attention of audiences but tended to dig himself into holes. The adviser, like Tetlock's foxes, avoided the holes, but couldn't retain audiences. Xerxes was right. If you try to anticipate everything, you'll risk not accomplishing anything. But so was Artabanus. If you fail to prepare for all that might happen, you'll ensure that some of it will.

VI.

Neither Xerxes nor Artabanus, therefore, would have passed F. Scott Fitzgerald's test, from 1936, for a first-rate intelligence: "the ability to hold two opposed ideas in the mind at the same time, and still retain the ability to function."[21] Fitzgerald may have intended nothing more than a reproach to himself. His writing career had stalled by then, and four years later he would die, of alcoholism, heart disease, and an obscurity made all the more painful by his earlier fame. He was only forty-four.[22] But the cryptic capaciousness of his aphorism, like Berlin's on foxes and hedgehogs, has made it immortal. The Delphic oracle would have been envious.[23]

One possible meaning for Fitzgerald's opposites could be taking the best from contradictory approaches while rejecting the worst: precisely the compromise that Xerxes and Artabanus failed to reach twenty-four centuries earlier. How, though, might you do that? It's easy to see how *two* minds can reach opposite conclusions, but can opposites coexist peacefully within *one*? They certainly didn't in Fitzgerald's, whose life was as tortured as Tolstoy's, and half the length.

The best answer to this question comes, paradoxically, from Berlin, who devoted much of his longer and happier life to reconciling conflicts within single minds. Ordinary experience, he pointed out, is filled with "ends equally ultimate . . . , the realization of some of which must inevitably involve the sacrifice of others." The choices facing us are less often between stark alternatives—good versus evil, for instance—than between good things we can't have simultaneously. "One can save one's soul, or one can found or maintain or serve a great and glorious State," Berlin wrote, "but not always both at once." Or, to put it in terms any kid would understand: you can't gobble all your treats on Halloween without throwing up.

We resolve these dilemmas by stretching them over time. We seek certain things now, put off others until later, and regard still others as unattainable. We select what fits where, and then decide which we can achieve when. The process can be difficult: Berlin emphasized the "necessity and agony of choice." But if such choices were to disappear, he added, so too would "the freedom to choose," and hence liberty itself.[24]

What, then, of Berlin's claim, in his Tolstoy essay, that foxes and hedgehogs divide "human beings in general"? Must we define ourselves as one or the other, as Tetlock asked his experts to do? Berlin admitted, shortly before his death, that this wasn't necessary. "Some people are neither foxes nor hedgehogs, some people are both." He'd just been playing an "intellectual game." Others took it too seriously.[25]

The explanation made sense within the larger framework of Berlin's thought, for what choices would we have if stuck within categories, mimicking animals, that mandated predictability?[26] If, as Fitzgerald argued, intelligence requires opposites—if freedom is choosing, as Berlin maintained—then priorities can't be predetermined. They'd have to reflect who we are, but also what we're experiencing: the first we could know in advance, but not always the second. We'd need to combine, within a single mind (our own), the hedgehog's sense of direction *and* the fox's sensitivity to surroundings. While retaining the ability to function.

VII.

Where, though—other than as a garbled Jane Austen title—might we find such sense *and* sensitivity? She offers a hint, for only narratives can show dilemmas across time. It's not enough to display choices like slivers on a microscope slide. We need to see change happen, and we can do that only by reconstituting the past as histories, biographies, poems, plays, novels, or films. The best of these sharpen and shade simultaneously: they compress what's happening in order to clarify, even as they blur, the line between instruction and entertainment. They are, in short, *dramatizations*. And a fundamental requirement of these is never to bore.

Steven Spielberg's 2012 film *Lincoln* is dramatization at its best. It shows the president, played by Daniel Day-Lewis, trying to make good on the claim, in the Declaration of Independence, that all men are created equal: what more praiseworthy cause could a hedgehog possibly pursue? But to abolish slavery, Lincoln must move the Thirteenth Amendment through a fractious House of Representatives, and here his maneuvers are as foxy as they come. He resorts to deals, bribes, flattery, arm-twisting, and outright lies—so much so that the movie reeks, visually if not literally, of smoke-filled rooms.[27]

When Thaddeus Stevens (Tommy Lee Jones) asks the president how he can reconcile so noble an aim with such malodorous methods, Lincoln recalls what his youthful years as a surveyor taught him:

> [A] compass . . . [will] point you true north from where you're
> standing, but it's got no advice about the swamps and deserts
> and chasms that you'll encounter along the way. If in pursuit
> of your destination, you plunge ahead, heedless of obstacles,
> and achieve nothing more than to sink in a swamp . . . , [then]
> what's the use of knowing true north?[28]

I had the spooky sense, when I saw the film, that Berlin was sitting next to me, and at the conclusion of this scene leaned over to
whisper triumphantly: "You see? Lincoln knows when to be a
hedgehog (consulting the compass) and when a fox (skirting the
swamp)!"

The real Lincoln, as far as I know, never said any of this, and the
real Berlin, sadly, never got to see Spielberg's film. But Tony Kushner's
screenplay shows Fitzgerald's linkage of intelligence, opposing ideas,
and the ability to function: Lincoln keeps long-term aspirations and
immediate necessities in mind at the same time. It reconciles Berlin's
foxes and hedgehogs with his insistence on the inevitability—and the
unpredictability—of choice: Lincoln can't know what deals he'll have
to cut until he's seen what the previous ones have accomplished. And
the film repeatedly connects big things with little ones: Lincoln understands that the vote in the House, and hence the future of slavery
in America, may well depend on who gets to be postmaster in some
village somewhere.

Spielberg's *Lincoln*, therefore, shows actions taken across time
(Berlin), the coexistence of opposites within a space (Fitzgerald),
and a shifting of scale that echoes—why not Tolstoy? For both Lin-
colns, the one portrayed and the one who lived, grasped intuitively
what Tolstoy tried to convey in his own colossal dramatization,

War and Peace: that everything relates to everything else. Perhaps that's why the great novelist, who rarely saw "greatness" in any leader, accorded that accolade posthumously to the martyred president.[29]

VIII.

The shifts of scale that take place in *War and Peace* still startle its readers. Tolstoy places us within the mind of Natasha at her first grand ball, within that of Pierre as he gets himself into and survives a duel, within those of Prince Bolkonsky and Count Rostov, the most difficult and indulgent fathers in modern literature. Yet Tolstoy zooms out from these intimacies to show us armies sweeping across Europe, then back in to focus on the emperors and officers who commanded them, then further in to portray the ordinary soldiers who lived, marched, and fought in them. He zooms out again after Borodino to show Moscow in flames, then in again to depict refugees from the burning city, among whom is the grievously wounded Prince Andrei, who dies in the arms of Natasha, with whom he'd fallen in love, three years and hundreds of pages earlier, at her first grand ball.

Whether we approach reality from the top down or the bottom up, Tolstoy seems to be saying, an infinite number of possibilities exist at an indeterminate number of levels, all simultaneously. Some are predictable, most aren't, and only dramatization—free from the scholar's enslavement to theory and archives—can begin to represent them.[30] But ordinary people, much of the time, manage nonetheless to make sense of them. Berlin tried to explain how in his Tolstoy essay:

History, only history, only the sum of the concrete events in time and space—the sum of the actual experience of actual men and women in their relation to one another and to an actual three-dimensional, empirically experienced, physical environment—this alone contained the truth, the material out of which genuine answers—answers needing for their apprehension no special sense or faculties which normal human beings did not possess—might be constructed.[31]

The passage is convoluted even for Berlin, who rarely saw simplicity as a virtue. But I think he's describing here an *ecological* sensitivity that *equally* respects time, space, and scale. Xerxes never had it, despite Artabanus' efforts. Tolstoy approximated it, if only in a novel. But Lincoln—who lacked an Artabanus and who didn't live to read *War and Peace*—seems somehow to have achieved it, by way of a common sense that's uncommon among great leaders.

IX.

I mean, by common sense, the ease with which most of us manage, most of the time. We generally know where we're going, but we're constantly adjusting our route to avoid the unexpected, including obstructions others place in our path while on *their* way to wherever *they're* going. My own students, for example, skillfully avoid collisions with lampposts, alarmed professors, and similarly preoccupied peers while compulsively consulting electronic devices permanently attached, it seems, to a hand or an ear. Not all of us are that agile, but there's nothing unusual about the simultaneous presence, within our minds, of a short-term sensitivity to surroundings and a long-term sense of direction. We live with these opposites every day.

The psychologist Daniel Kahneman attributes this proficiency to an unconscious reliance on two kinds of thinking. "Fast" thinking is intuitive, impulsive, and often emotional. It produces, when needed, instant action: it's what you do to keep from running into things, or to keep them from running into you. "Slow" thinking is deliberate, focused, and usually logical. It needn't result in action at all: it's how you learn in order to know. Tetlock sees a similarity in the human genome, and uses Berlin's animals to explain it:

> Foxes were better equipped to survive in rapidly changing environments in which those who abandoned bad ideas quickly held the advantage. Hedgehogs were better equipped to survive in static environments that rewarded persisting with tried-and-true formulas. Our species—homo sapiens—is better off for having both temperaments.[32]

We may owe our existence, then, to the dexterity with which we switch between fast and slow thinking—between the behavior of foxes and that of hedgehogs. For if we'd never gone beyond regarding ourselves as only one big thing, we'd have wound up, not just in one of Lincoln's swamps, but with the mammoths, in their tar pits.

Why, though, don't those in authority match this flexibility? How, at one end of history, could Xerxes and Artabanus have seen so little need for it? How, at the other end, could Tetlock's experts so readily have identified themselves as *either* foxes *or* hedgehogs, but not both? And why should we regard Lincoln's leadership as extraordinary if all he did was what ordinary people do every day? Common sense, in this sense, is like oxygen: the higher you go, the thinner it gets. "With great power comes great responsibility," Spider-Man's uncle Ben reminded him memorably[33]—but also the danger of doing dumb things.

X.

Which is what *grand strategy* is meant to prevent. I'll define that term, for the purposes of this book, as the alignment of potentially unlimited aspirations with necessarily limited capabilities. If you seek ends beyond your means, then sooner or later you'll have to scale back your ends to fit your means. Expanding means may attain more ends, but not all because ends can be infinite and means can never be. Whatever balance you strike, there'll be a link between what's real and what's imagined: between your current location and your intended destination. You won't have a strategy until you've connected these dots—dissimilar though they are—within the situation in which you're operating.

Where, then, does the adjective "grand" come in? It has to do, I think, with what's at stake. Your life as a student won't fundamentally change if you sleep for another twenty minutes tomorrow morning, at the cost of grabbing a cold bagel instead of a hot breakfast on your way to class. The stakes rise, though, as you consider what you're learning in that class, how that relates to the other courses you're taking, what your major and then your degree are going to be, how you might parlay these into a profession, and with whom you may fall in love along the way. Strategies become grander even as they remain within the beholder's eye. It's wrong to say, then, that states have grand strategies but that people don't. Alignments are necessary across time, space, *and* scale.

Grand strategies have traditionally been associated, however, with the planning and fighting of wars. That's not surprising, given the fact the first *recorded* relationships of aspirations with capabilities arose from the need to conduct military operations. "Put heads together," Homer has wise Nestor admonishing the Achaeans at a desperate moment in the long siege of Troy, "if strategy's any use."[34] The *necessity* for such alignment, however, goes back much further, probably to the first prehuman who figured out how to get something it wanted, using whatever means happened to be available.[35]

Short of life after death, the universal aspiration was surely survival. Beyond that strategies effloresced, from so simple a task as finding food, shelter, and clothing to such complex responsibilities as ruling great empires. Specifying success was never easy, but the finite nature of means helped. For although satisfaction, in the end, is a state of mind, achieving it requires real expenditures. It's in that fact that the need for alignment, and hence for strategy, has always arisen.

XI.

So is it possible to *teach* grand strategy, or at least the common sense that sustains it? If Lincoln, with as little formal education as any American president, learned what he needed to know from self-prescribed reading and self-assessed experience, can't we do the same?[36] The simple answer is that Lincoln was a genius and most of us aren't. Shakespeare, it appears, had no writing tutor. Does nobody else then need one?

It's worth remembering also that Lincoln—and Shakespeare—had a lifetime to become who they were. Young people today don't, because society so sharply segregates general education, professional training, ascent within an organization, responsibility for it, and then retirement. This worsens a problem Henry Kissinger identified long ago: that the "intellectual capital" leaders accumulate prior to reaching the top is all they'll be able to draw on while at the top.[37] There's less time now than Lincoln had to learn anything new.

That leaves it to the academy to shape the minds of its students while it has their attention, but the academic mind is itself divided. A gap has opened between the study of history and the construction of theory, both of which are needed if ends are to be aligned with means. Historians, knowing that their field rewards specialized research, tend to avoid the generalizations upon which theories depend: they thereby deny complexity the simplicities that guide us through it. Theorists, keen to be seen as social "scientists," seek "reproducibility" in results: that replaces complexity with simplicity in the pursuit of predictability. Both communities neglect *relationships* between the general and the particular—between universal and local knowledge—that nurture strategic thinking. And both, as if to add opacity to this insufficiency, too often write badly.[38]

There is an older way, though, in which history and theory have worked together. Machiavelli hints at it in the dedicatory letter to *The Prince*, where he values nothing so much "as the knowledge of the actions of great men, learned by me from long experience with modern things and a continuous reading of ancient ones." This he has distilled into "one small volume," meant to give "you [his patron Lorenzo de' Medici] the capacity to be able to understand in a very short time all that I [Machiavelli] have learned and understood in so many years and with so many hardships and dangers for myself."[39]

Carl von Clausewitz, in his monumental but incomplete classic

On War, develops Machiavelli's method more fully.[40] History alone, he argues, is just a long string of stories. That doesn't mean they're useless, though, because theory, when conceived of as distillation, keeps you from having to listen to them all again. There isn't time for that when you're about to go into combat, or any other fraught field of endeavor. But you can't just wander around either, like Tolstoy's Pierre at Borodino. This is where *training* comes in.

The well-trained soldier will surely perform better than one with no preparation at all, but what is "training," as Clausewitz understands it? It's being able to draw upon principles extending across time and space, so that you'll have a sense of what's worked before and what hasn't. You then apply these to the situation at hand: that's the role of scale. The result is a *plan,* informed by the past, linked to the present, for achieving some future goal.

The engagement, however, won't in all respects follow the plan. Not only will its outcome depend on what the other side does—the "known unknowns," of which former secretary of defense Donald Rumsfeld famously spoke[41]—but it will also reflect "unknown unknowns," which are all the things that can go wrong before you've even encountered an adversary. Together, these constitute what Clausewitz called "friction," the collision of theory with reality about which Artabanus tried to warn Xerxes, many centuries earlier at the Hellespont.

The only solution then is to improvise, but this is not just making it up as you go along. Maybe you'll stick to the plan, maybe you'll modify it, maybe you'll scrap it altogether. Like Lincoln, though, you'll know your compass heading, whatever the unknowns that lie between you and your destination. You'll have in your mind a range of options for dealing with these, based—as if from Machiavelli—upon hard-won lessons from those who've gone before. The rest is up to you.

XII.

Boats crossing the Hellespont these days still connect battlefields, as Xerxes' bridges once did: Troy lies just to the south on the Asian side; Gallipoli, on the European, is even closer. Now the vessels are ferries, though, and the armies they transport are tourists, taking advantage of the fact that thirty centuries separate sites only about thirty miles apart. There's even time, in a single day, to take in the Trojan Horse at Çanakkale—not the real one, of course, but the prop left over from the 2004 Brad Pitt movie.

The scene lacks the grandeur of what Xerxes saw from his promontory in 480 B.C.E., but it makes an important point: that combat experience is rarer even than in the recent past. For whatever reason—the fear that a world war could annihilate all its participants, the shift back to smaller wars that only partially engage societies conducting them, perhaps just good luck—fewer people find themselves on battlefields today fighting battles. The sightseers are taking over.

Clausewitz's concept of training, however, retains its relevance. It's the best protection we have against strategies getting stupider as they become grander, a recurring problem in peace as well as war. It's the only way to combine the *apparent* opposites of planning and improvisation: to teach the common sense that comes from knowing when to be a hedgehog and when a fox. Where, though, if not in the military and if only inadequately within the academy or on the job, can young people today get such an education?

"The Battle of Waterloo was won on the playing fields of Eton," the Duke of Wellington did *not* say—although as the Victorian era's principal supplier of epigrams, he certainly should have.[42] For apart from war and preparation for war, it's in competitive athletics that the Clausewitzian combination of a distilled past, a planned present, and an uncertain future most explicitly come together. With fitness more fashionable now than in the age of the great duke, there's more participation in games than ever before. But what does that get you, and what does it have to do with grand strategy?

You learn to play the game by having a coach, literally a "trainer," who does what drill instructors used to do when military service was mandatory: teach the basics, build stamina, enforce discipline, encourage collaboration, show you how to fail and to recover from failure. Once the game begins, though, your coach can only shout or sulk from the sidelines. You and your teammates are on your own. Still, you'll all do better for having been coached: it's not for nothing that coaches' salaries, at certain American universities, exceed those of the presidents who've recruited them.

Does any of this mean, though, that while playing the game you've been a hedgehog or a fox? You'd probably regard the question as silly because you'd been both: you had a hedgehog-like plan, you modified it as needed in a fox-like manner, and you won or lost depending on whether it worked or didn't. You'd find it hard to say, looking back, when you'd been which. Instead you held opposing ideas in your mind as you functioned.

It's much the same in most aspects of life, where we make such choices instinctively, or almost so. As authority increases, however, so does self-consciousness. With more people watching, practice becomes performance. Reputations now matter, narrowing the freedom to be flexible. Leaders who've reached the top—like Xerxes, or

Tetlock's experts—can become prisoners of their own preeminence: they lock themselves into roles from which they can't escape.

This, then, is a book about the *mental* Hellesponts that divide such leadership, on one shore, from common sense, on the other. There ought to be free and frequent crossings between them, for it's only with such exchanges that grand strategies—alignments of means with ends—become possible. But the currents are swift, the winds are untrustworthy, and the bridges are fragile. There's no further need now to intimidate or propitiate water, in the manner of Xerxes. But by analyzing how others since that monarch have managed oppositions of logic and leadership, we can perhaps coach ourselves for the crossings we'll sooner or later have to make.

CHAPTER TWO

LONG WALLS

S een from above, their shape would have resembled that of a giant bone, gnawed clean and tossed carelessly across southern Attica by some satiated god far to the north on Mount Olympus. One joint-like extremity rested on a rocky crag; the other just touched the water's edge. Total length was about six miles, but swellings at each end made the circumference seventeen. Four miles of implausibly thin shank connected them: set upright, the structure couldn't have borne its own weight. That wasn't its purpose, though, for these were walls, the longest ever built surrounding *two* cities.[1]

Athens, at the northeastern end, had some two hundred thousand inhabitants when the walls were finished in 457 B.C.E. Piraeus, to the southwest, had fewer people but more space: it was the Athenians' port for trade throughout the Mediterranean, as well as the construction, repair, and supply base for their navy, whose "wooden walls" had brought victory at Salamis twenty-three years earlier. Long after Athens lost the primacy it won on that occasion, Plutarch the historian found "a bloom of newness" in the city's buildings and public spaces, as if "some perennial spirit and undying vitality mingled in the composition of them." The rebuilt Acropolis, still bearing the scorches of Persian fires, presided over it all from its crag, as after many other afflictions it does even now.

The walls linking Athens and Piraeus were about five hundred feet apart: wide enough to accommodate a two-way flow of people, animals, carts, commodities, and treasure; narrow enough to make defense feasible. They were solid—some ten feet thick and twenty-five feet high—but strangely at odds with the elegance they guarded. Stones sat awkwardly in their mortar. Broken columns stuck out, as did the fragments of tombs. The explanation, officially, was memorialization: you were meant to recall the depredations of Xerxes as you walked the walls. Your ancestors were there to remind you.[2]

Xerxes had brought everything with him across the Hellespont except a grand strategy: if his aspirations *were* his capabilities, why bother to align them? He came to know scarcity only after the land, the sea, the weather, the Greeks, and their oracle introduced it to him. Believing himself strong in all respects, he held none in reserve: when one failed, others followed. And so he lost, it's been estimated, over nine hundred triremes, and a quarter of a million men.[3]

The Greeks, in contrast, knew only scarcity. Unlike the Persians, whose empire sprawled from the Aegean to India, they occupied a small rugged peninsula that fragmented resources and resisted authority. Towns and cities had to protect themselves: no King of Kings could do that for them. There were alliances, even colonies, but obligations were vague and loyalties often shifted. That made Greece a hothouse for rivalries, and hence for strategies.[4] Two stood out after Xerxes' defeat. They differed in all respects—excepting that scarcity required specialization.

I.

The Spartans, who fought to the last man at Thermopylae, had long been warriors. Bound to the Peloponnese but not as farmers—agriculture was left to slaves (*helots*)—their strategy was to make their army the best in Greece. Having no other objective, they failed to produce even respectable ruins. As military professionals, they trained constantly in order to fight infrequently: they'd missed the battle of Marathon in 490 because they'd been celebrating a moon festival. But when aroused, as by Xerxes' invasion, the Spartans' fury far exceeded their numbers. That's why, despite Thermopylae, Athens entrusted its land defenses to them. When these failed, Thucydides tells us, the Athenians "broke up their homes, threw themselves into their ships, and became a naval people."[5]

They were already a maritime people whose trading network stretched from the Atlantic to the Black Sea. The Athenians had also grown wealthy, extracting profits and protection payments from their dependencies, while mining silver in a nearby corner of Attica. That financed the fleet at Salamis, but Themistocles had more in mind than just seaworthy wooden walls. He wanted walls on the ground on a grand scale. By encircling Athens *and* Piraeus, these would make those cities an island—immune from attack by land, supplied in all necessities from the sea, poised to deploy a navy as formidable as the Spartans' army.[6]

Spartans and Athenians, therefore, became tigers and sharks, each dominant in its own domain.[7] Common sense might have called, at that point, for cooperation, since Persian dangers were still clear and present. Instead what happened made no sense. The Greeks embellished, unforgettably, the civilization they'd saved—after which they almost destroyed it.[8]

II.

The Peloponnesian War, fought between Athens, Sparta, and their respective allies from 431 to 404, resembled the much briefer Persian Wars in one respect: each had a great chronicler. Thucydides warned his readers, however, that he wouldn't be Herodotus. His history would refrain from attractiveness "at truth's expense." Its "absence of romance" might "detract somewhat from its interest," but he hoped for what Plutarch would later find in the remains of Athens: preservation from the effects of time, and hence, "a possession for all time." It would suffice, Thucydides wrote, to have his history judged useful by those seeking "*knowledge of the past as an aid to the understanding of the future, which in the course of human things must resemble if it does not reflect it.*"[9]

The past and future are no more equivalent, in Thucydides, than are capabilities and aspirations in strategy—they are, however, connected. The past we can know only from imperfect sources, including our own memories. The future we can't know, other than that it will originate in the past but then depart from it. Thucydides' distinction between resemblance and reflection—between *patterns* surviving *across* time and *repetitions* degraded *by* time—aligns the asymmetry, for it suggests that the past prepares us for the future only when, however imperfectly, it transfers. Just as capabilities restrict aspirations to what circumstances will allow.

To know one big thing or many little ones is, therefore, not enough: resemblances, which Thucydides insists *must* happen, can occur anywhere along the spectrum from hedgehogs to foxes and back again. So is he one or the other? It's as useless to ask as it would be, of an accomplished athlete, to try to say. Thucydides' "first-rate intelligence" accommodates opposing ideas so effortlessly that he entrusts us with hundreds in his history. He does so within time and space but also across scale: only Tolstoy rivals him, I think, in sensing significance where it seems not to be.

It's no stretch to say, then, that Thucydides *coaches* all who read him. For as his greatest modern interpreter (himself a sometime coach) has gently reminded us, the Greeks, despite their antiquity, "may have believed things we have either forgotten or never known; and we must keep open the possibility that in some respects, at least, they were wiser than we."[10]

III.

The Spartans never had a wall, trusting in their military prowess alone to deter adversaries. On hearing of Themistocles' plan to build one, they tried to convince the Athenians that no city should: such a ban would encourage unity among Greeks while denying the Persians fortifications in any future invasion. But the Spartans' real purpose, Thucydides argues, was to limit Athenian naval capabilities, which had proven so effective at Salamis. The absence of walls, with the resulting vulnerability of Athens and its port, would accomplish this.

Themistocles persuaded the Athenians to *appear* to welcome Sparta's proposal, even to the point of sending him there to conduct the negotiations. Meanwhile, Athens began a crash wall-building program. Men, women, and children all participated, using anything they could find: haste as much as memorialization, therefore, explains the walls' use of rubble. When the Spartans wondered why the talks were taking so long, Themistocles claimed to be waiting for inexplicably delayed colleagues. Eventually they arrived, but so did reports of what the Athenians were up to. If worried, Themistocles told the suspicious Spartans, they should send observers to Athens to see for themselves. He then secretly instructed the Athenians to detain their Spartan guests until the walls were nearing completion.

Once satisfied that they were, Themistocles abandoned all pretense: Athens, he announced, was now sufficiently walled to protect its people. Any future discussions would assume the Athenians' right to determine their own interests *and* those of other Greeks. The Spartans showed no anger; still, Thucydides notes, "the defeat of their wishes could not but cause them secret annoyance."[11] They'd been screwed—if such a thing is possible—by a wall.

IV.

All of this happened in 479–78, four and a half decades before the Peloponnesian War broke out. Thucydides makes it a flashback, unusual in his history. He wants us to see the connection, even if distant, between a great war and an almost comic collision of Spartan stolidity with Athenian trickery: small causes can have big consequences. It's not as though there was no turning back. Progress forward, however, would take place warily, for each aspect of the Athenian-Spartan relationship now carried multiple meanings.

Take, for example, the building of walls: was it a *defensive* or an *offensive* act? The Athenians intended their walls to secure their "island," the base from which, with their commerce and navy, they'd control the seas around Greece and much beyond. The Spartans saw safety in an absence of walls, but only because their army was and would remain the strongest in Greece. That, though, is why the Athenians thought they needed walls in the first place. The categories are too categorical.

Both Spartans and Athenians acted *strategically,* however, in that they were aligning aspirations with capabilities. Each sought security but by different paths; neither could afford to be, simultaneously, tigers *and* sharks. Collaboration, in theory, could have secured the sea and the land from all future dangers. That would have required, though, the extension of trust, a quality with strikingly shallow roots in the character of all Greeks.

Having outmaneuvered the Spartans, Themistocles returned in triumph to Athens, as he had after Salamis. But with the passage of time, his welcome wore thin: by 470 the Athenian assembly—which feared as much as it rewarded success in its leaders—had used its power of ostracism to ban him from the city. Ever resourceful, the organizer of victory over the Persians defected, in due course, to the Persians, spending the rest of his life in their service. And so the recently assassinated Xerxes, despite Aeschylus, got a kind of revenge after all.[12]

V.

One of the producers of *The Persians* was Pericles, an Athenian aristocrat who gave his name to the age that followed. Gracious, modest, but adept in attracting followers, he was a patron of the arts, an accomplished military commander, an experienced diplomat, an astute economist, a constitutional theorist of enduring originality, one of the finest orators ever, the rebuilder of Athens as we still know it, and for over a quarter century the leader of that city and the empire it ran.[13] Nonetheless it was Pericles who, more than anyone else, unleashed the Peloponnesian War—the unintended result of constructing a culture to support a strategy.

The Spartans needed no new culture because the Persian Wars had left their old one largely intact. That of the Athenians, however, was upside down. They'd shown their ability to fight on land by defeating the Persians (without the Spartans) at Marathon in 490, and (with the Spartans) at Plataea in 479. But Themistocles' "island" required relinquishing that proficiency: Athens, he feared, could never compete with Sparta's army.[14] By the mid-450s Pericles, who agreed, had finished the walls around Athens and Piraeus, allowing total reliance on the sea in any future war. The new strategy made sense, but it made the Athenians, as Thucydides saw, a different people.

Farmers, traditionally, had sustained Athens: their fields and vineyards supplied the city in peacetime, and their bodies filled the ranks of its infantry and cavalry when wars came. Now, though, their properties were expendable and their influence diminished. They'd become refugees if the Spartans invaded, crowding into the city to watch from its walls as their villas, crops, and olive trees were destroyed. Pericles, himself a landowner, promised as a show of resolve to torch his own. Eventually, he assumed, the Spartans, worried about unreliable *helots* on their own estates, would give up and go home—but not because of anything the former stabilizers of Athenian society had done. Meanwhile, ships operating out of Piraeus would support Athens from its overseas dependencies, while its navy would harass the Spartans' unprotected coastline, thereby hastening their departure.[15]

A merchant fleet and a navy, however, would be expensive. To fight on land, an Athenian hoplite—an infantryman—needed only a sword, a shield, a helmet, minimal armor, and absolute confidence in the man next to him, for Greek phalanxes advanced as a unit: improvisation ensured disaster. The navy, though, required port facilities, ships, sails, and banks of rowers willing to wallow in bilge water befouled by their own excretions (triremes rarely made pit stops), unable to see how the battle was going, at risk of drowning if it didn't go well. Something had to embolden them beyond visions of villas (which most had never possessed) or close order drill (impractical in smelly, slippery close quarters.)[16]

The need for motivation went well beyond rowing. Triremes were warships, useful only for ramming others. Their builders— whether private citizens or the public treasury—could hardly expect profits: there had to be less tangible benefits. Nor could the Athenians force their colonies to feed them: crops, livestock, and fish require encouragement, not instructions. Nor could the city pay women and children to work on walls: the interests of families would have to coincide with requirements of strategy. Massive enterprises must have major incentives. Somebody has to show everybody—or almost everybody—that sacrifices made now will bear fruit later. And the ones Pericles had in mind were not to the gods, as in earlier times,[17] but for a city that had become a state that was becoming an empire.

Which had to remain, nonetheless, a community. If Athens were to rely upon the ardor of *individuals,* then it would have to inspire classes within the city and peoples throughout the empire—even as it retained the cohesiveness of its rival Sparta, still in many ways a small town. That's why constructing a culture became, for Pericles, a priority.

VI.

Pericles used his "funeral oration," delivered in Athens at the end of the Peloponnesian War's first year, to explain what he hoped for. The dead had given their lives, he told the mourners, for the *universality of Athenian distinctiveness:* Athens imitated no one, but was a pattern for everyone. How, though, to reconcile these apparent opposites? Pericles' solution was to connect scale, space, and time: Athenian culture would appeal to the city, the empire, and the ages. Fortunately Thucydides, or someone he trusted, was there to take notes as the great man spoke.[18]

Since well before Pericles, Athens had been edging toward democracy, which he defined as favoring "the many instead of the few." By the time he took power, any adult male citizen who wasn't a slave could speak and vote in the Athenian assembly: with five to six thousand regular attendees, it was the largest deliberative body the world had—or still has—ever seen.[19] "[O]ur ordinary citizens," Pericles claimed in his speech, were "fair judges of public matters; for, unlike any other nation, we regard the citizen who takes no part in these duties . . . as useless." Discussion was "an indispensable preliminary to any wise action at all."

The assembly functioned by divorcing virtue from status. If a man wished to participate—a virtue—then "the obscurity of his condition"—status—wouldn't prevent his doing so. It followed that anyone who could strengthen a fortification, repair a boat, power an oar, pay others to do these things, or even bring up a child who might someday do them, would be serving the state. Experience was useful, but the specializations stratifying other societies were unnecessary. "I doubt if the world can produce a man," Pericles boasted, who "is equal to so many emergencies, and graced by so happy a versatility as the Athenian."

With their reliance on walls, ships, and rowers, the Athenians had democratized the waging of war. They'd have no warrior elites, trained from childhood in the manner of the fiercely hierarchical Spartans. But they would have more warriors, on whom the state could depend to protect *and* to determine its interests. "[W]here our rivals from their very cradles by a painful discipline seek after manliness, at Athens we live exactly as we please, and yet are just as ready to encounter every legitimate danger."

Democracy within the assembly would be a model for the city: what, though, of the empire? By contracting their commitments on land, the Athenians had expanded their need for control by sea. Some two hundred allies or subject states owed them allegiance as the Peloponnesian War began.[20] But circumstances, attitudes, and even languages varied widely: could Athens trust *other cultures* to sustain its own?

The city had acquired its "friends," Pericles acknowledged, by granting favors, "in order by continued kindness to keep the recipient in [its] debt; while the debtor [knows] that the return he makes will be a payment, not a free gift." Nevertheless, the Athenians had provided these benefits "not from calculations of expediency, but in the confidence of liberality." What he meant was that Athens would make its empire at once more powerful and more reassuring than that of any rival.[21]

It could in this way project democracy across cultures because insecure states, fearing worse, would freely align with Athens.[22]

Self-interest would become comfort and then affinity. Transparency, for this reason, was vital: "We throw open our city to the world, and never by alien acts exclude foreigners from any opportunity of learning or observing." Athenians found "the fruits of other countries" to be "as familiar a luxury as those of [their] own." The walls made their citizenship global.

Pericles' appeal to the future would be remembrance. The heroes he honored needed no markers: they "have the whole earth for their tomb." But their culture would construct memorials as "mighty proofs." These would include the architecture and adornment of cities, upon which Pericles lavished so much time and treasure. There would also be texts—the philosophical works, the plays, the histories, his own speeches—messages in bottles to distant ages confirming the singularity of his own. And ruins: "[W]e have forced every sea and land to be the highway of our daring, and everywhere, whether for evil or for good, have left imperishable monuments behind us."

As oratory, Pericles' speech compares only with Lincoln's at Gettysburg. But where Lincoln linked the costs of war to military success, Pericles was acknowledging strategic failure. He'd hoped, after all, to *avoid* a war with Sparta by balancing its land superiority against Athenian naval supremacy, while building a new kind of empire whose appeal would allay whatever suspicions it might provoke.[23] How, then, did Pericles find himself defining a culture meant to prevent a war after a great one had already broken out?

VII.

Thucydides provides three explanations. The first is that, in 435, the small and remote town of Epidamnus, facing civil war, sought help without success from its sponsor Corcyra, but did receive assistance from Corcyra's rival Corinth, thereby angering the Corcyrans, who sent a fleet to Epidamnus, provoking Corinth into dispatching its own ships as well as an army and settlers, after which both sides sought aid from the Athenians, who granted the Corcyrans a defensive alliance that dragged Athens into a naval battle with Corinth, leading the Athenians then to besiege Potidaea, a colony of the Corinthians, who at that point asked the Spartans to invade Attica, but they instead invited the Athenians and the Corinthians to justify their positions before the Spartan assembly. After which that body, moved less by the arguments it heard than by fear of "the growth of the power of the Athenians"—Thucydides' second and more succinct explanation—voted in 432 to declare war.[24]

The first account traces a causal chain in numbing detail. The second confirms that it was a chain, not a random assortment of events. Neither, however, reveals how "some damn foolish thing in the Balkans"[25]—Epidamnus is Durrës in modern Albania—provoked a war as devastating for Greeks as, proportionately, the Thirty Years' War was for Europeans in the seventeenth century, or the two world wars for all their participants in the twentieth.[26] To understand this, we need Thucydides' third explanation, which is that Pericles' reliance on reassurance had not reassured.

Thucydides provides it—more implicitly than explicitly—in his reconstruction of the debate at Sparta. This was, in effect, a "trial of Pericles," with the Corinthians prosecutors, the Athenians defenders, and the Spartans—the only speakers Thucydides names—serving as judges. At issue was how universal a distinctive culture could or should be.

The Corinthians began by blaming the *Spartans* for the Athenian long walls. Their "bluntness of perception" had allowed Themistocles' trickery decades earlier, from which Athens concluded that the Spartans "see, but do not care."

> You, Spartans, of all the Hellenes are alone inactive, and defend yourselves not by doing anything but by looking as if you would do something; you alone wait till the power of an enemy is becoming twice its original size, instead of crushing it in its infancy. And yet the world used to say that you were to be depended upon; but in your case, we fear, it said more than the truth.

The Athenians, in contrast, were "adventurous beyond their power, and daring beyond their judgment." The speed with which they acted enabled them "to call a thing hoped for a thing got." They "take no rest themselves and . . . give none to others." For these reasons, the Spartans should aid the Potidaeans by invading Attica. Not to do so would "drive the rest of us in despair to some other alliance."[27]

The Athenians responded by recalling the Persian Wars, even though "we are rather tired of continually bringing this subject forward." Despite the Spartans' sacrifice at Thermopylae, "we left behind us a city [Athens] that was a city no longer; and staked our lives for [one] that had existence only in desperate hope, and so bore our fair share in your deliverance and in ours." As for the empire, "[W]e acquired [it] not by violence, but because you were unwilling to prosecute to its conclusion the war against the barbarian, and because the allies attached themselves to us and spontaneously asked us to assume the command." The Athenians did, therefore, what anyone would have done. Given "the vast influence of accident in war," the Spartans should "[t]ake time" in deciding what they should do. It was all too common "to begin at the wrong end, to act first, and wait for disaster to discuss the matter."[28]

Archidamus, the Spartan king, supported the Athenians. War, he warned, required not so much arms as money, especially if between a continental and a maritime power. For "unless we can beat them at sea, or deprive them of the revenues which feed their navy, we shall meet with little but disaster." Diplomacy was the wiser course, leaving open the possibility, if it failed, of seizing parts of Attica but not laying them waste: that would benefit no one. Corinthian complaints about Spartan "slowness" neglected the likelihood that hastening a war would delay its conclusion, leaving it "as a legacy to our children."[29]

The Spartan assembly would make the final decision, however, and Sthenelaidas, one of several *ephors*—magistrates—carried the day. Because the Athenians had fought the Persians but mistreated the Spartans, he argued in loopy logic, they deserved "double punishment for having ceased to be good and become bad." More talk would do only more harm. "Vote therefore, Spartans, for war, as the honor of Sparta demands, and . . . with the gods let us advance against the aggressors." The yeas and nays were unclear, but when asked to stand and divide, the assembly supported Sthenelaidas. That was how, Thucydides repeats, "[t]he growth of the power of Athens, and the alarm which this inspired in Sparta, made war inevitable."[30]

VIII.

Pericles didn't attend his "trial" in Sparta, but he would have selected his spokesmen carefully. It's all the more striking, therefore, that their defense was so unpersuasive, even with the Spartan king's cautions about the dangers of war. Pericles had built his career and his city's culture on persuasion.[31] Something had gone badly wrong.

Perhaps his representatives lacked his eloquence, forcing them to fall back on the claim that all empires become oppressive instead of Pericles' insistence that his would liberate the human spirit. Perhaps Pericles himself would have wilted under the Corinthians' prosecutorial zeal: they made it clear that encounters with the Athenians hadn't liberated *their* spirit, and that the Spartans shouldn't expect that either. Perhaps also, though, there were loops in Pericles' logic, which the debate at Sparta brought out.

The Greeks thought of culture as character. It was predictability across scale: the behavior of a city, a state, or a people in small things, big things, and those in between.[32] Knowing who they were and what they wanted, the Spartans were wholly predictable. They saw no need to change themselves or anyone else. The Athenians' strategy of walling their cities, however, had reshaped their character, obliging them restlessly to roam the world. Because *they* had changed, they would have to change others—that's what having an empire means—but how many, to what extent, and by what means? No one, not even Pericles, could easily say.

Pericles was not Xerxes. "I am more afraid of our own blunders than of the enemy's devices," he admitted as war approached. Knowing that the Athenians' empire could not expand indefinitely, Pericles "unsparingly pruned and cut down their ever busy fancies," Plutarch explained, "supposing it would be quite enough for them to do, if they could keep the [Spartans] in check."[33] But as Pericles' agents acknowledged before the Spartan assembly, allowing the empire the equality he celebrated within the city could cause contraction, perhaps even collapse.

> [O]ur subjects are so habituated to associate with us as equals,
> that any defeat . . . that clashes with their notions of justice,
> whether it proceeds from a legal judgment or from the power
> which our empire gives us, makes them forget to be grateful
> for being allowed to retain most of their possessions, and
> more vexed at a part being taken, than if we had from the first
> cast law aside and openly gratified our covetousness.

The Persians had treated their empire more harshly, but that was in
the past and "the present always weighs heavily on the conquered"—
a strange word to use for Athenian "equals." If the Spartans were to
take over, then they too "would speedily lose the popularity with
which fear of us has invested you."[34]

Equality, then, was the loop in Pericles' logic. He saw both it and
empire as admirable, but was slow to sense that encouraging one
would diminish the other. His funeral address reflects the contradiction: he spoke of voluntary alliances pursuing a common good—but
he also congratulated the Athenians for having forced themselves on
"every sea and land . . . , whether for evil or for good." It's as if, instead
of holding opposing ideas simultaneously in his mind, he'd sequentially split his character: Dr. Jekyll gave way, in mid-speech, to Mr.
Hyde. Pericles' last years traced a similar trajectory.

IX.

A molehill made into a mountain shows how. Megara was—and is—
a small town at the northeastern end of the Corinthian isthmus, the
only land connection between the Peloponnese and the rest of

Greece. Its citizens had long feuded with the Athenians, while posing no military threat to the larger city. What the Megarians could do was join a hostile alliance: that of Corinth, close by, was the most likely. If this happened, others might follow, so in 433 Pericles persuaded the assembly to deny the Megarians trading privileges within Athens and to ban their use of harbors throughout the empire.

Megara had other options: indeed the ban seemed so pointless that Aristophanes made fun of it in his comedy *Acharnians,* produced a few years after Pericles' death. But the Megarian decree was meant to deter, not starve. It was an economic embargo designed to discourage future defections by nonmilitary means. Predictably, this innovation alarmed the Spartans, who made its revocation one of their conditions for avoiding war. Less predictably—because the edict's benefits seemed so much smaller than the risks of retaining it—Pericles refused.

His stubbornness was one of the sources of sourness in the Spartan assembly, but even after voting for war in 432, the Spartans were in no hurry to act. They sent three emissaries to Athens over the next year, each seeking compromise. Pericles, however, rejected every offer: "There is one principle, Athenians, which I hold to through everything, and that is the principle of no concession to the Peloponnesians."

The Megarian decree might look like "a trifle," but withdrawing it would be a slippery slope. "If you give way, you will instantly have to meet some greater demand." That ruled out diplomacy, leaving war the only alternative: it mattered not whether the cause "be great or small." Hadn't Themistocles vanquished the Persians with fewer resources than Athens had now? "We must . . . resist our enemies in any way and in every way, and attempt to hand down our power to our posterity unimpaired."[35]

In a reversal of the Athenians' advice to the Spartans, it was Pericles now who no longer took time. On his orders, presumably, the last Spartan emissary was not even received in Athens, but told to be out of Attica by nightfall. He's said to have remarked, as he crossed the border: "This day will be the beginning of great misfortunes to the Hellenes."[36]

X.

Pericles "was no longer the same man he had been before," Plutarch observed, "nor as tame and gentle and familiar as formerly with the populace, so as [ready] to yield to their pleasures and to comply with the desires of the multitude, as a steersman shifts with the winds." Thucydides sensed similar rigidity: Pericles "opposed the Spartans in everything, and . . . ever urged the Athenians on to war."[37] But why the change?

Perhaps he simply got old: flexibility is harder to maintain as that happens. Perhaps, Pericles' biographer has suggested, the accumulating crises of the late 430s intensified his emotions, reducing his willingness to compromise.[38] Perhaps also, though, there's an explanation in what it may mean to lead or, as Plutarch puts it, to "steer."

One way is to find flows you can go with. Having determined your destination, you set sails, motivate rowers, adjust for winds and currents, avoid shoals and rocks, allow for surprises, and expend finite energy efficiently. You control some things, but align yourself with others. You balance, while never forgetting that the reason you're balancing is to get from where you are to where you want to go. You're a fox *and* a hedgehog at the same time—even on water. That was the younger Pericles steering Athens: a polymath with a purpose.

Over time, though, Pericles began trying to control flows: the winds, the currents, the rowers, the rocks, the people, their enemies, and even fortune, he came to believe, would follow his orders. He could rely, therefore, on intricate causal chains: if A, then not only B, but inexorably C, D, and E. Plans, however complex, would go as planned. The older Pericles still steered Athens; now, however, he was a hedgehog trying to herd foxes, a different and more difficult enterprise.

The distinction clarifies what Thucydides keeps trying to tell us: that *fear* inspired by the *growth* of Athenian power caused the Peloponnesian War. There are, after all, two kinds of growth. One proceeds gradually, allowing adjustments to environments as environments adjust to whatever's new. Skillful growers can shape this process: cultivation, for them, is like navigation for Plutarch's steersmen—the *simultaneous* management of separate things. But no farmer or gardener can claim to anticipate, much less to control, all that may happen between the planting of seeds and the harvesting of crops.

The other kind of growth defies environments. It's inner-directed, and hence outwardly oblivious. It resists cultivation, setting its own direction, pace, and purpose. Anticipating no obstacles, it makes no compromises. Like an unchecked predator, an ineradicable weed, or a metastasizing cancer, it fails to see where it's going until it's too late. It *sequentially* consumes its surroundings, and ultimately itself.[39]

Pericles at first steered *with* flows—a strategy of persuasion. When not all were persuaded, though, he began steering *against* flows—a strategy of confrontation. Either way he challenged the status quo: Greece would not afterward be the same. But persuasion, pursued with patience, would have come closer to cultivation, and hence navigation, than the confrontations into which Pericles led the Athenians. That's the difference, fundamental in strategy, between respecting constraints and denying their existence.

Maybe he saw no choice. Once persuasion had failed, confrontation might have seemed the only way to keep to his course. Why, though, did he have to do that? Why not deviate, as Lincoln would later do, to avoid swamps, deserts, and chasms? Like Lincoln, Pericles looked ahead to the ages. He even left them monuments and sent them messages. But he didn't leave behind a functional state: it would take well over two millennia for democracy again to become a model with mass appeal. That's not farsightedness in a steersman. It's running your vessel onto rocks, with a long wait for rescuers to arrive.

XI.

The Spartans invaded Attica in the spring of 431 and the Athenians, as planned, evacuated their estates, crowding into the city to watch smoke again rise, on their horizons, in pursuit of their strategy. Their mood was not what it had been, however, when Themistocles ordered the evacuation of Athens half a century earlier. Then the victory at Salamis had come quickly. Now, no triumph was in sight. Pericles' funeral oration consoled the city but did little to lift its morale, and in 430 the Spartans returned—along with an ally no one could have foreseen.

The nature of the plague that struck Athens that summer remains a mystery: there's little doubt, though, that the "island" strategy amplified its effects. The Athenians had opened their city to the world, as Pericles boasted, but they also closed it off from its immediate surroundings. That made the long walls a mixing bowl in which bacteria from all over the empire found hosts from all over Attica—an unintended but deadly cosmopolitanism. Even the dogs and vultures that ate unburied corpses succumbed, Thucydides recalled, although he somehow survived. With their properties ravaged and now their bodies, the Athenians "began to find fault with Pericles, as the author of the war and the cause of all their misfortunes."[40]

He refused at first to convene the assembly, but then confronted it. His only mistake, Pericles insisted, had been to underestimate the city's resolve, for "the hand of Heaven must be borne with resignation, [and] that of the enemy with fortitude." Refugees from beyond the walls should praise the navy that protected them and the empire that sustained them: "[Y]ou may think it a great privation to lose the use of your land and houses, [but] you should really regard them [as] . . . accessories that embellish a great fortune," and hence, "of little moment."

Admittedly—and "to speak somewhat plainly"—that fortune required "a tyranny." To take the empire "perhaps was wrong, but to let it go is unsafe." Its subjects hated their masters now and, given the choice, would welcome others. Hatred, however, was "the lot of all who have aspired to rule." If incurred "for the highest objects," it would be "short-lived," for it was "the splendor of the present and the glory of the future [that] remains forever unforgotten."[41] And so Pericles again appealed to the ages to bail him out—as if he and his city could wait for ages for that to happen.

XII.

But Pericles died of the plague in 429, leaving Athens on the edge of a knife he'd sharpened. On one side was the democratic distinctiveness he hoped to make universal. On the other were the undistinctive brutalities that had hitherto run the world. In an age free from disease, fear, illogic, ambition, and deception, Pericles' successors might have balanced these opposites. Thucydides would not have expected this, though, "as long as the nature of mankind remains the same."[42] The rest of his history traces the Athenians' descent from an extraordinary to an ordinary culture. It's nowhere better illustrated than in two episodes twelve years apart, both of which involved rowing.

In 428 the inhabitants of Lesbos, an island just off the coast of Asia Minor, repudiated their alliance with Athens and sought Sparta's support. Fearing the example, the Athenians blockaded Mytilene, the principal port, and sent an army to wall off the city. The Spartans promised aid but—typically—failed to provide it, and the following summer the Mytilenians surrendered. Determined to deter any further defections, Cleon, now the most prominent Athenian, called for slaughtering the men while selling the women and children into slavery: "[I]f they were right in rebelling, you must be wrong in ruling." The assembly agreed, and a trireme sailed for Mytilene bearing these orders.

But then the assembly developed second thoughts. The Athenian empire, Cleon's rival Diodotus pointed out, was supposedly a "free community." Of course it would revolt if oppressed. It made no sense "to put to death, however justly, those whom it is our interest to keep alive." The assembly voted again and Diodotus narrowly prevailed. So a second trireme was sent to overtake the first and cancel the instructions it carried—but that would require vigorous rowing.

The first boat's rowers, Thucydides writes, made no haste "upon so horrid an errand." Those on the second, tasked with preventing a horror, had reason to hurry. Given special rations of wine and barley cakes, they ate while at oars and slept only when others replaced them. Having crossed the Aegean in record time, they reached Mytilene just as the Athenian occupiers were learning, from the slower first boat, what they were expected to do. Luckily they hadn't yet done it, and no massacre took place. The danger, Thucydides understates, "had indeed been great."[43]

Then, in 416, the Athenians sent an army to Melos, an island off the Peloponnesian peninsula that had long been a Spartan colony but remained neutral in the Peloponnesian War. The Melians should now submit to Athens, they were told, not because they were entitled to—only equals possessed rights—but because "the strong do what they can and the weak suffer what they must."

Shocked by this assertion (modern readers of Thucydides still tend to be), the Melians reminded the Athenians that they'd once had a reputation for fairness: if they were now repudiating it, that would be an example "for the world to meditate upon." They'd run that risk, the Athenians replied. They sought only the best for the Melians by seeking to subdue them.

Melians: And how, pray, could it turn out to be as good for us
    to serve as for you to rule?
Athenians: Because you would have the advantage of submit-
    ting before suffering the worst, and we should gain by not
    destroying you.

Was there, the Melians asked, no third way? What harm could there be in continued neutrality? As "masters of the sea," the Athenians responded, they required obedience, not friendship, from all islands. The Spartans, known for delay, wouldn't rush to rescue any of them.

Unwilling to relinquish their independence, placing faith in the hope that the world didn't really work this way, the Melians refused to yield. So the Athenians brought reinforcements and in 415—with no Spartan help in sight—Melos surrendered. The Athenians this time had no second thoughts and sent no second triremes. Instead, Thucydides records, they "put to death all the grown men whom they took, and sold the women and children for slaves, and subsequently sent out five hundred colonists and settled the place themselves."[44]

Spirits are indeed shadowy things, and Thucydides took them less seriously than did Herodotus. Still his history suggests that the spirit of Pericles shaped Athenian behavior toward *both* Mytilene and Melos. The younger man would have cheered the rowers racing across the Aegean fueled by wine and barley cakes: their energy in pursuit of a humane objective was what democratic universality was all about. But the older Pericles, fearing concessions, might well have applauded the inhumane mission to Melos. For as Thucydides grimly observes, war "brings most men's character to a level with their fortunes."[45] The greatest of the Athenians was no exception.

XIII.

Why, though, did Pericles fear concessions? The war had been one of choice, not necessity. Even after voting for it the Spartans offered ways out, none of which he took. Instead Pericles convinced himself that he couldn't concede a molehill—the Megarian decree—without a mountainous loss of credibility. But with the completion of the long walls a quarter century earlier, he'd conceded *all of Attica,* except for Athens and Piraeus, if a war with the Spartans ever broke out. What now made Megara worth that risk?

An explanation may lie in an American experience twenty-four centuries later. On January 12, 1950, Secretary of State Dean Acheson announced that the United States would henceforth rely on naval and air power to hold a "defensive perimeter" of offshore islands—Japan, Okinawa, the Philippines—in the western Pacific. With this decision, carefully considered at its highest levels, the Truman administration appeared to have conceded the rest of East Asia to the Soviet Union, the newly proclaimed People's Republic of China, and their dependencies.[46] These long walls were liquid, but they gave up more ground than Pericles could ever have imagined.

And yet, when the North Koreans invaded South Korea on June 25, 1950—Kim Il-sung and Stalin having read Acheson's speech— President Truman decided *within a day* to send American troops, under the command of General Douglas MacArthur, to defend that mainland position. MacArthur's successes brought China into the Korean War, which ended in a stalemate only in 1953. More than thirty-six thousand Americans died fighting for a country their government had openly deemed insignificant five months before starting to send them there.[47]

"Island" strategies require steady nerves. You have to be able to watch smoke rise on horizons you once controlled without losing your own self-confidence, or shaking that of allies, or strengthening that of adversaries. Building walls and proclaiming perimeters can be rational choices, for it makes little sense to pursue lost causes with limited resources. But strategy isn't always a rational enterprise.

Reassuring withdrawals, Clausewitz writes in *On War*, "are very rare." More often armies and nations fail to distinguish orderly disengagements from abject capitulations—or foresight from fear.

> There will be public concern and resentment at the fate of abandoned areas; the army will possibly lose confidence not only in its leaders but in itself, and never-ending, rear guard actions will only tend to confirm its fears. *These consequences* of retreat should not be underrated.[48]

That's what worried Pericles about the Megarian decree. No one in normal times would have thought it a test of Athenian resolve, but the escalations of 432–31 had made it so. Truman saw South Korea similarly. In itself, it was nothing. But when the North Koreans attacked—something they could have done only with Stalin's support—it became everything.

This, then, is how leaders dismantle walls they've built separating vital from peripheral interests. For the abstractions of strategy and the emotions of strategists can never be separated: they can only be balanced. The weight attached to each, however, will vary with circumstances. And the heat of emotions requires only an instant to melt abstractions drawn from years of cool reflection. Decades devoid of reflection may follow.

XIV.

Few historians would claim that Truman made the wrong choice in Korea; but Pericles' biographers have always wondered about the Megarian decree.[49] He had to *tell* the Athenians that their credibility was on the line: this would not otherwise have occurred to them. Truman didn't have to do that with the Americans and their allies. They *knew*.

The distinction is important. It's one thing for an enemy to test your resolve in a manner that all can see: you can then decide, in consultation with others, what to do, and you can usually determine when you've done it. It's quite another thing to test your nation's resolve against your own insecurities, for where do these stop? What prevents projecting anxieties onto indefinitely expanding screens? If the safety of Athens required retaining the Megarian decree, then why not suppressing the Mytilenians? Or killing the Melians? Or fighting a *land* war far from home against an enemy allied with the Spartan *navy*?

This last slope began slipping in the late 420s when Segesta and Selinus, two cities in western Sicily, revived an ancient quarrel. Syracuse, the largest city on the island, supported the Selinuntines, so the Segestans in 416–15 appealed to the Athenians, who'd earlier but vaguely promised protection. If Syracuse went unpunished, the Segestans insisted, it would take over all of Sicily, after which the Sicilians would join the Spartans and their allies, after which they'd together destroy the Athenian empire.[50]

The scenario echoed Epidamnus, Corcyra, and Corinth, but the logic seemed less plausible. Why would Syracuse, the only other democracy in the Mediterranean, align itself with the authoritarian Spartans? Even if it did, how could Athens defeat a city at least as large as itself on an island larger than the Peloponnese across eight hundred miles of ocean? Reputation wasn't at stake: having just slaughtered the nearby Melians, the Athenians would hardly seem weak abandoning the distant Segestans. And if Athens did rescue those precariously perched sparrows, how many others would demand equivalent care?

The Athenian assembly had always responded more to emotions than to abstractions, while relying on leaders to cool it off. Now, though, few were left. It dismissed protests from Nicias, the city's most experienced general, against being dragged into a war "with which we have nothing to do." It welcomed seduction by Alcibiades, better known for his dazzling looks and Olympics prowess than for his prudence. Sicily's defenders, this peacock claimed, were a rabble easily bribed. Their defeat would win Athens a western Mediterranean empire. Nor should anyone try to say where its expansion should stop, for "if we cease to rule others, we shall be in danger of being ruled ourselves." That, however, had been Pericles' defense of the Megarian decree.

Trapped now between the aura of Alcibiades and the ghost of Pericles, the desperate Nicias inflated his estimates of what the expedition would cost, but this only encouraged further enthusiasm. So the assembly sent him to Sicily in 415 with an immense armada—164 triremes and transport ships, 5,100 hoplites, 480 archers, 700 slingers, 30 horsemen—together with, as his co-commander, Alcibiades, who silkenly reminded everyone that "neither youth nor old age can do anything . . . without the other."[51]

Once there, though, neither youth nor age helped. Nicias was lethargic and often ill. Alcibiades, recalled to Athens to stand trial for debauchery, defected instead to the Spartans. Knowing the difficulties of sailing with horses, the Athenians hadn't brought enough: their adversaries had a surplus. The Sicilians fought bravely, more than matching Athenian reinforcements. Sensing opportunity, the Spartans for once acted quickly and imaginatively: they combined with the Corinthians to send a fleet of their own, which caught and sank that of the Athenians in the Syracusans' great harbor.

Unlike Xerxes after Salamis, the Athenians now had no way home. With morale deteriorating and discipline crumbling, they lost a critical battle by inadvertently revealing their password. They ran short of food and resorted to drinking bloody water. They abandoned their dead on the battlefield, an unheard-of sacrilege. They had no choice, in the end, but to surrender, only to be imprisoned for months within the Syracuse quarries, bereft of shade or sustenance, surrounded by rotting corpses. "[N]o single suffering to be apprehended by men," Thucydides laments, "was spared them."[52]

Strategy requires a sense of the whole that reveals the significance of respective parts. The Athenians lost this in Sicily. Well over half of their empire's military wound up there, but few returned. Meanwhile, as a modern historian has pointed out, "Spartans were camped thirteen miles from the walls of Athens, thousands of slaves were deserting from Attica, and tribute-paying allies from the Hellespont to the southern Aegean were on the verge of revolt."[53] The disproportions *approach* the inexplicable—but before leaving them there, it might be worth recalling Thucydides' reminders about the future.

XV.

Two thousand three hundred and eighty-two years after the Athenian surrender on Sicily the United States had 543,000 troops committed to the defense of what Henry Kissinger would later call "a small peninsula on a major continent."[54] By 1969, two hundred

Americans were being killed in Indochina each week: when South Vietnam surrendered in 1975, 58,213 Americans had died trying to save it.[55] That made Vietnam the fourth costliest war the United States has fought, the first it clearly lost, and in its rationale the most difficult to explain.

No Korea-like blitzkrieg began the war: the North Vietnamese ran it as a slowly escalating insurgency, resorting to conventional operations only as the Americans were withdrawing. Nor was Vietnam a proxy war for a larger power. Hanoi determined its outbreak, conduct, and settlement, with the Soviet Union and China providing irregular and at times even reluctant support.[56] Worried more about the possibility of war *with each other* during the late 1960s, both would soon seek *alignment* with Washington.[57]

Meanwhile, much was going on elsewhere. In 1969, the Soviet Union surpassed the United States in strategic missile capabilities. In 1968, it crushed the "Prague Spring," the most promising effort so far to reform Marxism-Leninism from within. In 1967, Israel reshaped the Middle East by defeating its Arab rivals and occupying the West Bank. In 1966, France withdrew its military forces from NATO, East and West Germany began diplomatic contacts, and China launched the Great Cultural Revolution. In 1965, race riots and antiwar protests in the United States reached levels not seen since the Civil War. And throughout the 1960s, a self-proclaimed Soviet satellite survived ninety miles off the coast of Florida, despite having hosted nuclear-tipped missiles that could have started—and perhaps ended—World War III.

Why, then, did the Americans invest so much in Vietnam when, in comparison with the whole of their interests at the time, so little was at stake there? Thucydidean resemblances, I think, suggest an answer. Megara might look like a trifle, Pericles told the Athenians in 432 B.C.E., but if they yielded on that small matter "you will instantly have to meet some greater demand." "Without the United States," John F. Kennedy warned a Texas audience on the morning of November 22, 1963, "South Viet-Nam would collapse overnight," and American alliances everywhere were equally vulnerable. There was no choice, Pericles insisted, but to "resist our enemies in any way and in every way." For, as Kennedy added: "We are still the keystone in the arch of freedom."[58]

However distant they may be in time and space, statements like these perch precariously across scale. For if credibility is always in doubt, then capabilities must become infinite or bluffs must become routine. Neither approach is sustainable: that's why walls exist in the first place. They buffer what's important from what's not. When one's own imprecisions pull walls down—as Pericles and Kennedy did when they dismissed the possibility of giving anything up—then fears become images, images become projections, and projections as they expand blur into indistinctiveness.

XVI.

Soon after Saigon fell, each officer assigned to the United States Naval War College for the 1975–76 academic year received a puzzling package in the mail. Inside was a thick paperback, with instructions to read it—all of it—before arrival in Newport. Most had served in Vietnam, some several times. All knew someone who'd been killed or wounded there. None wanted to talk about it, and there were as yet few histories to read. But we did now have Thucydides, and that was enough.

Although younger than all of my "students" and with no military experience, I'd been recruited to co-teach "Strategy and Policy" by Admiral Stansfield Turner, a man with flexible views on credentials but firm ones on the relevance of the classics to contemporary affairs.[59] He was determined that we would cover Vietnam—we were, after all, a war college and he was its president—even if we had to get there by a 2,500-year detour. And so I began discussing, with my seminar, an ancient Greek previously known to me only as a stern piece of statuary.

In the spirit of Thucydides, we were soon reflecting on resemblances, at first in general terms—walls, armies, navies, ideologies, empires—and then more specifically on strategies: did the Athenians or the Spartans better adapt objectives to capabilities? And then analogies: did this tell us anything about the Cold War? And then democracies: did the one in Athens defeat itself? And then: what could the Athenians have been thinking when they sent an *army* to, of all places, *Sicily*? At which point there was silence, followed by a falling away of all constraints. Vietnam was not only up for discussion: it was for weeks all we talked about. We were doing post-traumatic stress therapy before it had a name. Thucydides trained us.

It took me decades to figure out why this worked. The answer at last came in another seminar, for newly arrived Yale freshmen, in the fall of 2008. These students were young enough to have been grandchildren of the officers I'd known at Newport. None had any experience of war. They did, however, have Tolstoy, for in the spirit of Admiral Turner, I'd required them to read every line of *War and Peace*. They not only did so, but began bringing it up even on days when I hadn't assigned it. One day I asked what connection Prince Andrei, Natasha, and the bumbling Pierre could possibly have to their very different lives? There was, as at Newport, a moment of silence. Then three students simultaneously said the same thing: "They make us feel less lonely."

Thucydides wouldn't have put it in that way, but I suspect this is what he meant when he encouraged his readers to seek "knowledge of the past as an aid to the understanding of the future, which in the course of human things must resemble if it does not reflect it." For without some sense of the past the future can be only loneliness: amnesia is a solitary affliction. But to know the past only in static terms—as moments frozen in time and space—would be almost as disabling, because we're the progeny of progressions *across* time and space that *shift* from small scales to big ones and back again. We know these through narratives, whether historical or fictional or a combination of both. Thucydides and Tolstoy are, therefore, closer than you might think, and we're fortunate to be able to attend *their* seminars whenever we like.

CHAPTER THREE

TEACHERS AND TETHERS

Half a world away from the Hellespont bridges and the Athenian long walls, the ancient Chinese, knowing nothing of Xerxes or Pericles, were preparing a manual on aligning aspirations with capabilities. Sun Tzu may have been one person or many and *The Art of War* could have been compiled over several centuries: in that sense, it's more like Homer than Herodotus or Thucydides. But the Greek epics and histories depict distinctive events and individuals. They leave it to us to draw lessons.

Sun Tzu, in contrast, sets forth *principles,* selected for validity across time and space, and then connects them to *practices,* bound by time and space. *The Art of War,* therefore, is neither history nor biography. It's a compilation of precepts, procedures—and categorical claims: "If a general who heeds my strategy is employed, he is certain to win. Retain him! When one who refuses to listen to my strategy is employed, he is certain to be defeated. Dismiss him!"

That's straightforward enough, but what's the strategy? "The nature of water is that it avoids heights and hastens to the lowlands," Master Sun tells us. "[T]he nature of logs and stones is that on stable ground they are static; on unstable ground, they move. If square, they stop; if round, they roll." And, more succinctly: "Do not gobble proffered baits." Sun Tzu might as well have advised us, with Shakespeare's Polonius, to "neither a borrower nor a lender be." Or, from Marketing 101, to "buy low and sell high."

Except that history is full of borrowers and lenders who bought high but had to sell low. They disengaged their practices from their principles. They couldn't resist proffered baits. What look like platitudes, in *The Art of War*, are in fact *tethers*, meant to prevent such separations. "[T]he shape of an army resembles water," Sun Tzu goes on to explain. If you attack where your enemy least expects it—if you "avoid his strength and strike his emptiness"—then, "like water, none can oppose you." Logs and stones illustrate leverage: "[O]ne need use but little strength to achieve much." And on proffering: "The fish which covets bait is caught; troops who covet bait are defeated."[1]

Polonius's pontifications float freely above landscapes, which is why Hamlet mocks him:

Hamlet: Do you see yonder cloud that's almost in shape of a camel?

Polonius: By the mass, and 'tis like a camel indeed.

Hamlet: Methinks it is like a weasel.

Polonius: It is backed like a weasel.

Hamlet: Or like a whale.

Polonius: Very like a whale.[2]

Sun Tzu would never put up with this. He lures lightning from thunderstorms with kite, string, and key. He grounds each precept in some crackling sharp reality. He tethers what's obvious to what's much less so: how states, without defeating themselves, can win wars.

"Having paid heed to the advantages of my plans," Master Sun advises, generals "should act expediently in accordance with what is advantageous." The tautology itself tethers, for the "advantages" of which he writes lie in the "advantageous" situations that make leverage possible. Wise leaders will seek these out. They'll sail with winds, not against them. They'll skirt swamps, not slog through them. They'll avoid battles until they're sure they can win them. They'll try to benefit from the absence in life—if not in games—of level playing fields. They'll understand the futility, as my Naval War College students used to like to put it, of "shoveling shit uphill."

"War is a matter of vital importance to the State," Sun Tzu warns, not to be embarked upon "without due reflection." Xerxes and Alcibiades didn't reflect. Artabanus and Nicias did so unduly. Master Sun reflects but then acts, deploying maximum leverage against minimal resistance. Success comes as quickly as the least expenditure of resources and lives allows. "Know the enemy, know yourself," *The Art of War* exhorts. "Know the ground, know the weather. Your victory will *then* be total."[3]

But wouldn't that require knowing everything before you could do anything? Artabanus had no answer when Xerxes asked, but Sun Tzu does: simplicity, he shows, coexists with complexity and can guide us through it.

The musical notes are only five in number, but their melodies are so numerous that one cannot hear them all. The primary colors are only five in number but their combinations are so infinite that one cannot visualize them all. The flavors are only five in number but their blends are so various that one cannot taste them all. In battle there are only the normal and extraordinary forces, but their combinations are limitless; none can comprehend them all.[4]

No one can anticipate everything that might happen. Sensing possibilities, though, is better than having no sense at all of what to expect. Sun Tzu seeks sense—even common sense—by tethering principles, which are few, to practices, which are many. He fits the mix to the moment, as if setting sound levels on a synthesizer, or color combinations on a computer screen. He leaves enough options to satisfy any fox, while retaining the purposefulness of a hedgehog. He keeps opposing ideas in his mind by projecting them across time, space, *and* scale.

Leadership in *The Art of War*, then, is seeing simplicities in complexity. Some realities are as easily grasped as Sun Tzu's five fundamental sounds, colors, and flavors: that's how we know their nature. But when simplicities mix, complexities become endless. No matter how thoroughly we prepare, they'll always surprise us. If tethered to principles, however, they need not paralyze us. And how might you learn to tether? By having great teachers, I think, for tethering is what they have us do.

I.

For someone with so many names—Caius Octavius Thurinus, Caius Julius Caesar Octavianus, Imperator Caesar *Divi Filius*, Imperator

Caesar Augustus *Divi Filius*, Imperator Caesar Augustus *Divi Filius Pater Patriae*—he started out with relatively little. He was born into the family of a respectable but forgettable Roman senator in 63 B.C.E. By the time he was twenty, he was a third of a ruling triumvirate. He became at thirty-two the most powerful man in the "western" world. He died peacefully at seventy-six in a bed he'd selected, an extraordinary accomplishment for an emperor of that era—all the more so for his never having used that title. His life fed rumors, long before his death, that strange signs had preceded his birth: even an unusual if not immaculate conception (something about a snake). In fact, though—apart from a teacher's timely launch—the kid made it mostly on his own.[5]

The Greeks had Chiron the centaur instructing Achilles and other epic heroes: the Romans got by, well enough, with Julius Caesar. His conquests had doubled, within two decades, the size of their "republic's" empire.[6] His histories, two thousand years later, elicit readership and respect. After crossing the Rubicon— the real one—in 49, he became Rome's paramount leader, determined to restore order after a half century of civil wars. But Caesar, then in his fifties, had little time left, as Plutarch puts it, to "outdo his past actions by his future." His haste made him, on March 15, 44, the most famous assassination victim ever. Caesar's life *and* death, therefore, were exemplary. He taught what to do *and* what not to do.[7]

Caesar had no living legitimate children, but he did have Octavian, a promising great-nephew, to whom he'd awarded the Roman equivalent of an internship. Octavian's assignment was to "shadow" Caesar around Rome, then join him in Spain on what turned out to be his last military campaign. The young man handled the proximity well, always observing, never presuming, building his résumé and stamina—his health was always delicate—for what Caesar might next have in mind. Octavian was training for an offensive against the Parthians when word reached him, in Macedonia, of the murder in Rome two weeks earlier. He was only eighteen. "We will talk later," the novelist John Williams imagines him telling disconsolate friends. "Now I must think of what this will mean."[8]

His first decision was to return to Rome without knowing who was in charge or how he'd be received. The stakes skyrocketed when he learned, after landing near Brundisium, that Caesar's will had made him an heir and—by adoption—a son. He reached the capital as Caius Julius Caesar Octavianus,[9] and out of respect for their martyred leader the legions he encountered took his new status seriously. Octavian could have blown the opportunity by coming across as a twerp. But he saw the difference, even then, between inheriting a title and mastering the art of command. The first can happen overnight. The second can take a lifetime.

Octavian never explained how he learned this, but with the privilege of closely observing the greatest of all commanders, he'd had to have been a blockhead not to pick up something. Sun Tzu, untranslated in Europe for another eighteen centuries, suggests what it might have been:

> If wise, a commander is able to recognize changing circumstances and to act expediently. If sincere, his men will have no doubt of the certainty of rewards and punishments. If humane, he loves mankind, sympathizes with others, and appreciates their industry and toil. If courageous, he gains victory by seizing opportunity without hesitation. If strict, his troops are disciplined because they are in awe of him and are afraid of punishment.[10]

Caesar, in turn, appears never to have explained to Octavian why he was being taught.[11] That spared him the hang-ups of knowing he'd be son, heir, and commander. Rome's Chiron tethered a student who had little sense of being tethered. The constraint conveyed instruction *and* liberation.[12]

II.

Octavian would need both if he were to go beyond just taking the cheers of his great-uncle's legions. His own stepfather thought it too dangerous to accept Caesar's inheritance or title. Cicero, the famous orator and a family friend, considered both undeserved. Even Mark Antony, who made Rome uncomfortable for Caesar's assassins, tried to do the same for the "boy" who had taken Caesar's name. In his capacity as consul, Antony withheld the bequest Caesar had left to the citizens of the city, and kept Octavian waiting when—without success—he came to protest.

His response was to leverage limited assets. Octavian pledged his own wealth to the Romans and, when this proved insufficient, borrowed to provide more. The risk paid off, making Antony look cheap. It was easier to turn Cicero, a well-known weather vane. He loved flattery and Octavian gave it freely, even though Cicero had welcomed Caesar's assassination. For Cicero also hated Antony, and it was useful to have him denouncing the consul on a more epic scale— the *Philippics,* fourteen furious speeches in the Roman senate—than Octavian could ever have managed. His chief preoccupation during the summer of 44 was staging Caesar's funeral games, unexpectedly under a comet. It was not a bad omen, Octavian acrobatically assured the Romans: it was his great-uncle's soul ascending to immortality.[13]

Agility too, however, could go only so far: Octavian's longer-term prospects required retaining the loyalty of Caesar's armies and he'd as yet little military experience. Antony was no Caesar, but he had a lot. What he lacked was Octavian's skill in taking initiatives, setting up sequences, and benefiting accordingly.[14] Drawing on his Macedonian ties, Octavian seized the funds Caesar had reserved for the offensive—now canceled—against the Parthians. He then sent agents with bonuses to greet troops disembarking at Brundisium. Caught off guard, Antony rushed there, failed to match the largesse, lost his temper, and ordered decimations: arbitrary executions of every tenth man in several units. The bloodshed restored discipline, but with such resentment that the Macedonian legions defected, as soon as they got the chance, to the man they were now coming to regard, in name and in fact, as the new Caesar.[15]

Octavian was less than half Antony's age, but he was the far shrewder judge of character. He made himself a foil for the older man's flaws: massive debts, sexual promiscuity, public drunkenness, explosive volatility.[16] Caesar's heir was no prude and he certainly had a temper, but he sensed the need for self-control—Antony rarely did. Nor was Antony ever quite sure what he wanted. He'd known of, but not participated in, the assassination plot. He hoped to rule Rome, but hadn't decided what he'd do with it if he had it. He allowed drift and depravities to deprive him of purpose. Octavian in contrast focused, from the moment Caesar's will let him know who he was, on avenging his "father's" death, on completing Rome's rehabilitation, and on *not* winding up in a bloody heap on the senate floor.[17]

III.

That required self-assessment, a skill not even Caesar mastered—
hence the bloody heap—which Octavian with difficulty acquired.
Shortly after his return from Macedonia he mistook the acclaim of
Caesar's veterans for a mandate to march on Rome, as the great general himself had earlier done. But Octavian's Rubicon was not yet in
sight: his troops refused to fight Antony's, and the Romans weren't
ready to welcome a teenage dictator. The fiasco humiliated Octavian. He'd try harder, henceforth, to keep his enthusiasms within
his competencies.

He'd known, since childhood, that he got sick easily. What he
hadn't known, until it was almost too late, was that something like
this also happened before battles.[18] Perhaps it was physical, perhaps
psychological, but it looked like cowardice. Octavian first experienced the problem at the first battle in which he participated, near
Mutina, in northern Italy, in April 43. He'd merged his forces with
those supporting Cicero and the senate to take on Antony, still a
formidable figure. Rome's new consuls Hirtius and Pansa led their
legions courageously and would die from their wounds, as would
many of Octavian's men. He on the first day, however, was conspic-
uously invisible. No one, even now, is sure why.

Octavian recognized quickly, though, that this wouldn't do. And
so on the second day he rallied himself and his troops, led them
through enemy lines, retrieved Hirtius' body as well as a lost standard, and forced Antony to withdraw. With one consul dead, the
other dying, and his adversary fleeing, Octavian achieved, through
sheer will, a victory worthy of Caesar himself. He didn't rush back
to Rome, however, to claim his triumph. He waited until he was

sure of support from the deceased consuls' legions—and until Antony, now in Gaul, had had time to regroup. Then Octavian crossed his Rubicon with an army that respected him, reinforced by another, more distant, that Cicero and his fellow senators had reason to fear. Octavian only at that point claimed the consulship, the most powerful position in Rome. He was not yet twenty.[19]

From this position of strength, Octavian worried about his *weaknesses*. To run Rome was not to control its empire. Antony, despite Mutina, remained unchallenged in Gaul. Caesar's assassins Cassius and Marcus Brutus were recruiting armies in Syria and Macedonia. Sextus Pompeius, the son of Caesar's old adversary Pompey, had seized Sicily. The Roman senate itself, where the conspiracy against Caesar had been hatched, could do anything if not carefully watched. Self-assessment for the triumphant Octavian, then, suggested the need for help, even if from distasteful sources. For as one of his biographers has pointed out: "To remove a rival was to remove a potential ally."[20]

IV.

He started with Antony, on an island in a river near Mutina, in the fall of 43. Octavian, with his legions, marched north from Rome while Antony, with his, proceeded south from Gaul, bringing along Lepidus, a complaisant former consul.[21] Together they had more troops than Octavian, but he demanded equal treatment. And so, as their guards watched warily from both banks, the three warlords— one barely beyond adolescence—divided most of the world they knew.[22]

To Octavian's disadvantage, it might at first seem. Antony got the best parts of Gaul, Lepidus took Spain and the routes from Italy to it, and Octavian had to content himself with Sardinia, Sicily, and the African coast, where he'd have to fight Sextus Pompeius. Octavian also gave up his consulship, allowing the triumvirate to rule Rome. At this stage, however, status meant more than substance. He preferred, from an inferior position, to be one of three: ruling alone could await superiority. Meanwhile, there were scores to settle.

While on the island, Antony, Lepidus, and Octavian exchanged names of prominent Romans to be killed, their properties seized, and their families exiled. The most prominent of those "proscribed" was Cicero, who'd always talked too much. Despite his sensitivity to the way winds blew, he'd infuriated Antony with the *Philippics.* That triumvir didn't just have the orator executed: he had Cicero's head, along with the hand that had drafted the speeches, nailed to the rostrum in the Roman Forum.[23]

It's unlikely that Octavian would have ordered such a display, but it's equally unlikely that he tried to prevent it. Cicero had swung around to praising him publicly as a promising youth, but couldn't help hinting privately that so inexperienced a leader could always be discarded if necessary. The suggestion got back to Octavian, who filed it for future reference.[24] With Antony now an ally, he had no further need for Cicero's *Philippics,* or his applause, or his indiscretions. Which is to say that Octavian had no further need of Cicero.

The triumvirate's next priority was to proscribe Brutus and Cassius, but that would require their military defeat. In a strange echo of Cicero, the battle took place at Philippi, in Thrace, in the fall of 42.[25] Antony commanded for the triumvirate while Lepidus stayed behind to run Rome. Octavian disembarked his legions in Macedonia but immediately fell ill, reaching the battlefield only on a litter. From an unfavorable position and against fortified lines, Antony surprised Cassius and then Brutus, leading each to commit suicide. The only triumvir capable of commanding had achieved a complete victory.

Furious with himself, Octavian lashed out at others. He humiliated and even executed captives. After Antony honored Brutus' corpse, Octavian is said to have desecrated it, sending the head back to Rome to be placed before his great-uncle's statue—fortunately it sank in a shipwreck on the way. Octavian himself, upon his return, found the city's citizens cowering, for fear of what he might do next. Too old now to be an immature tyrant, he was nonetheless behaving like one.[26]

V.

But Octavian regained self-control, partly through an improvised show of resolve, partly by getting help, and partly with a more disciplined resort to brutality. Antony stayed in the east after Philippi, ostensibly to resume Caesar's campaign against the Parthians, but probably also to dodge the responsibility of distributing land, in Italy, to soldiers whose service was no longer needed. That task fell to Octavian, and there was no way he could perform it without infuriating the landowners displaced or the veterans disappointed. Meanwhile, Sextus Pompeius, from his Sicilian base, was slowly shutting down Rome's grain supply from across the Mediterranean.

The crunch came one day in 41 when Octavian was late for a meeting with recently discharged soldiers. Angered by the delay, they slaughtered a centurion who'd tried to keep order. Octavian arrived, viewed the body, asked the men to behave better in the future, and proceeded to hand out allocations. His calm so shamed the former troops that they demanded the murderers' punishment. Octavian agreed, but only on the condition that the perpetrators acknowledge their guilt, and that the veterans approve their sentences. He'd called forth courage and composure in a dangerous situation—qualities not evident after Philippi—and so began his own reputational rehabilitation.[27]

That led Antony's wife Fulvia and his brother Lucius to try to depose Octavian before he won too much support. Lucius seized the fortified town of Perusia in central Italy, while Fulvia recruited troops in and around Rome. Still in the east, Antony knew what was happening but was distracted, having proclaimed himself the new Dionysius, dressed the part, and fallen in love with Cleopatra of Egypt, with whom Caesar had had a protracted affair. Antony claimed to be raising funds for the offensive against the Parthians and to be securing Rome's food: Egypt had no shortage of gold or grain.[28] But he handed Octavian an opportunity.

Knowing now that he was no battlefield commander, Octavian turned over the siege at Perusia to Quintus Salvidienus Rufus and Marcus Vipsanius Agrippa, two friends who'd been with him in Macedonia at the time of Caesar's assassination. They quickly forced Lucius' surrender, while Fulvia's armies simply melted away. Octavian had the sense this time to delegate his authority, not to try to exercise it where he doubted his own competence.[29]

He had no such doubts when it came to deterrence. Determined to prevent any further rebellions, Octavian brought three hundred senatorial-rank prisoners back to Rome, condemned them to death, and had them sacrificed on the site of Caesar's cremation. Such practices had long been suppressed, but Octavian broke the rules to make two points. He'd tolerate no further opposition from within the city. And he himself, by shedding blood in the center of Rome, could claim at last to have avenged Julius Caesar's murder.[30]

VI.

The empire was now a duopoly—Octavian and Antony had side-tracked Lepidus in Africa—but its halves weren't run in the same way. Octavian, in Rome, was learning what to do with power once he had it. Antony, still in the east and after Philippi the stronger of the two, was forgetting what he'd known about the same thing. Each still disliked the other; each trusted the other even less. One, however, retained a purpose and acted accordingly. The other, when he acted at all, reacted. It was no longer much of a contest.

Perusia revealed the pattern. Octavian first reconstituted respect in Rome by navigating the treacherous currents of land redistribution. He then won a battle by entrusting its conduct to others with superior military skills. Finally, he fortified his authority against further insurrections by publicly executing prominent rebels, an act of violence sufficiently precise in its victims and clear in its intentions that it prevented more violence. Octavian was thinking ahead: how one decision can be made to affect what happens next.

Antony wasn't. The latest division of the empire had given him all of Gaul, but he was in Greece, preparing to move—in the opposite direction—against the Parthians. Suddenly his governor in Gaul died. Octavian, who from Rome was much closer, rushed there and took command of eleven legions. It was a direct challenge to Antony, who put off the Parthians, ordered his armies back to Italy, and began arranging with Sextus Pompeius a land and sea offensive that would wipe out Octavian altogether.

But Antony brought more ships than he needed and not enough men, for Octavian had also occupied Brundisium. He again fell ill before any battles took place, but this allowed time for troops on both sides to fraternize, and then to demand that their commanders make peace. At that point, Antony lost the resolve that had propelled him across the Adriatic: he abandoned Sextus, acknowledged Octavian's authority in Gaul, and returned his attention to the Parthians. Not, however, before securing—or so he thought—the new settlement. His wife Fulvia having died shortly after her failed coup, Antony now married Octavia, the beloved sister of the "boy" with "only a name."[31]

There's no way Octavian could have planned all of this.[32] He couldn't have anticipated that angry veterans would kill a centurion, or that Fulvia and Lucius would rebel without Antony's support, or that the governor of Gaul would die, or that Antony would miscalculate his logistics, or that his troops and Octavian's would refuse to fight, or that Antony would reverse course and wed his sister. Unlike Pericles, Octavian never tried to forge, from contingent events, causal chains.[33]

Instead he seized opportunities while retaining objectives. He saw next steps where Antony stumbled. Octavian stuck to his compass heading while avoiding swamps: it's almost as if Antony sought out swamps, sank into them, and then got bored with them. He was, Plutarch concludes, "full of empty flourishes and unsteady efforts for glory."[34]

VII.

Which could hardly be said of Sextus Pompeius, the most formidable enemy Octavian ever faced. His father Pompey's greatest achievement had been to suppress piracy throughout the Mediterranean, but Sextus saw its political uses and could revive it, from Sicily, whenever he wanted. That endangered Rome, because the city and its surroundings relied so heavily on food imports, mostly from Egypt. Sextus had the Romans, if not by their necks, then by their stomachs.

Antony's reconciliation with Octavian gave Sextus a grievance, and by the end of 40, he'd blockaded Italy. That provoked a riot in Rome, which Octavian, recalling his success with the angry veterans, tried again to stare down. This time, though, he was pelted with stones and might have been killed had not Antony rushed in soldiers to rescue him. No one could doubt, any longer, Octavian's bravery. But in proving it he'd risked his life—to be saved only by Antony's lack of foresight. For this was his last chance to rid himself of, without assassinating, an exasperating rival.[35]

Negotiations with Sextus having failed, Octavian decided to invade Sicily and secure the supply routes permanently. He knew nothing about navies, though, and Sextus easily defeated the Roman fleets, one of which Octavian commanded. And so the ruler of half the empire found himself shipwrecked on the Italian side of the Strait of Messina with only a few other survivors, no food or supplies, and no means of summoning help except by lighting fires in the hills, hoping for the best. Fortunately a passing legion saw these and rescued Octavian, in time for him to watch a storm, on the next day, complete the destruction of his armada.[36]

But he appears not to have fallen ill, or to have despaired, or to have rethought taking Sicily. Instead he regrouped, secured the Italian coast against raids by Sextus, and placed Agrippa—just back from pacifying the Gauls—in charge of the next offensive. Twenty-four at the time, he had no greater nautical experience than Octavian. But

where Octavian had come to rely, in crises, on simply showing resolve, Agrippa prepared on a scale worthy of Xerxes. He rearranged
topography by linking two lakes, hidden by forested mountains, to
the sea. The forests provided wood to build warships, the lakes became training facilities for crews, and the mountains hid it all from
Sextus, who could only guess what was happening from offshore.[37]

It took two years, but by 36 Agrippa was ready. Three fleets
would converge on Sicily: his own, another formed from ships
Antony had supplied, and a third commanded by Lepidus sailing
from Africa. The first two ran into storms, however, and only
Lepidus successfully landed troops—whereupon he began collabo-
rating with Sextus. Who had, again, surprised and humiliated
Octavian: he wound up stranded this time on the Sicilian coast
until his armies could find him. It was Octavian's third rescue in as
many years.

Agrippa, however, retained enough of his fleet to overwhelm
that of Sextus, driving him into exile while leaving Lepidus, who
had again switched sides, in charge of Sicily. Having suffered a long-
overdue physical collapse, Octavian played no part in this battle,
but he recovered in time to claim a symbolic victory. Suspecting
that Lepidus had flipped once too often, Octavian appeared at his
camp one day, alone and unarmed. He took some blows, shed blood,
and began to retreat, but found the men following because they admired his audacity: this time he required no rescue. Lepidus could
only surrender.[38]

So Octavian triumphed in Sicily after all, but more by show than
through strategy: he repeatedly risked his life, while relying on
Agrippa's steady hand. Once he'd prevailed, though, Octavian stead-
ied himself. He forced Lepidus from the triumvirate but allowed a
dignified retirement—there were no executions or exhibitions of

body parts. That left only Antony to contest Octavian's rule over the Roman world. And Octavian had the good sense, this time, to let his adversary defeat himself.

VIII.

Having promised so often to fight the Parthians, Antony could no longer delay doing so.[39] He began his campaign in 36, as Octavian and Agrippa were completing their conquest of Sicily. Antony relied, for supplies and funds, on his former and future lover Cleopatra, a greater delicacy than it might have been had he not married Octavian's sister. Reasons of state could justify both relationships but only awkwardly, another problem Antony appears not to have anticipated. That he and Cleopatra had had twins made the situation no simpler. Nor did Cleopatra's claim, probably true, that she was the mother of Julius Caesar's only biological son: the young man's name, dangerously, was Caesarion.[40]

If Antony juggled mistresses, matrimony, and politics badly, the same was true of his military operations against the Parthians. He started too late to finish before winter, then accidentally revealed his plans to a spy, then failed to ensure the loyalty of allies along the way, and finally left his supply train so inadequately guarded that the Parthians destroyed it. He had no choice, at that point, but to order a costly retreat through snowstorms to the Syrian coast, where Cleopatra took her time re-equipping him. Antony reported to Rome, though, that all was well.

Octavian didn't believe this, but took Antony at his word. He ordered victory celebrations, knowing that these would discredit his rival all the more than if he seemed to be welcoming Antony's defeats. He then withheld reinforcements, citing Antony's dispatches as evidence that he didn't need them. Octavian did send Octavia with supplies from Greece, though, counting on her arrival alongside those from Cleopatra to complicate the situation still further. Antony took the replenishments but ordered Octavia back to Rome, fueling rumors of a revived affair with the Egyptian queen. Octavian chose not to deflate these, trusting that Antony, through self-inflation, would confirm them soon enough.[41]

That happened when the word got out that Antony had deposited a will—supposedly inviolately—with Rome's vestal virgins. Octavian demanded that they hand it over, and when they refused he seized it. The breach of tradition was shocking: Octavian gambled, however, that the will's contents would be even more so, and he was right. It recognized Caesarion as Julius Caesar's son and it conveyed Antony's request, even if he died in Italy, to be buried beside Cleopatra in Egypt.

Antony was no longer Roman in the eyes of Romans: if he should ever rule the empire, they feared, it would cease to be Roman too.[42] That was the final break. Octavian arranged it, Antony blundered into it, and it remained only for war to settle. This required a single significant battle, at sea off the Greek coast near Actium, in September of 31. Antony and Cleopatra placed their ships and armies in and around the harbor, but Octavian and Agrippa bottled them up, preventing resupply. Plagued by desertions, Antony lost most of his fleet trying to break out: he and Cleopatra then fled to Egypt with no further means of defense. Antony had given up everything, Plutarch records, "to follow her that so well had begun his ruin and would hereafter accomplish it."[43]

Octavian took his time in pursuit, but in the summer of 30, he occupied Alexandria, meeting little resistance. Antony and Cleopatra committed suicide—he, clumsily, by dagger; she elegantly (if the legend is accurate) by asp.[44] It remained only for Octavian to execute the unfortunate Caesarion, still a teenager, and to tour the great city, then much more impressive than Rome.[45] To bring history full circle, Octavian paid his respects at the tomb of Alexander the Great. The coffin was opened, but while placing a crown on the embalmed corpse, the new ruler of the known world inadvertently knocked off the former ruler's nose.[46] The miscalculation didn't much matter.

IX.

For Octavian never modeled himself on Alexander.[47] The Macedonian learned limits only through failures. His troops had to tell him, just short of the Himalayas, that they could go no further. Octavian saw constraints while seeking successes, and on those few occasions when he did lose sight of them, quickly self-corrected. Strategy, therefore, came naturally: he rarely confused aspirations with capabilities. Alexander spent his life doing so, and didn't long survive the realization that they weren't the same. He died in Babylon—from exhaustion, illness, and disappointment—at thirty-three.[48] Octavian was that age but only a third of the way through his career on the day in Alexandria, almost three centuries later, when he saw and subtracted from what was left of Alexander.

Octavian was fortunate, of course, to have survived his own illnesses and the many risks he ran, but he was also more careful than Alexander in deploying strengths and in compensating for weaknesses. "He who knows the art of the direct and the indirect approach will be victorious," Sun Tzu writes, appearing as usual to cover all possibilities. But then he tethers: "Such is the art of maneuvering."[49]

Direct approaches work, Master Sun suggests, only when capabilities approximate aspirations. Abundance allows all you want: there's little need for maneuver. Most of the time, though, capabilities fall short—that was Octavian's problem. Insufficiency demands indirection, and that, Sun Tzu insists, requires maneuver:

> [W]hen capable, feign incapacity; when active, inactivity. When near, make it appear that you are far; when far away, that you are near. Offer an enemy a bait to lure him; feign disorder and strike him. . . . When he concentrates, prepare against him; where he is strong, avoid him. . . . Pretend inferiority and encourage his arrogance. . . . Keep him under a strain and wear him down.

Opposites held in mind simultaneously, thus, are "the strategist's keys to victory." It's as if Sun Tzu pre-channels, however improbably, F. Scott Fitzgerald. But then the sage adds, as if to oppose—and tether—himself: "It is not possible to discuss them beforehand."[50]

Victories must connect: otherwise they won't lead anywhere. They can't be foreseen, though, because they arise from unforeseen opportunities. Maneuvering, thus, requires planning, but also improvisation. Small triumphs in a single arena set up larger ones elsewhere, allowing weaker contenders to become stronger.[51] And that brings us back to the young Octavian running circles around the befuddled Antony, leveraging limited assets until he could switch, at Actium, to a more direct approach.

X.

"[W]e have come a great long way," a poet told Octavian, shortly after his return from Alexandria in the year 29. "The time has come to unyoke our steaming horses."[52] The poet was Virgil, the poem was the *Georgics,* and Octavian is said to have listened as the author and a few friends read it aloud, over several days, all 2,118 hexameters.[53] This was no epic—*The Aeneid* would come later—and the occasion has so puzzled Octavian's recent biographers that they've passed over it. Why would the most powerful man in the world sit still for instruction, at such length, on the rotation of crops, the nurturing of vines, the breeding of cattle, and the keeping of bees? John Buchan, an earlier biographer, suggested that Octavian was ready to slow down, to look around, and to think about how to use power now that he had no rivals. He was shifting from navigation to cultivation.[54]

The rising Octavian had spent a decade and a half fending off, buying out, circumventing, eliminating, or capitalizing on threats posed by Antony, Cicero, Cassius, Brutus, Fulvia, Lucius, Sextus, Lepidus, Cleopatra, and Caesarion, as well as Rome's senate, its mobs, his sicknesses, storms and shipwrecks, even a comet. He did so resourcefully, but he wasn't setting the pace. He kept seizing the initiative, losing it, and having to regain it. He couldn't keep this up. No steaming horse runs forever.

After Actium, Octavian began controlling events, rather than letting them control him. He put off any new campaign against the Parthians. He placed local rulers—Herod in Judea was an example—in charge of difficult provinces. He settled veterans by giving them land and long-term support. He pleased Rome by accepting triumphs,

staging games, and starting a building program meant to match Alexandria's. But knowing the dangers of arrogance, he also affected
modesty. He rushed through his triumphs instead of stretching them
out, maintained less than luxurious living arrangements, and when
returning from travel crept into the city to avoid elaborate welcomes.
He secured authority by appearing to renounce it, most dramatically
on the first day of 27 when he unexpectedly gave up all his responsibilities. The surprised senate had no choice but to forbid this and to
award Octavian the title of *princeps* ("first citizen")—as well as a new
name: Augustus.[55]

What he was really doing was giving up the republic, but so
gradually and with such tact—while displaying at every stage such
self-evident benefits—that the Romans would adapt to and even
embrace their new environment, hardly noticing how much it had
changed. They themselves would become crops, vines, cattle, and
bees. For unlike Xerxes, Pericles, Alexander, and Julius Caesar—not
the least of whose gifts to Octavian had been to start him early—
Caesar Augustus saw time as an ally. As the historian Mary Beard
has pointed out, he didn't need to abolish anything. He used time to
grow things.[56]

One was a constitutional settlement renewing respect for the senate and the rule of law while retaining, as if in a soft glove, an iron
fist. Another was imperial stabilization: the empire, Augustus announced, was large enough. Beyond a few boundary adjustments, it
needn't expand further. Still another was a national epic. Rome had
no Homer, so the *princeps* provided one. *The Aeneid,* unlike *The
Iliad* and *The Odyssey,* is a commissioned work. Augustus encouraged its composition, subsidized its author, and saved the manuscript from the flames when the dissatisfied Virgil, on his deathbed,
asked to have it burned.

Aeneas is a prince of Troy who, after fleeing those flames and surviving countless tests, founds Rome, a city that becomes an empire favored by gods. He could be Octavian on his path to power, "his thoughts racing, here, there, probing his options, / shifting to this plan, that—as quick as flickering light."[57] But apart from a famous prophecy—"Son of a god, he will bring back the Age of Gold"[58]— Virgil says little about how Augustus might use power. *The Aeneid* looks to Rome's past, not its future. It celebrates navigation, not cultivation.

Why, then, did the *princeps* see such value in planting—and preserving—this very long poem? "[T]he greatness of poetic perception," the novelist Hermann Broch has him say to the dying poet, "and therefore your greatness, Virgil, lies in being able to grasp all of life . . . in a single survey, in a single work, in a single glance." So are strategy and statecraft the ability to grasp interconnections? To know where you've been in order to see where you're going? It's hard to understand, otherwise, how an indirect approach—whether Odysseus' twists and turns or Octavian's probes and shifts—can ever reach Ithaca, or anywhere else. "[I]t will yet be part of my future fame," Broch's Augustus correctly concludes, "that I was the friend of Virgil."[59]

XI.

There were some things, though, that even Augustus couldn't control: one, sadly, was his own family. He understood, as had his great-uncle, that abandoning the republic would subject the empire to the uncertainties of inheritance. It seemed a reasonable bargain at the time, for Rome was more tolerant of divorce and adoption than most monarchies would later become. That would allow the cultivation of heirs—and opportunities to tether the most promising—without having to depend on who'd given birth to whom.[60]

Misfortune caught up with Augustus, though, in the breeding (the word isn't too strong) of his own family. He married four times, but only his third wife produced a child, Julia, who for all her brilliance and self-assurance could not, as a woman, succeed him.[61] That left adoption as an alternative, and a major priority for Augustus as *princeps* was to grow a new Octavian. His first choice was Marcellus, the much-admired son of his sister Octavia by her first marriage.[62] Augustus had him marry Julia when she was only fourteen, but Marcellus died of a sudden illness at twenty-one, in time for Virgil to portray him poignantly as a lost spirit in *The Aeneid*.[63] The next possibilities were Tiberius and Drusus, the sons by a previous marriage of Augustus' last and longtime wife, Livia. Drusus died at twenty-nine, though, from injuries sustained in a riding accident. Tiberius stayed healthy, but he and the *princeps* distrusted each other—owing to still more maneuvers on the latter's part to secure a successor.

Hoping to expand his options, Augustus forced Julia, after the death of Marcellus, to marry the much older Agrippa, his own contemporary and the genius behind so many of his military victories. They had five children with three males among them, but Gaius and Lucius died young and the third, Agrippa Posthumus—born after his father's death—became, as a teenager, a vicious thug. So Augustus, now desperate, demanded that Tiberius divorce his wife, whom he loved, and marry Agrippa's widow, whom he hated. Julia reciprocated, and the unhappy union produced only a child who died in infancy, after which Tiberius—defying Augustus—exiled himself to the island of Rhodes. From there, he divorced Julia, whose sexual escapades had begun shocking even the Romans, leading Augustus to exile her to the smaller and more desolate island of Pandateria, off the Italian coast. Hoping for the best, Augustus then adopted Tiberius and Agrippa Posthumus, in 4 C.E. and at the age of sixty-seven, but with little confidence in either.[64]

Five years later—far too old, by the standards of his era, to be running anything—the *princeps* suffered his worst military defeat. He'd long opposed expanding the empire, but this didn't preclude straightening its perimeters. He therefore approved an extension of Roman rule from the Rhine to the Elbe, which would, with the Danube, shorten the mostly riverine boundary running from the North to the Black Sea.[65] It looked good on maps, but it required pacifying Germania, a heavily forested region of which the Romans knew little. The task fell to Publius Quinctilius Varus, who promptly led three legions, at Teutoburg, into a catastrophic ambush. Some fifteen thousand men were enslaved or killed—surviving relics suggest by particularly gruesome means—and Augustus lost a tenth of his entire army almost overnight.[66]

He's said to have raged for months, banging his head against walls, talking to himself, refusing to shave, seeing no one: Lear-like, but without a heath, a storm, or the consolations of a fool. He eventually pulled himself together, knowing though that, despite his long life, he'd secured neither his empire nor his succession. The best he could manage, when he knew he was dying, was to surprise Agrippa Posthumus on the island to which *he'd* been exiled and—after determining that the young man hadn't changed—to have him slain, with no greater regret than Octavian had felt for Caesarion almost half a century earlier. The embittered Tiberius, it was now understood, would become—untethered—the new Caesar.

Augustus died, just short of his seventy-seventh birthday, in the same house in which his real father had done so, near Naples: the date was August 19, 14. Characteristically, he'd prepared last words: "I found Rome built of clay: I leave it to you in marble." But then he asked, with the lightness that, for all his troubles, never quite left him: "Have I played my part in the farce of life creditably enough?" And then he added, as if Shakespeare had staged his curtain call:

> If I have pleased you, kindly signify
> Appreciation with a warm goodbye.[67]

In his great novel on the life of Augustus, John Williams has Julia recall asking her father, when they were still speaking: "[H]as it been worth it? . . . [T]his Rome that you have saved, this Rome that you have built? Has it been worth all that you have had to do?" The *princeps* looks at her for a long time and then looks away. "I must believe that it has," he finally replies. "We both must believe that it has."[68]

XII.

Perhaps it was. Rome's subsequent history set standards unsurpassed since for dysfunctional ruling families and exposed imperial perimeters: still, by the strictest reckoning, the empire survived for four and a half centuries after Augustus' death. Rome didn't "fall" until 476. The Byzantine empire, founded by Constantine, would last for another thousand years; and his role in Christianizing the Roman empire would be at least as consequential as that of Augustus in establishing it. The Holy Roman empire, a European remnant of Roman rule, originated in 800 with Charlemagne—one of whose titles was "most serene Augustus"—and held itself together for its own thousand years, until Napoleon swept it aside. Even he knew better than to try that with the Roman Catholic Church, founded in the age of Augustus, which seems likely to endure for as far into our future as anyone can foresee, under the rule of a *pontifex maximus,* a position dating back to the ancient kings of Rome some six centuries before Octavian was born.

Longevity, for empires, is by no means automatic. Most have risen, fallen, and been forgotten. Others may be remembered for the legends they inspired, the arts they produced, or the ruins they left behind, but not for much else: who today would model a state on Xerxes' Persia, or Pericles' Athens, or Alexander's Macedonia? Rome, though, is different—as is China. Their legacies—in language, religious belief, political institutions, legal principles, technological innovation, and imperial administration—have survived repeated "collapses" of regimes that gave rise to them. If the post–Cold War era is indeed to witness a contest between the "West" and the "East," then that will reflect the durability of Roman and Chinese *cultures*—empires of mind[69] *cultivated*, through many crises, over a very long time.

Augustus was Rome's most skillful cultivator. Having navigated himself into unchallenged authority, he used it to turn a failing republic—as if it were a Virgilian vine—into an empire that flourishes, in more ways than most of us realize, even now. Plants aren't aware that they're being made to mature in a certain way, but if firmly rooted and carefully tended they'll cooperate. The *princeps* was fortunate to have been given the time such horticulture requires. He employed it productively while cultivating, within himself, a purpose for planting as well as, in harvesting, self-restraint.

He feared, at the end, that he'd failed, and in one sense he had:

he never got to train a successor in the way Julius Caesar had trained him. Had the dying Augustus foreseen his heirs' abuses, he'd have been horrified: Nero was only forty years into the future.[70] But Rome was robust enough, as China has also been, to survive terrifyingly bad rulers.[71] Both have done so through diversification: dependent on no single variety of power, they grew into ecosystems, as robust gardens and forests tend to do.

It's all the more interesting, then, that Augustus understood so much of Sun Tzu while knowing nothing of him. The explanation may lie in a logic of strategy that undergirds cultures—much as grammar does languages—over vast stretches of time, space, and scale. If so, common sense, when confronting uncommon circumstances, may itself be another of the contradictions held simultaneously in the minds of first-rate intelligences. For the practice of principles must *precede* their derivation, articulation, and institutionalization. You may be looking at clouds, like Polonius, but you'll need to have both feet firmly planted on the ground.

CHAPTER FOUR

SOULS AND STATES

Shortly after the Civil War ended, a young American spent two arduous years among the peoples of northeastern Siberia. He was George Kennan, the distant relative of a better-known twentieth-century namesake, George F. Kennan, who would devise the Cold War strategy of "containment." The first Kennan, twenty at the time, was surveying routes for a telegraph that would link the United States with Europe: underwater cables were as yet unreliable, so the possibility of a land line through British Columbia, Russian Alaska, Siberia, and European Russia, requiring only a crossing of the Bering Strait, seemed worth exploring. The project collapsed when, in 1866, the Atlantic cable at last started working, but it took Kennan months to get the word. He wound up without a future in long-distance telegraphy, and with a personal religious crisis.

In his 1870 book, *Tent-Life in Siberia,* Kennan admitted how easily he might have slipped from the Ohio Presbyterianism in which he'd been raised into "the worship of evil spirits who are supposed to be embodied in all the mysterious powers and manifestations of Nature, such as epidemic and contagious diseases, severe storms, famines, eclipses, and brilliant Auroras." Christianity in adversity was surprisingly shallow.

> No one who has ever lived with the Siberian natives, studied their character, subjected himself to the same influences that surround them, and put himself as far as possible in their places, will ever doubt the sincerity of either priests or followers, or wonder that the worship of evil spirits should be their only religion. It is the only religion possible for such men in such circumstances.

Even Russians, steeped in Orthodoxy and with long experience in the region, could find their God distant and malevolent forces near: "[T]hey sacrificed a dog, like very pagans, to propitiate the diabolical wrath of which the storm was an evidence." The actions of man, Kennan concluded, "are governed not so much by what he intellectually believes as by what he vividly realizes."[1]

This fear of what's beyond understanding roots religion in all the great cultures of which we know. Atheism has little historical continuity. But as long as religions were polytheistic—when each calamity was the caprice of a particular god—faiths posed few problems for the running of states. Gods spent so much time quarreling with one another that mortals maintained a kind of balance among them. Men could respect or neglect gods, even on occasion make or unmake them, an art at which the Romans especially excelled.[2] No single set of beliefs challenged official authority.

Except among Jews, for whom feuds among gods were the ambivalences of a single God, who'd complicated things further by choosing them to form a state.[3] The history of Israel became a jagged disputation between this deity, acting through angels and prophets, and His designees, reacting as kings, priests, and even in one instance an old man scraping scabs on an ash heap.[4] But as Edward Gibbon, the first great modern historian of Rome, pointed out, Judaism was an exclusionary religion. Having been "chosen," Jews sought few converts, so their state never had the imperial aspirations of Rome's empire.[5] Augustus could govern it as he did Gaul, Spain, or Pannonia, without fearing that he was raising a rival.

The *princeps* couldn't have known that another monotheism, this one inclusionary, had appeared during his reign: "[A] pure and humble religion," Gibbon wrote, that "gently insinuated itself into the minds of men, grew up in silence and obscurity, derived new vigor from opposition, and finally erected the triumphant banner of the Cross on the ruins of the Capitol." Covering himself carefully, Gibbon attributed Christianity's rise to its proselytizing zeal, its flexibility about ritual, its claims of miracles, its promise of an afterlife, and of course, "the convincing evidence of the doctrine itself, and . . . the ruling providence of its great Author."[6] It would take centuries, but this empire would be the first to flourish—as Rome's never did—on a global scale.

Not, however, without a recurring dilemma: what did its subjects owe to Caesar and what to God?[7] Could Christianity survive in the absence of state protection? Could the state claim legitimacy without Christianity's sanction? Resolving these issues would consume the attention of medieval and early modern minds. Nor is it clear, even now, whether Christianity caused Rome's "fall"—as Gibbon believed—or—as the legacies of Augustus suggest—secured Rome's institutional immortalities. These opposites have shaped "western" civilization ever since. Not least by giving rise to two truly grand strategies, parallel in their purposes but devised a thousand years apart by—as we've come to think of them—one of the greatest of saints and one of the gravest of sinners.

I.

Augustine never regarded himself as a saint. Born in 354 C.E. in the small North African town of Thagaste, he's notorious within the annals of autobiography—a genre he largely invented—for portraying himself, even at his mother's breast, as a ravenous parasite: "[I]f babies are innocent, it is not for lack of will to do harm, but for lack of strength." He grew up not learning Greek because forced to try, enthralled with *The Aeneid* but not arithmetic, weeping for Dido but not God. He wasted time cheating at games. He failed to worry about worrying his parents. He sought pleasure, beauty, and truth only in worldly things: "I was a great sinner for so small a boy."[8]

And that was before he, as a teenager, discovered sex. "I was inflamed with desire. . . . I ran wild with lust. . . . I was foul to the core, yet I was pleased with my own condition." "So tell us more," readers throughout the ages have furtively whispered. So he does:

> [A]dolescent sex welling within me exuded mists which clouded over and obscured my heart. . . . Love and lust together seethed within me. . . . I was tossed and spilled, floundering in the broiling sea of my fornication. . . . One day at the public baths [my father] saw the signs of active virility coming to life in me and . . . was happy to tell my mother about it, for . . .

Enough already! But Augustine, unembarrassed, plows on: he devotes pages of his *Confessions* to a single pear tree, from which he and his gang knocked off all the fruit—sour anyway—and fed it to pigs. "For the sake of a laugh, a little sport, I was glad to do harm . . . because we are ashamed to hold back when others say 'Come on! Let's do it!'"[9]

It's the second most famous fruit-bearing tree in the Judeo-Christian tradition, and Augustine uses it and much else in this strange work—why publish a confession made privately to God?[10]— to ask how an omnipotent deity can, within the world He created, allow imperfections of any kind. Jupiter "punishes the wicked with his thunderbolts and yet commits adultery himself," Augustine impertinently points out. "The two roles are quite incompatible."[11] Where, though, does that leave Christianity's God?

The question was urgent for Augustine's age, because the emperor Constantine had legalized all religions in 313—an improbable miracle, it seemed, when Christians had so recently suffered Diocletian's persecutions—but Rome's fortunes, even with Christianity as its official religion, had hardly improved. Imperial succession remained unpredictable. Boundaries were overstretched and underdefended. "Barbarians," no better understood than Kennan's Siberians, crashed against outposts in waves from the fathomless reaches of Asia. Visigoths sacked Rome itself in 410, when Augustine was fifty-six, and two decades later he would die, besieged literally by Vandals, in the North African port of Hippo Regius, where he'd long been bishop.[12]

Augustine wrote the *Confessions* soon after taking that position, for which he thought himself ill prepared. He'd spent most of his twenties as a Manichean, seeking to explain evil by limiting God's power. This at last proved too simple, and under the influence of a formidable mother, Monica, and an imposing mentor, Ambrose, the bishop of Milan, Augustine underwent a slow and painful conversion to Christianity, which he describes vividly. Even then, he hoped only to establish a monastery until the Christians in Hippo, where he wanted to put it, forcibly ordained him as a priest, and then promoted him to episcopal status.[13]

It seems an odd way of proceeding—recruiting bishops as draft choices, like professional athletes—but it reflected a desperate search for authority as Roman rule was receding. Bishops provided spiritual guidance while also serving as magistrates, law enforcers, and community organizers. Theological training was less important than firmness of will, persuasiveness in rhetoric, and the pragmatism necessary to get things done. The mature Augustine possessed these qualities, but he had something else his flock couldn't have anticipated: the capacity to make the most of an opportunity. From this perch he hadn't chosen on the periphery of a crumbling Roman world, Augustine set out to reconcile faith with reason in worlds to come. The *Confessions* began the journey with a self-imposed public humiliation, leaving all the more room for his subsequent work to soar.[14]

II.

The City of God, Augustine's magnum opus, composed over many years and completed shortly before his death, isn't about differences between Heaven and earth, as is often supposed, but rather overlapping terrestrial jurisdictions. To oversimplify vastly,[15] there is one God and there can be only one Caesar. Men owe allegiance to both while on earth. How they balance these loyalties determines prospects for eternal life, but the demands of Caesar and the judgments of God reflect circumstances as well as certainties. The unexpected may not surprise God: Augustine has the humility to be unsure. It cannot, though, be anticipated by man.

Man, therefore, must manage unknowns, for God has endowed him—or cursed him—with free will. That's the price paid for original sin, but it's also the opportunity that allows hope: human existence need not be pointless; man isn't at the mercy of capricious gods. Determining obligations to Caesar and God becomes, then, the grandest of strategic tasks, for it requires aligning limited human capabilities with an aspiration—an afterlife—that has no limits.

Unfortunately, *City* lacks the clarity of the *Confessions*. It's a loose, baggy literary leviathan—a *Moby-Dick* of theology—in which cycles and epicycles, angels and demons, myths and histories jostle one another in no particular order. Making it a manual for strategy, much less for salvation, is devilishly difficult. Strangely though, miraculously almost, Augustine benefits from being taken *out* of context. You can pull together topics from where he's left them, free them from the qualifications and digressions with which he's surrounded them, and they'll usually make sense. His style obscures inner logic, nowhere more so than on the issue of war and peace.[16]

When is a Christian justified in *not* turning the other cheek but in fighting and if necessary killing? What obligations can a Christian ruler impose, in defense of his rule, on those he rules? How, if at all, might a state be saved without endangering souls? Why bother if, as Augustine maintains, Caesar's world is corrupt and God's is perfect? And what in Augustine's answers—themselves imperfect, as he acknowledges—has made them soar, influencing thinking on "just war" ever since?

III.

The genius of Augustine is that he concerns himself more with tensions than with their sources: order *versus* justice, war *versus* peace, Caesar *versus* God. He treats polarities as gravitational forces without trying to say what gravity is. Man's choices lie between the polarities, but no formulae reveal what those choices should be. For every "thou shalt not kill," Augustine finds commendations, within sacred texts, of opposite behavior.[17] He questions authorial intent centuries before post-structuralism. He's comfortable, up to a point, with contradictions.

That makes his teachings procedural, not absolute. While respecting the Neoplatonism that influenced early Christianity, Augustine shows that reality always falls short of the ideal: one can strive toward it, but never expect to achieve it. Seeking, therefore, is the best man can manage in a fallen world, and what he seeks is his choice. Nevertheless, not all ends are legitimate; not all means are appropriate. Augustine seeks, therefore, to guide choice by respecting choice. He does this through an appeal to reason: one might even say to common sense.

Take, for example, the question of why states are necessary: if God is all-powerful, who needs Caesars? Without Caesars, Augustine replies, there'd be no Christians, and that can't be God's will. To be a Christian is itself to choose, freely, to follow Christ; but that choice would have left little behind if all Christians had been fed to lions. Caesars rarely did that, however: the Roman empire over the three centuries from Jesus' death to Constantine's was, despite repressive intervals, a surprisingly hospitable space for the new religion.[18] Which is one of the reasons Augustine and his fellow

Christians found the fourth- and fifth-century "decline" of Rome so unnerving.

It followed then, as a generalization derived from observation, that order must precede justice, for what rights can exist under constant terror?[19] A peaceful faith—the only source of justice for Christians—can't flourish without protection, whether through toleration, as in pre-Constantine Rome, or by formal edict, as afterward.[20] The City of God is a fragile structure within the sinful City of Man.

It's this that leads Christians to entrust authority to selected sinners—we call it "politics"—and Augustine, for all his piety, is a *political* philosopher. Just as he also became, as Rome's authority waned, an authoritarian bishop, prepared to embrace lesser evils (or, as he put it, "benevolent harshness"[21]) in order to ward off greater ones.[22] Augustine's targets were deviations from orthodoxy, which he attacked with an almost Leninist zeal as if the only way to advance a faith is to purge it of all nuance. His mind was larger than his persecutions, however: the implications of his thinking were more sweeping, more lasting, and ultimately more humane.

Augustine concluded that war, if necessary to save the state, could be a lesser evil than peace—*and that the procedural prerequisites for necessity could be stated.* Had provocation occurred? Had competent authority exhausted peaceful alternatives? Would the resort to violence be a means chosen, not an end in itself? Was the expenditure of force proportionate to its purposes, so that it wouldn't destroy what it was meant to defend? Could these human decisions—for Augustine never doubted that they were that—advance some divine purpose? So that cities of God and Man could coexist without fracturing a flawed world?

IV.

There were, of course, precedents for questioning the wisdom of war: Artabanus, Archidamus, and Nicias had all done that, if unsuccessfully, and Thucydides' doomed Melians had raised timeless misgivings about the conduct of wars once started. No one before Augustine, however, had set standards to be met by states in choosing war. This could be done only within an inclusionary monotheism, for only a God claiming universal authority could judge the souls of earthly rulers. And only Augustine, in his era, spoke so self-confidently for Him. The cringing author of the *Confessions* had come a long way.

Augustine framed his standards as a checklist, not as commandments. He knew how often prophets had thundered prohibitions, only to reverse them in the face of necessity or new instructions from On High.[23] For all of his harshness in rooting out heretics, Augustine preferred persuasion on issues of war and peace: "have you thought about this?" or "wouldn't it make sense to do that?" He saw no need, within this realm, to threaten, and that gained him followers over time.[24]

That's because checklists adapt better to change than commandments. Sailors rely on them before going to sea. Soldiers employ them in planning missions. Surgeons demand them, to make sure they'll have the instruments they need and that they'll leave none behind. Pilots run through them, to ensure taking off safely and landing smoothly—preferably at the intended airport. Parents deploy them against all that can go wrong in transporting small children. Checklists pose common questions in situations that *may* surprise: the idea is to approach these having, as much as possible, reduced the likelihood that they will.

Augustine's great uncertainty was the status of souls in the City of Man, for only the fittest could hope to enter the City of God. Pre-Christian deities had rarely made such distinctions: the pagan afterlife was equally grim for heroes, scoundrels, and all in between.[25] Not so, though, with the Christian God: behavior in life would make a huge difference in death. It was vital, then, to fight wars within rules. The stakes could hardly be higher.

V.

There were problems, however, with Augustine's checklists. If the need to fight wars by rules was so great, why did he squirrel away so much of what he wrote on that subject in the manner of that creature? So that it took centuries for others—Aquinas, Gratian, Grotius, Luther, Calvin, Locke, Kant—to locate, excavate, codify, and apply Augustine's insights to the realm of statecraft?[26] How could he hope to save states or souls by hiding the means of doing so? The *Confessions* had shown Augustine to be capable of luminous clarity, as had the thousands of sermons he delivered as a working bishop, many of which we can still sample.[27] But maybe that was the difficulty.

Augustine had heavy episcopal responsibilities throughout the last half of his career. These entitled him to scribes, who relied on shorthand to record his ideas,[28] but that in turn imposed the burden of volume, for who had the time to go through it all, organize it, and make it readable? Augustine's pronouncements, like Nixon's tapes, swamped their originator. So while Augustine's checklists would influence *thinking about* war for hundreds of years to come—thinkers can take the time to ferret out obscure texts—it's less clear that these moderated the actual *conduct of* wars to come.[29]

Perhaps, though, there's a larger issue that even clear presentation might not have resolved. It's that Augustine was never wholeheartedly a monotheist.[30] He worshipped Reason as much as he worshipped God, but he never showed God to be any more bound by Reason than Jupiter had been: "The two roles are quite incompatible." This is where Augustine was *uncomfortable* with contradictions.

Why do wars happen in the first place? They reflect, of course, man's sinfulness, resulting from his fallen state. But because God is all-powerful, wars must also accord with His will—even though Augustine holds that God's actions consistently manifest His love for man. So man must in some way benefit from war, perhaps by being punished, like a child, for his own good, or if dead transported to a better world. How, though, if this is the case, can some wars be just and some not? Why have standards at all? They illuminate the path, Augustine suggests, by which the righteous within the City of Man make their way to the City of God, leaving the unrighteous behind.

What, though, distinguishes these qualities? Not pacifism, for Augustine regards military service as necessary to sustain the state without which Christianity can't survive. Nor is such service conditional: Christian soldiers must obey orders, he insists, and can only hope that these will meet the standards of justice. Whether they do or not reflects circumstances that only God can determine. Thus even unjust wars, if fought for Christ, can become just.[31] Augustine could have been with the Athenians on Melos. He's a theological Dr. Pangloss,[32] seeing in the worst that can happen the best that's possible.

Or so it might seem. But perhaps a compromise lies where Augustine's checklists leave you, when you do have room to maneuver. You lean, bend, or tilt in a certain direction when choosing between order and justice, war and peace, Caesar and God. You're aligning aspirations with capabilities, for in Augustine's thinking justice, peace, and God fit the first category, while order, war, and Caesar inhabit the second.

Alignment, in turn, implies interdependence. Justice is unattainable in the absence of order, peace may require the fighting of wars, Caesar must be propitiated—perhaps even, like Constantine, converted—if man is to reach God. Each capability brings an aspiration within reach, much as Sun Tzu's practices tether his principles, but what's the nature of the tether? I think it's *proportionality*: the means employed must be appropriate to—or at least not corrupt—the end envisaged. This, then, is Augustine's tilt: toward a logic of strategy transcending time, place, culture, circumstance, and the differences between saints and sinners.

VI.

It's long been assumed that Machiavelli is in Hell and—worse—content to be there.[33] That possibility would not have occurred to Augustine or to many, if any, of his contemporaries. Hippo Regius and Florence, where Niccolò Machiavelli was born in 1469 and spent most of his life, weren't that far apart geographically: both had been near-peripheries of a much farther-flung Roman empire. By the late fifteenth century, though, Rome's situation had greatly changed. Its emperors had become popes managing strikingly different empires: an all too worldly City of Man confined to the

papal states of central Italy, and the Roman Catholic Church, a supposedly universal City of God coexisting uneasily with secular sovereignties throughout central and western Europe—some of which
were now extending their rule, under the pope's semi-supervision,
to the edges of South and Southeast Asia, and to newly discovered
lands to be known soon as America.

From his office high above the Piazza della Signoria in Florence,
the young Machiavelli, a rising functionary in the city-state's government, could have seen celebrations honoring Amerigo Vespucci:
the Vespuccis were Florentines, and he knew the family. The first
sentence of Machiavelli's *Discourses on the First Ten Books of Titus
Livius,* which he began writing in 1515 after falling from favor, finds
it "no less dangerous to discover new ways and methods than to set
out in search of new seas and unknown lands." This is not, however,
because of God's wrath, but human envy. Augustine worried about
both. Machiavelli, recently imprisoned and tortured, fears God less
than he does man.[34]

Not that he disbelieved, or was disrespectful. His writings refer
often to God, as was customary in the culture from which he came.
But the gods of the ancients and the Christian God, Machiavelli
slyly suggests, could have been the same. He attends mass rarely
enough to cause comment—even jokes—among his friends. And
Machiavelli never takes it upon himself to speak for or to try to explain God, as did Augustine. Except for a single significant sentence
in *The Prince,* the book that's supposed to have sent Machiavelli to
Hell: "God does not want to do everything."[35]

It's hard to see why this was controversial, for Machiavelli is careful to add: "so as not to take free will from us and that part of the
glory that falls to us." Wasn't free will God's idea? Wasn't it supposed

to lead to redemption, which would be glorious for those who achieved it? Questions like these, in Augustine's thinking, had run up against his belief in God's omnipotence: how could freedom exist in a predetermined world? Uneasy with these opposites, he tried but failed, on an epic scale, to reconcile them.[36] Machiavelli, in contrast, is more relaxed. If God said free will, then he must have meant it. Isn't it arrogant to try to constrain Him within the limits of reason? Wouldn't it be liberating, for man, not to try?

You might conclude from this, following Isaiah Berlin, that Augustine was a hedgehog and Machiavelli a fox. You might acknowledge, emboldened by F. Scott Fitzgerald, that Machiavelli had a first-rate intelligence—holding opposites in mind while functioning—and that Augustine, for all his diligence, fell short. Neither view seems implausible. But a more revealing distinction may lie in temperament: to borrow from Milan Kundera,[37] Machiavelli found "lightness of being" bearable. For Augustine—perhaps because traumatized as a youth by a pear tree—it was unendurable.

VII.

So what is "lightness of being"? My students would say that it's learning not to "sweat it," and Machiavelli, from behind several hedges, uses that very verb:

> [M]any have held and hold the opinion that worldly things are so governed by fortune and by God, that men cannot correct them with their prudence, indeed that they have no remedy at all; and on account of this they might judge that one

> need not sweat much over things but let oneself be governed
> by chance. . . . When I have thought about this sometimes, I
> have been in some part inclined to their opinion.

In the end, though, he resists being blown about like a feather. "I judge that it might be true that fortune is arbiter of half our actions, but also that she leaves the other half, or close to it, for us to govern." Fifty percent fortune, fifty percent man—but zero percent God. Man is, however precariously, on his own.[38]

Machiavelli knows from Florence's experience with the Arno that rivers, when flooding, can cause great destruction. But men, if farsighted, can lessen the danger by building dikes and dams.[39] God may approve, but no longer Himself does hydraulics. States, Machiavelli suggests, operate similarly. If governed badly, men's rapacity will soon overwhelm them, whether through internal rebellion or external war. But if run with *virtù*—his untranslatable term for planning without praying[40]—states can constrain, if not in all ways control, the workings of fortune, or chance.

The skills needed are those of imitation, adaptation, and approximation. Machiavelli commends the study of history, "for since men almost always walk on paths beaten by others and proceed in their actions by imitation . . . , a prudent man should always enter upon the paths beaten by great men, and imitate those who have been most excellent, so that if his own virtue does not reach that far, it is at least in the odor of it." That's adaptation: Machiavelli's "odor" is Thucydides' distinction between reflection and resemblance, which the passage of time sharpens. And approximation? "[P]rudent archers," Machiavelli points out, knowing the strength of their bow, "set their aim much higher than the place intended, not to reach such height with their arrow, but to be able with the aid of so high an aim to achieve their plan."[41] For there will be deflection—certainly from gravity, perhaps from wind, who knows from what else? And the target itself will probably be moving.

Eternal truths have little to do with any of this, beyond the assurance that circumstances will change. Machiavelli knows, as did Augustine, that what makes sense in one situation may not in the next. They differ, though, in that Machiavelli, expecting to go to Hell, doesn't attempt to resolve such disparities. Augustine, hoping for Heaven, feels personally responsible for them. Despite his afflictions, Machiavelli often sees comedy.[42] Despite his privileges, Augustine carries a tragic burden of guilt. Machiavelli sweats, but not all the time. Augustine never stops.

"Lightness of being," then, is the ability, if not to find the good in bad things, then at least to remain afloat among them, perhaps to swim or to sail through them, possibly even to take precautions that can keep you dry. It's not to locate logic in misfortunes, or to show that they're for the best because they reflect God's will. That's for Augustine the hedgehog, the ponderous Pangloss of his day.

VIII.

Despite these differences, Augustine and Machiavelli agree that wars should be fought—indeed that states should be run—by pre-specifiable procedures. Both know that aspirations aren't capabilities. Both prefer to connect them through checklists, not commandments.[43] But where Augustine, who had a job, could spend years explaining divine rationality, Machiavelli was out of a job and trying to get one. So he had to be clear, brief, and humble.

He wrote *The Prince* soon after his release from prison in 1513, his shoulders still sore from his having been dropped—at least six times—by a rope tied to his wrists behind his back. These were among the "hardships and dangers" to which Machiavelli referred in his dedicatory letter to Lorenzo de' Medici, but he made fun of his torture in his letters to friends.[44] Whistling in darkness was a specialty.

Lorenzo probably never read *The Prince*[45]—he wasn't his age's brightest lightbulb—nor would it have done him much good if he had because he died in 1519. Machiavelli himself followed in 1527, five years before *The Prince* was published, in 1532. By then it was ecumenically notorious. It's said to have justified both the Protestant Reformation and the Catholic Counter-Reformation. It made the first papal Index of Prohibited Books, in 1559. It inspired sneers in Shakespeare but sympathy in John Locke and the American Founding Fathers. It created, for better or for worse, the contemporary discipline of "political science." And it keeps my own students awake nights: "Is *this* what I'll have to do after I graduate?"[46] If Augustine was a great sinner for so small a boy, *The Prince* is a great shocker, even now, for so small a book.

IX.

Its most memorable scene takes place in the piazza at Cesena early one morning in 1502, where the local governor, Remirro de Orco, is found in two pieces, with a bloody knife and a block of wood between them. "The ferocity of the spectacle," Machiavelli recalls, "left the people at once satisfied and stupefied." Cesare Borgia had made Remirro the governor of Romagna with instructions to pacify the rebellious province. This he did, but so brutally that he'd never have the loyalty of its people. So Borgia didn't just sack his subordinate: he disassembled him and displayed the pieces. The shock and awe accomplished its purpose: at the cost of one life, others were saved that would have been lost if a new revolt had broken out. "I would not know," Machiavelli concludes of Borgia, "how to reproach him."[47]

It's easy to assume, but wrong to be certain, that Augustine would have objected: if no parent had ever punished a child, he asks, "which of us would not have grown up intolerable"?[48] Such "benevolent harshness" seeks some greater good: the act may be violent—it was for Remirro, and it can seem so to a child—but it isn't, or shouldn't be, indiscriminate. The principle, for both Augustine and Machiavelli, reflects common sense: if you have to use force, don't destroy what you're trying to preserve.[49]

There was thus a gruesome proportionality in Borgia's exhibition of body parts—they came from only a single body—and the idea shows up elsewhere in *The Prince*. Machiavelli praises rulers who used violence as a means to an end—examples include Moses, Cyrus, Romulus, and Theseus—but he despises Agathocles of Sicily, who so loved violence that he made it an end in itself: "[O]ne cannot call it virtue to kill one's citizens, betray one's friends, to be without faith, without mercy, without religion; these modes can enable one to acquire empire, but not glory."[50]

The "higher glory," Augustine reminds us, is "to stay war itself with a word, than to slay men with a sword." But Machiavelli points out how rarely this is possible, for "a man who wants to make a profession of good in all regards must come to ruin among so many who are not good." They are indeed many, Augustine admits, which is why good men may have to seek peace by shedding blood. The greater privilege, however, is to avert "that calamity which others are under the necessity of producing." Machiavelli agrees, but notes that a prince so infrequently has this privilege that if he wishes to remain in power he must "learn to be able not to be good," and to use this proficiency or not use it "according to necessity."[51] As fits man's fallen state, Augustine sighs. As befits man, Machiavelli simplifies. "Don't sweat it. Move on."

Both this saint and this sinner, then, see proportionality as a pathway. For Augustine, it shows rulers, however deeply into iniquity they may have descended, the way back from the City of Man to the City of God. Machiavelli doesn't imagine communities "that have never been seen or known to exist,"[52] but he does seek *virtù,* by which he means doing what's required when facing necessity but not in all respects at its mercy. It's here that he's most original—and most brave.

As Machiavelli's finest translator has put it: "[J]ustice is no more reasonable than what a person's prudence tells him he must acquire for himself, or must submit to, because *men cannot afford justice in any sense that transcends their own preservation.*"[53] The cagey Florentine might have appreciated, for its literary qualities, Charles Dickens's *A Tale of Two Cities.* But he'd have thought it careless in the extreme for Sydney Carton, that novel's hero, to submit so gallantly at the end, to the sound of knitting, to his own disassembly.[54]

X.

States can't afford such irresponsibility, which is why they require strategies. These can't depend, Machiavelli insists, on discerning the will of God: it's "presumptuous and foolhardy" even to try.[55] Man must manage on his own, but for that he needs princes and princes need advisers. The adviser can't tell the prince what to do, but he can suggest what the prince should know. For Machiavelli this means seeking patterns—across time, space, and status—by shifting perspectives. "[J]ust as those who sketch landscapes place themselves down in the plain to consider the nature of mountains . . . and to consider the nature of low places place themselves high atop mountains, similarly, to know well the nature of peoples one needs to be prince, and to know well the nature of princes one needs to be of the people."[56]

Sketches, as Machiavelli sees them, convey complexity usably. They're not reality. They're not even finished representations of it. But they can transmit essential if incomplete information on short notice. They thus enhance, although they never replace, good judgment. Like Augustine's checklists, they show the directions in which a prince might lean, bend, or tilt while balancing opposites. They tether practices to principles in unknown futures by showing how these were tethered in known pasts.

You can conquer a country, Machiavelli argues, by "ruining" its regime and by "eliminating" the ruling family's "bloodline." You can move there and run it yourself. Or you can let its people "live by their laws, taking tribute from them and creating within them an oligarchical state which keeps them friendly to you." This makes the most sense, for "a city used to living free may be held more easily by means of its own citizens than in any other mode, if one wants to preserve it."[57]

Machiavelli doesn't favor democracy in any modern sense. But he does incline away from brutality and toward consent. The "great," he points out—he means the nobility—will always wish to oppress the people. The people will wish not to be oppressed. So where, within these polarities, should a prince be? Machiavelli's answer is simple, even quantifiable: "[A] prince can never secure himself against a hostile people, as they are too many; against the great, he can secure himself, as they are few."[58]

That doesn't mean courting popularity: it is, on the whole, "much safer to be feared than loved." For love "is held by a chain of obligation, which, because men are wicked, is broken at every opportunity . . . , but fear is held by a dread of punishment that never forsakes you." Cruelties, however, should be swiftly administered—hence the logic of shock and awe—while benefits should be distributed slowly "so that they may be tasted better." That's why a prince must learn *when* not to be good: timing is everything.[59]

Machiavelli embraces, then, a *utilitarian* morality: you proportion your actions to your objective, not to progress from one nebulous city to another, but because some things have been shown to work and others haven't.[60] Where Augustine is a closeted polytheist, uneasily juggling incompatibilities of God and Reason, Machiavelli outs his own monotheism by seeking, above all, to minimize mess. If he praises duplicity, it's because it's efficient: how else, if you're not going to pray, can you reconcile, within your own mind or policy, contradictions? Machiavelli is always honest, if less often tactful. He is, one of his biographers has written, "the least Machiavellian of men."[61]

XI.

What, though, *is* the objective? I think it's Augustine's vision of justice, which order must precede. Only a state can provide stability, but Augustine's reports only to his God. Machiavelli is no atheist, but his God doesn't run states. That the Roman Catholic Church still has one—if much diminished from that of the Christian Roman emperors—interests, exasperates, and sometimes amuses Machiavelli, but it's not the future. Indeed he blames the church for keeping Italy divided when states elsewhere are organizing, not by cities or regions, but rather cultures, languages, and emergent civilizations.[62]

Who, then, will oversee them? They'll do it themselves, Machiavelli replies, by balancing power. First, there'll be a balance *among* states, unlike older Roman and Catholic traditions of universality. Machiavelli anticipates the statecraft of Richelieu, Metternich, Bismarck, the second Kennan, and Henry Kissinger. Enshrined formally in the 1648 Treaty of Westphalia, it saw little significance in the internal configuration of states: what mattered was their external behavior.[63]

But Machiavelli understands balancing in a second and subtler sense, conveyed more explicitly in *The Discourses* than in *The Prince:*

> [I]t is only in republics that the common good is looked to properly in that all that promotes it is carried out; and, however much this or that private person may be the loser on this account, there are so many who benefit thereby that the common good can be realized in spite of those few who suffer in consequence.[64]

This idea of an *internal* equilibrium within which competition strengthens community wouldn't appear again until Adam Smith unveiled an "invisible hand" in *The Wealth of Nations* (1776), until the American Founding Fathers drafted and in *The Federalist* justified constitutional checks and balances (1787–88), and until Immanuel Kant linked republics, however distantly, with *Perpetual*

Peace (1795). From all of this would emerge the twentieth-century idea of an international system consistent with order *and* justice, [65] although Augustine had foreseen it long before.

This is not to claim that Augustine influenced Machiavelli, who influenced Westphalia, which influenced Woodrow Wilson: history doesn't require direct inheritances. But this sixteen-hundred-year search for justice—an aspiration—by way of order—a capability—suggests a persisting pattern: Thucydides might have regarded it as one of his recurring resemblances, human nature being what it is.

It followed, then, that distillations of these, if sharply focused and succinctly presented, could prepare states for the future. Machiavelli most closely met this standard: *The Prince,* to paraphrase Pangloss, is the best of all policy briefs. All the more so for its author's having never, ever confused power with PowerPoint™.

XII.

The first Kennan's Siberians, the saintly Augustine, and the sinful Machiavelli devised strategies for salvation: the Siberians from blizzards, earthquakes, diseases, famines, and shimmering lights in the night sky; the saint from disorder on earth and fires in Hell; the sinner from incompetent rulers and the failed states they ran. The Siberians sacrificed animals to satisfy gods. The saint sought Reason in a single God. The sinner did without gods—and God—altogether. Siberians had unwritten rituals of propitiation. Augustine mapped imaginary cities in a big book. Machiavelli prepared a brief for a prince whose attention span in no way matched that of its subsequent readers.

All prescribed procedures: "Do this, now do that." All related the past to the future: "This worked before—it's worth trying again." All employed checklists: "Before you do anything, be sure of what you're trying to do and make sure you have what you'll need." You can't and shouldn't do everything, though, so you'll also select: "Here's what we can afford," or "Here's what's right." You *proportion* aspirations to capabilities. These are opposites—the first being free from limits and the second bound by them—but they must connect. That happens only when you hold both in mind simultaneously.

It's not easy. Augustine failed to show how God's omnipotence could coexist with man's freedom. Machiavelli solved that problem— God didn't want to do everything—but created another by leaving God with little to do. These loose ends remained, uncomfortably, until 1953—when Isaiah Berlin gave a lecture.[66] He called it "The Originality of Machiavelli," but the essay it became rebuilt Augustine's cities. Without ever mentioning them.

Why, Berlin asked, had Machiavelli upset so many people over so many years? The Elizabethans alone condemned him in print some four hundred times[67]—my sleepless students follow a long tradition. Machiavelli indeed lacked tact, but he'd trigger-warned, in *The Prince*, that he wouldn't "ornament" his prose.[68] He had few illusions: it was Hobbes, however, who called life "solitary, poore, nasty, brutish, and short."[69] Nor did Machiavelli disguise unpleasant realities. It was Augustine, though, who said of babies that they did no harm only through "lack of strength."[70]

Machiavelli's great transgression, Berlin concluded, was to confirm what everyone knows but no one will admit: that ideals "cannot be attained." Statecraft, therefore, can never balance realism against idealism: there are only competing realisms. There is no contest, in governing, between politics and morality: there is only politics. And no state respects Christian teaching on saving souls.

The incompatibilities are irreconcilable. To deny this is, in Berlin's words but in Machiavelli's mind, to "vacillate, fall between two stools, and end in weakness and failure."[71]

What, then, to do? It helped that Machiavelli and Berlin had lightness of being, for their answer is the same: don't sweat it. Learn to live with the contradictions. Machiavelli shows "no trace of agony," Berlin points out, and he doesn't either: "anchorites" can always "practice their virtues in the desert," while "martyrs will obtain their reward hereafter." Machiavelli "is interested in public affairs; in security, independence, success, glory, strength, vigour, felicity on earth, not in heaven; in the present and future as well as the past; in the real world, not an imaginary one."[72]

And so, except for monks on parched poles, Augustine's City of God no longer exists on earth. The City of Man, which survives, has no single path to salvation. "[T]he belief that the correct, objectively valid solution to the question of how men should live can in principle be discovered," Berlin finds, "is itself in principle not true." Machiavelli thus split open the rock "upon which Western beliefs and lives had been founded." It was he "who lit the fatal fuse."[73]

XIII.

But fatal to what? Faith in single solutions, Berlin shows, has led "both Catholics and Protestants, both conservatives and Communists, [to defend] enormities which freeze the blood of ordinary men."[74] Machiavelli's blood ran colder than was ordinary: he praised Cesare Borgia, for example, and he refused to condemn torture despite having suffered it (Augustine, never tortured, took a similar position).[75] Machiavelli was careful, however, to *apportion* enormities:

they should only forestall greater horrors—violent revolution, defeat in war, descent into anarchy, mass killing, or what we would today call "genocide."

Berlin sees in this an "economy of violence," by which he means holding a "reserve of force always in the background to keep things going in such a way that the *virtues* admired by [Machiavelli] and by the classical thinkers to whom he appeals can be protected and allowed to flower."[76] It's no accident that Berlin uses the plural. For it comes closer than the singular, in English, to Machiavelli's *virtù*, implying no single standard by which men must live.

"[T]here are many different ends that men may seek and still be fully rational," Berlin insists, "capable of understanding . . . and deriving light from each other." Otherwise, civilizations would exist in "impenetrable bubble[s]," incomprehensible to anyone on the outside. "Intercommunication between cultures in time and space is possible only because what makes men human is common to them, and acts as a bridge between them. But our values are ours, and theirs are theirs."

Herein lie, then, the roots of toleration, "historically the product of the realisation of the irreconcilability of equally dogmatic faiths, and the practical improbability of complete victory of one over the other." These extend to the painful stretch, as if on a rack, between what public life demands and what private life allows: only anchorites, on their poles, are above politics.

Perhaps there are other worlds in which all principles are harmonized, but "it is on earth that we live, and it is here that we must believe and act."[77] By shattering certainty, Machiavelli showed how. "[T]he dilemma has never given men peace since it came to light," Berlin lightly concludes, "but we have learnt to live with it."[78]

CHAPTER FIVE

PRINCES AS PIVOTS

M y dictionary defines a "pivot" as "a pin, point, or short shaft on the end of which something rests and turns, or upon and about which something rotates or oscillates."[1] Posterity has long regarded Augustine and Machiavelli as pivots in the history of "western" thought because each, with enduring effects, shifted long-standing relationships between souls and states. Neither, however, could have known that this would happen. They'd have found it surprising to have eclipsed, in posthumous prominence, the princes they served.

For whom obscurity, during *their* lifetimes, was impossible. Their lowliest subjects would have heard of them. The loftiest lords quailed before them. The health, mental stability, and reproductive prowess of princes could cause faiths to rise and nations to fall: they were the international celebrities of their time. Societies for centuries pivoted on them.[2] But not in just the same way.

Somewhere in England, sometime in the late sixteenth century, a young nobleman arrives late for a banquet. Still panting from having run, he kneels before the guest of honor, bows his head in embarrassment, and offers a bowl of rose water.

> Such was his shyness that he saw no more of her than her ringed hand, . . . but it was enough. It was a memorable hand; a thin hand with long fingers always curling as if round orb or sceptre; a nervous, crabbed, sickly hand; a commanding hand; a hand that had only to raise itself for a head to fall; a hand, he guessed, attached to an old body that smelt like a cupboard in which furs are kept in camphor; which body was yet caparisoned in all sorts of brocades and gems; and held itself very upright though perhaps in pain from sciatica; and never flinched though strung together by a thousand fears; and the Queen's eyes were light yellow.

For it is she, Elizabeth R as she styles herself, and even though the occasion is imagined—the youth will remain youthful, owing possibly to an unexpected gender transformation, well into the twentieth century—this passage from Virginia Woolf's biography/novel *Orlando* brings us as close to the great aging queen as we, from this distance, are likely to get.[3]

Meanwhile, in Spain a dead king is being remembered, at his funeral, as a hand-loom weaver. That profession might seem easy, the eulogist insists, "but in reality [it] is very hard." Extremities must coordinate while eyes remain focused and the brain keeps track, for any of innumerable threads may at any moment unravel, tangle, or break.

> Such is the life of a king: writing with his hands, traveling with his feet, his heart attached to threads—one to Flanders,

> another to Italy, another to Africa, another to Peru, another
> to Mexico, another to the English Catholics, another to pre-
> serving peace among Christian princes, another to the prob-
> lems of the Holy Roman Empire. . . . Is the thread to the
> Indies broken? Hurry up and tie it! Is the thread to Flanders
> broken? Run and fix it! Such a busy life, divided among so
> many threads. . . . Oh what excellent regal qualities, found in
> no one else.

The king was Philip II, the date is 1598, and Dr. Aguilar de Ter-
rones's sermon, unlike Orlando's obeisance, is real.[4] His metaphor
matches Woolf's, however, in its evocation of character—and, by
implication, of divergent pivoting in princely rule.

Philip rushes from crisis to crisis, rarely resting, never fully in
control. He's whacking moles, and they pop up everywhere. Elizabeth, in contrast, refuses to hurry. She'll whack when she has to—the
raised hand can indeed remove a head—but she sets times and places.
She resists unnecessary expenditures of resources, energy, reputation,
and—unusually in a monarch—virginity. For like Penelope in *The
Odyssey,* she's beset by suitors. Unlike Penelope, however, Elizabeth
weaves strategies, not shrouds.[5]

The king, an Augustinian, sees his empire as a shroud connecting the City of Man to the City of God, no part of which is dispens-
able. "[R]ather than prejudice the Faith or God's service in the
slightest way," he pledges at one point, "I will lose all my dominions
and a hundred lives if I had them."[6] The queen, more Machiavellian,
regards her state (not yet an empire) as a stage for performance
rather than as a holy relic.[7] "[B]e ye ensured," she tells Londoners at
her coronation, "that I will be as good unto you as ever queen
was . . . [and] that for the safety and quietness of you all, I will not

spare, if need be, to spend my blood."[8] Philip promises obedience to God, not his subjects. Elizabeth serves her subjects, fitting God to their interests. The king, looking to Heaven, venerates. The queen, feet on earth, calculates. The differences test the ideas of Augustine and Machiavelli against the demands of statecraft at the dawn of the modern age.

I.

Both monarchs would have absorbed Augustine from Catholic doctrine—Philip avidly, Elizabeth grudgingly (she was, unmistakably, Henry VIII's daughter)—and both may have read Machiavelli. Philip's father, the Holy Roman emperor Charles V, carefully studied *The Prince,* and the Florentine's works were in Philip's library, even though marked as on the pope's list of prohibited books. Translations made Machiavelli infamous in England as Elizabeth was growing up, but she, skilled at languages, could have read him in the original Italian.[9] Neither she nor Philip left commentaries. Where they placed themselves within the two traditions, though, is clear enough.

Princess Elizabeth, not yet twenty, grumbled openly when forced to attend mass following the accession to the throne of her Catholic half-sister Mary in 1553.[10] After becoming queen five years later, Elizabeth stalked out of services she disliked, and loudly corrected sermons she'd stayed to hear. She reinstated, as one of her first acts, her godfather Thomas Cranmer's *Book of Common Prayer,* for which Mary had burned him at the stake. Like her real father, Elizabeth sought not to abolish English Catholicism, but to *nationalize* it by denying papal authority over the state she ruled. It was after all—apart from an already fractious Irish colony—the only one she had.[11]

When Charles V abdicated in 1555–56, he ruled more states than he could easily remember: Spain and its "new world" territories of Mexico and Peru, the Netherlands, Burgundy, large portions of Italy, Austria, Hungary, and Bohemia, as well as scattered outposts along the North African coast and in what would become the Philippines. King Philip II inherited most of this,[12] along with an apology from his father for the "extreme" gap he'd left between revenues and expenses. The new monarch must give up nothing, though, for "honor and reputation" were everything. In squaring this circle, Philip should place his faith in "what is most certain, which is God."[13] To whom it would fall to find a way.

"NON SUFFICIT ORBIS," a medal struck for Philip proclaimed in 1583, after he'd taken over Portugal and its overseas colonies: "The World Is Not Enough."[14] The phrase dates from Alexander the Great, but it couldn't have been said of his empire, as it was now of Spain's, that the sun never set on it. How, though, could one king rule it? With Philip's lands that much more extensive than Elizabeth's, he should have found delegation easier than she. Their practice, however, was just the opposite.

Elizabeth readily yielded authority,[15] whether to court favorites, complaisant clerics, wealthy nobles, enterprising sea captains, or to all of her subjects over the inner makeup, on matters of faith, of their own minds. She didn't even design her own palace: she simply took over, or borrowed, the ones she fancied. In this she followed Machiavelli, for if God didn't want to do everything, why should she? It was enough to awe, to set limits, and, like Augustus, to let things grow—while retaining, deftly if possible, fiercely if necessary, her own autonomy.[16]

Philip, like Augustine, saw God's hand in all that happened. That made God's interests and those of the king, His agent, inseparable. Authority, hence, could hardly be shared, despite the months required for orders in a global empire to produce actions. And palaces? Philip personally designed the Escorial, the grandest monastery any monarch would ever inhabit. He then filled it with relics and sequestered himself among them, unable to see beyond the responsibilities that engulfed him and, as a consequence, the paperwork that swamped him.[17]

The ruler of a microstate who macromanaged, therefore, coexisted in time with the ruler of a macrostate who micromanaged. This made no sense in terms of geography, logistics, or communications. But as a reflection of royal *minds*—and, through them, of contrasting *philosophies* on the alignment of souls with states—it made perfect sense, so much so that the future of the world Europe would soon rule pivoted on the distinction.

II.

Philip was once, and wanted again to be, England's king. Queen Mary had married him in 1554, hoping for an heir while linking her state with the Catholic great powers of Europe. Charles V, still Holy Roman emperor, favored the union and Philip, not yet king of Spain, dutifully agreed. But Mary's only pregnancy turned out to be false, and Philip, whose authority in England was only matrimonial, spent little time there. Marriage to a foreign prince made Mary unpopular: she became more so by sending hundreds of other "heretics" into the flames that consumed Cranmer, and by losing Calais, England's last continental outpost, to the French in 1558. Mary died, little mourned, later that year. With her death Philip, now the fully empowered ruler of an earth-circling empire, lost his nominal power in a small, sun-deprived island.[18]

Elizabeth's position, while Mary ruled, had been precarious. As the daughter of Anne Boleyn, whom Henry VIII had married, disavowed, and beheaded, she had no clear claim to the throne. She showed little respect for the Roman Catholicism Mary was reimposing. She knew of, even if she didn't participate in, plots to overthrow the queen. The principal danger Elizabeth posed, though, was popularity: ever the performer, the princess played the contrast for all it was worth.[19] Mary kept her in limbo, at times receiving her warmly, at others holding her at a distance under house (actually castle) arrest, and at one point imprisoning her in the Tower of London, causing Elizabeth to fear her mother's fate.

Her most influential protector was Philip. If Mary were to die without issue—or if childbirth were to kill her, as it did so many women in her time[20]—he preferred having Elizabeth as queen instead of her cousin Mary Stuart, presumptive heir to the throne of Scotland. This Mary had grown up in France, Spain's greatest rival, and had long been betrothed to Francis, the son of King Henry II. There was also the possibility, if Elizabeth did rule, that the widowed Philip could marry her. As Queen Mary's health worsened, England teetered between French and Spanish spheres of influence. Philip knew which way he wanted it to go.[21]

And what of Elizabeth? She professed satisfaction, as princess, with her single state,[22] but after becoming queen in November 1558, she was widely expected to follow Mary's example, take a husband, and if more fortunate give birth to an heir. Their father, after all, had made succession by bloodline his central (if brutal) priority. The Roman alternative of adoption, which might have saved him a lot of trouble, had long since fallen into disuse: with few exceptions,[23] legitimacy now required royal births.

Rarely as yet, though, of ruling queens. Marriages, however risky for Henry's consorts, had never put *his* life in danger, but Elizabeth's, with each pregnancy, would be. Even if these went well, independence, which she valued no less than her father, would collide with the near-universal presumption that wives should defer to husbands: Mary, with the sole right to rule, had nonetheless allowed Philip to drag her into the war with France that lost Calais. "Looks" too could be a problem. Elizabeth preferred eye-pleasing men, but couldn't marry an English favorite without enraging others. A foreign marriage would avoid that: distance made it difficult, however, for royal couples to see each other before deals were done, and pre-photographic images could mislead disastrously. Recalling Henry VIII's revulsion on meeting his fourth wife, Anne of Cleves, only days before their wedding, Elizabeth wisely insisted that she wouldn't "trust portrait painters."[24]

She'd seen Philip when he was in England, though, and she knew—even if she didn't like to acknowledge—that he'd tried to keep her safe.[25] Philip wasted no time after Mary's death in proposing to Elizabeth, but the new queen turned him down, noting politely that their realms could have the amicable relations he said he wanted without a wedding. The king's real purpose, he revealed privately, had been to "prevent that lady from making the changes in religion that she has in mind, and so to serve God." Hers was to modify religion, in order to reclaim independence from Rome. The disparity became clear within months of Elizabeth's accession, at which point Philip proposed to Isabel of France, the daughter of Henry II, who became his new wife.[26]

Elizabeth would entertain, over the next quarter century, well over a dozen suitors,[27] each of whom, after varying degrees of dalliance, she spurned. Her motives remain unclear. Perhaps she feared sex, or childbirth. Perhaps her father's marriages haunted her. Perhaps she wished to share her throne with no rival, however titular. Perhaps she put off a decision until it was too late: she was juggling proposals well into her forties.[28] But the most likely explanation is that Elizabeth prized pivoting. Her strategy, the historian Garrett Mattingly has explained,

> was to arrange the courtiers and counselors around her, the diplomats and envoys, the kings and powers of the Continent in an elaborate interlocked design so cunningly and delicately balanced that each part should counteract another and she herself should always be free.[29]

The price, to be sure, was loneliness: Woolf's uprightness "strung together by a thousand fears." But as Philip's interests corresponded, in his mind, with those of God, so Elizabeth's paralleled those of her modest but potentially pivotal island state.

III.

Philip found himself more often a pincushion than a pivot, stuck on multiple points at once. He was repelling a French attack on the Netherlands when he learned of Mary's death, as well as that of his father, the recently abdicated Charles V, in Spain. What happened in England would determine Catholicism's future there, but Philip had for too long neglected his Spanish homeland. It would dishearten the Dutch, however, to leave without making peace, "although my presence here does nothing to win them over. . . . I think they would be happy with any sovereign except me." They'd confirmed this by reducing his income, while his sister Juana, serving as regent in Spain, so flatly rejected his request to her for additional funds that Philip feared he was being laughed at. And yet, the king insisted, as an absolute monarch he need not acknowledge "any temporal superior on this earth."[30]

How could Philip have no superior but be paralyzed by constraints? One reason is that his family, the ubiquitous Hapsburgs, had long privileged dynastic ties over geographic, economic, or cultural affinities: they conquered, it was said, by marrying. As a result, Philip ruled—and depended on revenues from—a patchwork of peoples owing him little loyalty.[31] Noncontiguous boundaries compounded the problem, as did the king's dislike of delegating authority. His mind could be in multiple places at once, hence his multiple dilemmas. Placing Philip's body in that position, however, was beyond even God's capabilities.

The Romans managed more of Europe than Philip and populations at least as diverse, arguably with greater efficiency. But their lands adjoined one another, their administrators didn't see delegation as religious dereliction, and their only competitors were barbarians who took centuries to wear their victims down. Philip had to contend with the French, the English, the Dutch, the Portuguese, the Holy Roman empire, the Ottomans, the papacy, and—most unnervingly—the Protestant Reformation, which was spreading its heresies throughout much of the continent. With this many moles to whack, it's hardly surprising that the king was at war somewhere for all but six months of his forty-three years on the throne.[32]

From a secular standpoint, he didn't do badly: Philip lost none of the territories Charles V left him. Spain wouldn't give up the

Netherlands until half a century after Philip's death, and Portugal with its overseas possessions would remain Spanish for six decades. Spain's own "new world" dominions, extending eventually from mid–North America to Tierra del Fuego, survived into the early nineteenth century and in fragments until 1898, a longevity rivaling that of the British empire.[33] Even Philip's debts, about which he complained constantly and on which he defaulted repeatedly, may have been, by modern standards, sustainable.[34]

Philip judged himself, though, on a loftier scale. He sought to serve God, and the empire only to the extent that it advanced God's interests. All other goals required "shut[ting] your ears, and even your eyes," for they were by definition unworthy. "Believe me: this is the simplest, least stressful and most sure path for everything." No doubt it was as long as God provided the means to achieve His ends. To Philip's bewilderment, however, God could be as parsimonious as the difficult Dutch. Since all depended on His will, Philip wrote in 1559,

> I can only wait for whatever He is pleased to grant. . . . I hope
> that [He will] provide me with the means to hold on to my
> dominions, and not let them be lost because I lack the means
> to hold on to them, which would be the saddest thing for me
> and something I would regret more than anything else one
> can think of—and much more than if I lost them in battle.

"My only aim is to get it right," the king lamented. "[B]ut I am so unlucky that when I want something . . . , it often turns out badly. This is how the world works."[35]

What Philip wanted was loyalty from his subjects, prosperity within his provinces, credibility among his competitors, a return to orthodoxy where it had been endangered—and, more vaguely, a world that was "not enough." He failed to see incompatibles, and hence the need to pursue certain objectives at the expense of others. The king resisted prioritizing ends, even though God Himself had chosen selectively to provide means.

Instead Philip lashed himself with Augustinian anxieties. How could a world working against God's agent—which Philip believed he was—reflect God's intentions—which Philip believed it must? God couldn't be inconsistent, like Jupiter, or evil, like Satan. But He could, Augustine had suggested, be *instructional:* God could make men fail in order to better themselves, whether in this world or the next. That became the basis for Philip's grand strategy: not to plan with a view to pivoting but, in the manner of saintly pincushioned martyrs, to suffer. "Pray God that in heaven," he wrote lugubriously in 1569, "we shall be treated better."[36]

IV.

Elizabeth, like Machiavelli, neither expected nor needed reassurance. She thanked God—not Philip—for her survival as princess, but as queen rarely sought instruction from anyone, terrestrial or divine. "She is a very strange sort of woman," Count de Feria, Spain's ambassador, reported after finding the new monarch relaxed, even laughing, as if she were reading his mind. "She must have been thoroughly schooled in the manner in which her father conducted his affairs. She is determined to be governed by no one."[37]

Feria was among the first, but by no means the last, of Elizabeth's perplexed interlocutors. She could be childlike or canny, forthright or devious, brave or risk-averse, forgiving or vindictive, serene or volcanic, even feminine or masculine: "I have the body but of a weak, feeble woman," she told her troops as the Spanish Armada sailed for home in 1588, "but I have the heart and stomach of a king, and of a king of England too." Relishing opposites, the queen was constant only in her patriotism, her insistence on keeping ends within means, and her determination—a requirement for pivoting—never to be pinned down.[38]

Her hopes for religion reflected this. Knowing the upheavals her country had undergone—Henry VIII's expulsion of the pope from English Catholicism, the shift to strict Protestantism in Edward VI's brief reign, the harsh reversion to Rome under Mary—Elizabeth wanted a single church with multiple ways of worship. There was, she pointed out, "only one Jesus Christ." Why couldn't there be different paths to Him? Theological quarrels were "trifles," or, more tartly, "ropes of sand or sea-slime leading to the Moon."[39]

Until they affected national sovereignty. God's church, under Elizabeth, would be staunchly English: whether "Catholic" or "Protestant" mattered less than loyalty. This was, in one sense, toleration, for the new queen cared little what her subjects believed. She would watch like a hawk, though, what they did. "Her Majesty seems to me incomparably more feared than her sister," Feria warned Philip— which was saying something since that lady had been "bloody" Mary. "We have lost a kingdom, body and soul."[40]

Diplomacy and defense too would be self-reliant. Blessed with an island, not Philip's scattered provinces, Elizabeth could avoid the costs of a standing army, adapt her navy for protection or provocation, and align her state as necessary—never permanently—with the continental enemies of her enemies. God's gift to England was geography, which piety wouldn't augment, or its absence diminish.

Ireland and Scotland (the latter still an independent country) remained running sores: the French and Spanish attempted to exploit unrest in both territories. But Elizabeth's rebels never caused her the trouble Philip had in trying to suppress the Dutch, who from 1572 were in revolt—with England's help when the queen chose to give it. By resisting military commitments while enforcing domestic economies, Elizabeth balanced revenues and expenses during most of her reign, even running a surplus in its second and third decades. In contrast to Philip, she never declared bankruptcy.[41]

We don't usually connect fiscal responsibility with lightness of being, but in Elizabeth they aligned. Lightness allowed flirtation, which cost less than obligation, whether to suitors or to their realms. It eased delegation: the queen loved performing, but also others' performances.[42] It facilitated strategic mischief: when short of funds, Elizabeth allowed her navy to raid Philip's treasure ships returning from America—perhaps, she suggested in response to his protests, they'd been the victims of pirates?[43]

The queen's lightness also upended courtiers, leaving her in control. A memorable victim was the Earl of Oxford,[44] who, one day while bowing respectfully, farted loudly. Elizabeth said nothing and seemed not to notice, but Oxford, humiliated, went into exile for seven years. At last he reappeared, bowed again, this time silently, and waited anxiously. "My Lord," the queen responded (I like to think after a slight pause), "I had forgot the fart."[45]

Pivoting requires gyroscopes, and Elizabeth's were the best of her era. She balanced purposefulness with imagination, guile, humor, timing, and an *economy* in movement that, however extravagant her display, kept her steady on the tightrope she walked. Philip's gyroscopes, if he had any, malfunctioned constantly. She, without visible effort, retained the initiative in all she did. He exhausted himself regaining it in one place while losing it somewhere else. She deftly turned adversaries against each other. He ponderously united them against himself. She, running a poor state, kept it solvent. He, running a rich one, begged and borrowed. She never felt not up to her role. He worried repeatedly that he was not up to his.

Machiavelli, thinking gyroscopically, advised his prince to be a lion *and* a fox, the former to frighten wolves, the latter to detect snares. Elizabeth went him one better by being lion, fox, and female, a combination the crafty Italian might have learned to appreciate. Philip was a grand lion, but he was *only* a lion. Such princes can through conscientiousness, Machiavelli warned, become trapped. For a wise ruler "cannot observe faith, nor should he, when such observance turns against him, and the causes that made him promise have been eliminated. . . . Nor does a prince ever lack legitimate causes to color his failure to observe faith."[46] Philip, reporting to an all-seeing God, found coloring beyond his capabilities: maybe that's why he always wore black.[47] Elizabeth, reporting only to herself, dazzled: "Age [could] not wither her, nor custom stale / Her infinite variety."[48]

V.

When Machiavelli wrote of faith in this context, he didn't necessarily mean religious conviction. His point was simply that circumstances change, and that princes shouldn't impose old promises on new situations. He wasn't anticipating the Protestant Reformation: he'd hardly had time, before dying in 1527, to become aware of Martin Luther.[49] Half a century later, though, the conduct of statecraft couldn't so easily dismiss religious differences. Elizabeth and Philip had to decide where the observance of faith coincided—and didn't—with the obligations of princely rule.

They managed a wary demarcation through most of the 1560s. Philip was consolidating his position in Spain and securing the Mediterranean from the Ottoman Turks. Elizabeth was expanding England's influence in Scotland, where a French civil war had deprived Mary Stuart, now Queen of Scots, of external support. But an Anglo-Spanish détente would require insulation from religion, and growing Protestant unrest in the Netherlands—a strategic sensitivity for both monarchs—was making that increasingly unlikely.

It forced Philip into costly military campaigns that threatened but also tempted Elizabeth. Spain's success would entrench a Catholic superpower dangerously close on the English Channel. Not, however, without vast costs, which only American gold and silver could cover. Elizabeth's navy could intercept Spanish ships anywhere along their long route, leaving her free—because distance delayed communications—to avow or disavow its actions. Closer to home but with similar slipperiness, she could hide Dutch pirates in English ports. She thus had a choke hold, annoying if not lethal, on Philip's northern European foothold.[50]

Religion was also undermining diplomacy. Elizabeth's ambassador got himself banned from the Spanish court for mocking the pope and conducting Protestant services; citing diplomatic immunity, she refused to replace him. Meanwhile, Philip's emissary in London was secretly communicating with Mary Stuart, now deposed as Scotland's queen, who'd fled to England and sought Elizabeth's protection. Philip himself, in 1569, assured Mary of his sympathy and support as long as she remained—she'd been known to waver—a resolute Catholic.

With the French having abandoned Mary, Philip no longer feared her alignment with them. And so he returned to the project he'd suspended a decade earlier: reviving Roman Catholicism in England. Then he'd hoped for Elizabeth's help, perhaps even through marriage. Now he'd written her off: "God must be allowing . . . her sins and unfaithfulness, so that she will be lost." It was clear, therefore, "that, after my special obligation to maintain my own states in our holy faith, I am bound to make every effort in order to restore and preserve it in England as in former times."[51]

Philip placed his plan within a larger revival of Catholic crusading, aimed this time at liberating Canterbury, not Jerusalem. The Augustinian obligation to serve the state had evolved into a papal obligation to serve the church, no longer by ridding the Holy Land of infidels—that was a lost cause—but by killing European Christians who'd rejected Rome's authority. Henry VIII had made England a prime target, and in 1570 Pope Pius V did his part by excommunicating Elizabeth, in effect licensing the faithful not only to overthrow, but to assassinate her.[52]

The Duke of Alba, commander of Philip's armies in the Netherlands, found all of these ideas impractical: "Even though the principal means must come from God, as your Majesty very virtuously and piously suggests, it seems necessary to examine what human resources would be needed to carry out your wishes." He had no confidence that he could launch a cross-Channel attack, or if he did that it would succeed, or if it did that Elizabeth's Catholics would betray her, or if they did that the English—whatever their faith—would accept Mary as their new queen. The piled-up contingencies alarmed Alba, for whom pacifying the Dutch, in a much smaller country, had proven difficult enough. Philip ordered him, nonetheless, to proceed: "I am so attached to [the invasion] in my heart, and I am so convinced that

God our Savior must embrace it as His own cause, that I cannot be dissuaded. Nor can I accept or believe the contrary."[53]

Having told God what to do, however, Philip lost track of what *he* had to do: micromanaging an empire on which the sun never set tended to blur his vision. To Alba's relief, but to the exasperation of Pius V and even more to that of his successor, Gregory XIII, the king allowed his great scheme to drift. All that Philip accomplished in the end was to alert Elizabeth, who saw that she could no longer afford toleration. She may not have been, when she became queen, as feared as "bloody" Mary, but she now knew that she had to be.

VI.

The pope's edict made it impossible, Elizabeth's biographer Anne Somerset has written, "to be both a good Catholic and a good Englishman."[54] For with Philip to the south conspiring with Mary Stuart in the north, England was theologically, if not yet militarily, under siege. Hawk-like vigilance, even vengeance, was necessary.

Elizabeth had already unleashed the latter in 1569 in the aftermath of an anti-Protestant rebellion—badly run and quickly suppressed—in northern England. Worried that its leaders might free the former Queen of Scots, under castle arrest nearby, Elizabeth turned viciously on their followers, ordering more executions for a single uprising than Henry VIII or Mary Tudor had ever done. She insisted on killing "the meaner sort of rebels," for "the terror of others," presumably their betters. The poor, the queen explained, must "worthily [suffer] death."[55]

Vigilance paid off with the discovery, in 1571, of the most elaborate plot yet to invade England, depose Elizabeth, and put Mary

Stuart on the throne. A Florentine banker, Roberto Ridolfi, had made himself the link connecting Pius V, Mary, Philip, and the Duke of Alba, the only conspirator who questioned the feasibility of what he proposed. Ridolfi proved him right by talking too much, allowing Elizabeth's spymasters to track what was happening and, at the right moment, expose it. Mary was lucky, after this, to retain her head; but it was henceforth precariously positioned.[56]

Like many leaders who like to think they're loved, Elizabeth professed indifference to her own security.[57] This worried her counselors, keenly aware that she hadn't produced or designated an heir. But here delegation paid off. In 1573 she made Sir Francis Walsingham her secretary of state, with orders to do whatever was necessary—she needn't know what—to guard queen and country. This Elizabeth could accept, for she'd made the two the same.

Convinced that there was "less danger in fearing too much than too little," Walsingham took counterespionage, or "spiery," as it was then known, to unprecedented extremes. Using bribery, theft, entrapment, blackmail, and torture, he built a network of informants stretching across Europe. It's hard to say that it wasn't needed: the pope was routinely encouraging assassination now, and Philip himself had approved Elizabeth's murder if it would make Mary Stuart queen.[58]

What we like to recall as the Elizabethan "golden age" survived only through surveillance and terror: that was another of its contradictions, maintained regretfully with resignation.[59] The queen's instincts were more humane than those of her predecessors, but too many contemporaries were trying to kill her. "Unlike her sister, Elizabeth never burned men for their faith," her recent biographer Lisa Hilton has written. "She tortured and hanged them for treason."[60] Toleration, Machiavelli might have said, had turned against

Elizabeth. She wanted to be loved—who wouldn't? It was definitely safer for princes, though, to be feared.

VII.

Philip gave Elizabeth more to fear when he took over Portugal in 1580. That country had pioneered long-distance ocean navigation a century earlier: now its ships and sailing skills served Spain.[61] Elizabeth had made the most of her smaller navy by sending Sir Francis Drake on a three-year voyage around the world—the first since Magellan's—showing that no seas were safe for Spanish treasure. But although profitable in the extreme for Drake, his queen, and his investors, the expedition didn't change the fact that if Philip ever combined his fleet with his army in the Netherlands—acknowledged to be the best anywhere and now under the command of Alba's successor, the Duke of Parma—it might be difficult indeed to save England. [62]

Elizabeth responded with more pinpricks, none painful enough to reverse the unfavorably shifting balance of power. She increased subsidies to the Dutch rebels and, for the first time, sent English troops to fight alongside them: these measures did little, though, to hinder Parma. She dispatched Drake, also with infantry, to the West Indies, where he raided ports and captured more booty, but failed to hold any permanent base.[63] Meanwhile, plots against the queen continued, any one of which, if successful, could leave no alternative to Mary Stuart. Walsingham's agents turned up three in as many years between 1583 and 1585.[64]

After Parliament made conversion to Catholicism treasonable, priests were regularly executed in England. Mary remained, however, a Counter-Reformation center of gravity, "the instrument whereby the perils do grow," as Elizabeth's adviser Lord Burghley put it. Still the queen's prisoner in northern England, Mary hadn't abandoned her faith, her ambitions, or her appetite for conspiracy.[65] That left Elizabeth in an awkward position.

To kill a priest was one thing; to kill a former and possibly future queen was quite another. Elizabeth abhorred regicide, knowing its violent role in English history. Its use now would make her more bloodthirsty than "bloody" Mary, who'd allowed the young Elizabeth to live. It would equate her morally with papal efforts to enforce orthodoxy by assassination. And it would risk an uncertain succession, for what was to prevent Mary Stuart's son James VI, now King of Scots and brought up as a Protestant, from converting to Catholicism if he believed his mother to have been unjustly murdered?

In the end, Elizabeth maneuvered masterfully. She bribed James to repudiate his mother, while approving a parliamentary ban on any future Catholic monarch. She let Walsingham implicate Mary by forging documents in another plot that was real enough: Mary, unwisely, took the bait. After the conspirators were arrested, Elizabeth insisted on prolonged public executions. She then had Mary convicted of treason, expressed dismay at the verdict, and asked Parliament if the rogue queen's death was really necessary. Assured that it was, Elizabeth delayed approving the warrant until her councilors, in desperation, slipped it among a stack of papers awaiting her signature. She signed it casually, but made it clear later that she knew perfectly well what they thought they'd tricked her into doing.

Fearing that Elizabeth would change her mind, they rushed the warrant north to Fotheringhay, where Mary was being held. Her execution followed quickly—the date was February 8, 1587—and Elizabeth was quickly informed. She appeared at first undisturbed, but then pulled off one of the greatest public performances of her life, weeping hysterically, protesting that she'd been deceived, threatening to hang those responsible, and appearing for weeks to mourn the dead queen. It was like allowing, then disavowing, Drake. Now, though, with more craft and greater consequence, she had allowed and disavowed herself.[66]

VIII.

Mary's execution didn't dissuade Philip, however, from preparing to invade England. One reason was the acquisition of Portugal: "[I]f the Romans were able to rule the world simply by ruling the Mediterranean," the king's chaplain reminded him, "what of the man who rules the Atlantic and Pacific oceans, since they surround the world?" Another was the ease with which Philip's admiral, the Marquis of Santa Cruz, had ejected French, English, and rebel Portuguese forces from the Azores in 1582–83, thereby seeming to show the feasibility of amphibious operations. Still another came from a new pope, Sixtus V, who insisted as adamantly as his predecessors that it was Philip's divinely inspired duty to restore Catholicism in England.[67]

Philip found the papal pressure exasperating: didn't the pope realize that suppressing Dutch rebels was also a holy cause? God should do His part by first securing that victory, after which Spain could conquer England. It wasn't possible to do everything at once. But then Elizabeth went beyond pinpricks: having picked up rumors of an impending invasion, she authorized Drake to begin raiding Spain itself. His brief landing in Galicia in the fall of 1585 shocked Philip, who saw that it could be the first of many. Facing the prospect of having to defend the entire Iberian coastline, he convinced himself that the only way to defeat Drake would be to attack his home base. With this in mind, Philip focused, without further distraction, on the "Enterprise of England." Mary's death made no difference—other than to convince him that God now wanted *him* to succeed Elizabeth.[68]

God failed again, though, to provide the resources, circumstances, and organizational efficiency that this would require. Philip's micromanagement delayed preparations, as did Drake's continuing raids. Secrecy had long been lost, eliminating any hope of surprise. Strategy was unclear: how would the "Armada"—commanded now not by the experienced Santa Cruz, who'd died, but by the Duke of Medina Sidonia, who lacked seafaring skills—link up with Parma's army in the Netherlands to make the Channel crossing? The largest naval force ever assembled sailed from Lisbon in May 1588, only to run into a storm that scattered it, forcing repairs and resupply in the northern Spanish port of Corunna. Philip was undaunted: "If this were an unjust war, one could indeed take the tempest as a sign from Our Lord to cease offending Him," he admonished the demoralized duke. But "I have dedicated this enterprise to God. . . . Pull yourself together, then, and do your part."[69]

"The world was never so dangerous, nor never so full of treasons and treacheries as at this day," one of Elizabeth's favorites, the Earl of Leicester, had written her from the Netherlands a few months earlier.[70] Her ports were better prepared for commerce than defense. She had no way of knowing how many of her subjects remained quietly Catholic. Parma was close to crushing the Dutch rebels. And Elizabeth's navy, however well trained, was no match numerically for Medina Sidonia's massive fleet, which appeared off Cornwall on July 29.[71] The queen did, however, have a strategy.

She'd first brought Drake home, knowing that her admirals could best confront the Armada in the English Channel, where they knew it would have to be. She foresaw no great battle, as at Salamis or Actium: instead her fleet would follow the Spanish ships, picking them off one by one while awaiting more promising opportunities—which Philip obligingly provided. Medina Sidonia's warships were supposed to protect Parma's barges as they carried his army to England. But the king's orders said nothing about timing, or the means by which the admiral and the general would communicate, or how the winds and tides could bring the two fleets together from opposite directions and then, at just the right moment, propel them in the same direction toward England. That was a lot to leave in God's hands.

Medina Sidonia anchored off Calais on August 6, having heard nothing from Parma; he, just up the coast in Flanders, was surprised to learn on the next day of the Armada's arrival. He hurried his troops onto their barges, only to discover that Sir Charles Howard, Elizabeth's lord admiral, had that night taken advantage of a favorable wind to rig fireships, forcing the Armada, in panic, to cut its anchor cables and disperse. Off Gravelines, on the next day, Howard's fleet battered the disorganized Spanish: Parma could only watch, in frustration, from the beaches. England, overnight, was again safe. Howard had improvised, knowing that his queen would approve.

The English didn't defeat the Armada, but they wore it down, which amounted to the same thing. Reliant, throughout their voyage, on supplies taken on weeks earlier in Corunna, with no possibility now of replenishment in any friendly port, the Spanish had no option but to sail home the long way: across the North Sea, around the Shetlands, and down the inhospitable west coasts of Scotland and Ireland. The first ships didn't reach Spain until the third week in September:

of the 129 that left at the end of July, at least 50 were lost, and many of those returning had to be scrapped. Half the men who embarked for England died, most from wrecks, starvation, or disease: the toll may have been 15,000. The English, in contrast, lost only the eight vessels sacrificed to the flames at Calais, and about 150 men.[72]

IX.

"I hope that God has not permitted so much evil," Philip wrote after the first reports of the disaster reached him, "for everything has been done for His service." Soon, though, he was planning a new invasion,[73] convinced that God, by inflicting adversity, had been only testing him. "I undertake to deal with everything necessary to achieve all this. . . . I shall never fail to stand up for the cause of God."[74] Augustine, of course, had made a similar argument, but what God would test, he'd insisted, was *proportionality* in aligning ends with means. There was never, in Augustine, an injunction *indiscriminately* to expend earthly lives and treasure for heavenly purposes.

"To invade by sea upon a perilous coast, being neither in possession of any port, nor succoured by any party, may better fit a prince presuming on his fortune than enriched with understanding," Sir Walter Raleigh observed after the Armada had failed.[75] Machiavelli could have said this. Augustine could have too, with the substitution of "God" for "fortune." What made Philip, then, so persistently *dis*proportionate?

Geoffrey Parker, his best biographer, finds an answer in late twentieth-century "prospect" theory: leaders, it suggests, risk more to avoid losses than to achieve gains.[76] Given the empire Philip inherited and then expanded, he had a lot to lose. What's strange, though, are the risks he ran to *regain* territories he hadn't lost. It wasn't Philip's fault that Henry VIII broke with Rome, or that Mary Tudor failed to reverse his heresy. These misfortunes, together with the Protestant Reformation, could even have been God's punishment for centuries of papal excesses. Philip didn't see it that way, though. He was sure that God had entrusted him not just with the task of losing nothing more, but also with that of recovering for the church its ancient and medieval universality.

"[I]f God had placed Your Majesty under an obligation to remedy all the troubles of the world," Philip's private secretary suggested in 1591, "he would have given you the money and strength to do so." "I know you are moved by the great zeal you have for my service," the king replied, "but you must also understand that these are not matters that can be abandoned by a person who is as conscientious about his responsibilities as you know me to be. . . . The cause of religion must take precedence over everything else."[77]

It was one of many occasions on which Philip resorted to what Parker calls "spiritual blackmail."[78] When warned that his objectives exceeded his capabilities, the king would claim that those doing the warning themselves lacked faith: God would close the gap. When God didn't, Philip insisted that *he* would remain faithful, even if God's attention had wandered. God did indeed test Philip. But Philip didn't put himself beneath testing God.

X.

Elizabeth tested God too, but for English patriotism, not Catholic universality. "[T]he shining glory of princely authority hath not so dazzled [our] eyes," she assured Parliament shortly before she died, "but that we well know and remember that we also are to yield an account of our actions before the great judge." She showed no sign, though, of fearing the verdict: she "delighted that God hath made me His instrument to maintain His truth and glory and to defend this kingdom."[79] If queen and country were the same in her mind, so too, in God's, were "truth and glory" and defending "this kingdom."

Certainty, however, never required haste. From the moment Elizabeth became queen, the historian A. N. Wilson has pointed out, "her advisers and courtiers had been urging her to make decisions: to be Catholic or to be Protestant; to marry; to fight a decisive and expensive war in Ireland or the Low Countries. In almost all cases, Elizabeth had dithered, Hamlet-like; and dithering had been, if not the right policy, then at least not the wrong policy." For "Elizabeth, like Hamlet, could see the calamitous effects of too great a precision and too great a decisiveness in political life."

They hardly at first seem similar. Shakespeare's prince, dressed like Philip always in black, lacks Elizabeth's lightness—except in his mad scenes, where he feigns irresponsibility, even lunacy, to smoke out his enemies. Elizabeth used dithering, which looks irresponsible, in something like the same way: to remind her advisers for whom they worked; to hold off her suitors, thus balancing their states; and, when the balance at last turned against her, to lure the Spanish Armada into the English Channel where, by trusting her admirals, she sprang a massive mousetrap. Precision and decisiveness, in each of these situations, could have entrapped her. "This god-daughter of Cranmer, the liturgical master of hendiadys," Wilson concludes, "had seen the wisdom of double-think."[80]

My dictionary defines "hendiadys" as "a complex idea expressed by two words connected by a copulative conjunction." Or, less lustily, how two things can be, or become, one. How, for example, could a new religion, conceived in the lust of an English king, replace a faith souls had followed for a thousand years? Perhaps by speaking to them, without condescension, in their own tongue. Cranmer's *Book of Common Prayer*, Wilson shows, rolls out majestic hendiadys, bringing unforgettable clarity to a language still young enough to be growing:

> Almighty and most merciful father; We have erred and strayed from thy ways like lost sheep. We have followed too much the devices and desires of our own hearts. . . . Behold our most gracious sovereign lady Queen Elizabeth . . . grant her in health and wealth long to live; strengthen her that she may vanquish and overcome all her enemies; and finally after this life she may attain everlasting joy and felicity.

Hendiadys can seem to say the same thing: "erred and strayed," "devices and desires," "health and wealth," "vanquish and overcome," "joy and felicity." But their combinations can also introduce, so deftly that one hardly notices, contradictions: "almighty and most merciful father," or "our most gracious sovereign lady."

Raising the possibility that a father may forgive, that a lady may rule—and that a virgin queen may save a state and leave a legacy. These were new possibilities, which Elizabeth opened triumphantly. As, from a distance, she encouraged Shakespeare, who peppered his plays and poems not just with new words, but with such rich redundancies—"How weary, stale, flat and unprofitable / Seem to me all the uses of this world!"—that, as Wilson puts it, he "stretched and expanded the English language," thereby giving to all who spoke it "a larger vocabulary and hence a larger capacity to describe experience."[81]

And, hence, to manage it. For if, as Thucydides warned two thousand years earlier, words in crises can lose their meaning, leaving in the "ability to see all sides of a question [an] incapacity to act on any,"[82] then Shakespeare and his Great Queen found safety in multiple meanings, some repetitive, some opposed, but all so implanted as to make them unforeseeably applicable. Hendiadys positioned a culture against paralysis in a world that was to come.

XI.

"[O]n a warm July evening of the year 1588, in the royal palace of Greenwich, . . . a woman lay dying, an assassin's bullets lodged in abdomen and chest. Her face was lined, her teeth blackened, and death lent her no dignity; but her last breath started echoes that ran out to shake a hemisphere." The word reached the great ships, and for a day Medina Sidonia paced the decks. "Then his decision was made; and one by one the galleons and carracks, the galleys and the lumbering urcas turned northward towards the land. Towards Hastings . . . , where history had been made once centuries before."

Philip II becomes again king of England, the Protestant Reformation collapses throughout Europe, Spain rules all of South *and* North America, Captain Cook plants the papal flag in Australia. "To some the years that passed were years of fulfillment, of the final flowering of God's Design; to others they were a new Dark Age, haunted by things dead and others best forgotten. . . . Over all, the long arm of the Popes reached out to punish and reward; the Church Militant remained supreme."[83]

Keith Roberts's 1968 novel *Pavane* portrays what might have happened had history pivoted, 380 years earlier, in only a slightly different way. His 1960s—it's then that he sets his tale—is an England of transportation by steam tractors, illumination by candles, and communication by semaphores, for Rome has banned petroleum, electricity, and telegraphy. Radio, allowed only to a secretive guild, is otherwise necromancy. Politics are authoritarian, education is limited, and memory is dim. "One of those minor Elizabethans," a character explains, having recalled, unexpectedly, a few lines from *Richard III*. "We had him at school. I forget his name; I thought he was rather good."[84]

Pavane seems sufficiently anti-Catholic to have made the papal index if it hadn't been abolished in 1966—until another character advises, also unexpectedly: "Do not despise your Church; for she has a wisdom beyond your understanding." Rome, it turns out, has had modern technology, even nuclear expertise, all along, but has held it back until civilization catches up and can use it wisely. "Did she hang and burn? A little, yes. But there was no Belsen. No Buchenwald. No Passchendaele." Only an ancient—but real—Armageddon from which this knowledge came.[85]

This last twist makes Roberts's novel hendyadic: the church, more than anyone suspects, masters contradictions and therefore links the cities of God and Man. It's *only*, of course, a novel. But counterfactuals, like ghosts, should haunt historians. It's all very well to say that Augustine is in Heaven and Machiavelli is in Hell: where, though, is Philip? If there's a God and He's really Catholic, then the king, ever faithful, ranks among the grandest strategists of all time.[86] And Elizabeth? Machiavelli would for her, for eternity, at least be good company.

CHAPTER SIX

NEW WORLDS

It's not counterfactual to claim that the *real* events of 1588 in the English Channel echoed loudly and long enough "to shake a hemisphere."[1] The previous century had seen the Portuguese and the Spanish, neither hitherto seismically significant, exploiting a new understanding of ships, sails, winds, and currents to explore and conquer immensities of strange new things.[2] "NON SUFFICIT ORBIS," Philip II's motto for his Iberian kingdoms and the empire they'd acquired, was eloquently apt: Eurasia, the old world into which all earlier empires had fit, had indeed not been enough. As the Armada left Lisbon that summer, few from whom it faded from sight would have anticipated anything other than enduring Catholic monarchies throughout what had become known as America.

For how could God *not* be on the side of the Christian kingdoms of Castile and Aragon that had, in the single year 1492, expelled their Muslim neighbors, ejected their Jews, and almost as an aside expanded the size of the earth? Or, in the year that followed, gained title to the new territories, together with Portugal, by papal edict? Or, as Spain, required only three years to conquer Mexico and not many more to control Peru, thereby ensuring apparently endless supplies of gold and silver? Or, using these riches, imposed administrative and even architectural uniformity on two unfamiliar continents? Or mapped out, for their diverse inhabitants, a single path to salvation? Accomplishments on this scale require more than self-confidence: they presume knowledge of, and correspondence with, God's will.

Two hundred and thirty-five years after the Armada sailed, however, a staunchly *Protestant* statesman, in the swampy new capital of a *secular* state, was drafting an equally presumptuous proclamation for his *republican* sovereign: "that the American continents, by the free and independent condition which they have assumed and maintain, are henceforth not to be considered as subjects for future colonization by any European powers." When Secretary of State John Quincy Adams made the Monroe Doctrine a motto for the "United States of America" in 1823, that country lacked the means of securing the "new world" against its "old" masters. It had the self-confidence, though, of Spain in its prime, and that, Adams saw, would suffice.[3]

"The failure of the Spanish Armada," Geoffrey Parker has argued, "laid the American continent open to invasion and colonization by northern Europeans, and thus made possible the creation of the United States." If that's right, then the future pivoted on a single evening—August 7, 1588—owing to a favorable wind, a clever lord admiral, and a few fiery ships. Had he succeeded, Philip would have required Elizabeth to end all English voyages to America.[4] But from the moment his captains cut their anchor cables, Spain began a slow decline, and a new world order its gradual ascendancy.

I.

The English, at the time of the Armada, had barely begun overseas expansion. The word "colony" to them meant Ireland. "Newfoundland," whose shores they'd visited, meant fish. "Exploration" meant joint-stock companies, the first of which had a grand title—"The Mystery, Company, and Fellowship of Merchant Adventurers for the Discovery of Unknown Lands &c"[5]—but an ill-conceived mission: it directed its energies, in an age of global cooling, toward finding trade routes to China through Hudson's Bay and around northern Russia. Drake's circumnavigation of 1577–80 signaled Elizabeth's curiosity about wider worlds: by then, though, Spain had for half a century controlled the Caribbean, Mexico, and large portions of South America. Sir Walter Raleigh's Roanoke, the first English settlement in North America, came only in 1584–85, but quickly and humiliatingly failed.[6]

Despite Spain's lead, Elizabeth refused to rush. She let her merchants risk *their* ships and settlers, but not *her* navy or treasury. She encouraged Drake to spook the Spanish, while under no illusion that his raids alone could secure her state. She sought self-sufficiency in overseas enterprises, sensing the shortcomings of Philip's micromanagement. She took interest only when convinced that others had interests, chiefly though not exclusively commercial. She set the template, thereby, for British America: a hodgepodge of colonies lacking common purpose, bound more to the sea and to England than to each other, strung out thinly along a thousand miles of coastline from Massachusetts to Georgia, and for the most part lightly—even absentmindedly—administered.[7]

Spanish America, by the 1750s, had six times the population and many more times the size and wealth of its northern counterpart. Its great cities, serviceable roads, and standard practices rivaled those of the Roman empire: there was nothing absentminded about it. The historian John Elliott has pointed out that a Mexico City gentleman visiting Lima, twenty-six hundred miles to the south, would have felt entirely at home: "Civic institutions were identical; the forms of worship the same." This wouldn't have happened in the British colonies, "where differing local backgrounds, differing motives for emigration and differing religious beliefs and practices created a mosaic of communities settled at a diversity of times and in a diversity of ways."[8] Imagine the young John Adams—John Quincy's father—among the planters of Virginia or the slave owners of South Carolina: the clash of cultures would have been almost as great as if *he'd* been in Lima.

Spain, like Rome, imposed uniformities on particularities. This could produce impressive results: it's unlikely, otherwise, that either empire would have expanded so far so fast. The price, though, was shallow roots, which allowed adversity to shake authority.[9] The English spread their influence more slowly, but adapted more easily, especially in North America. Where when trouble came, it brought a republican revolutionary *transfer* of authority, not a collapse, the example of which, over the next two centuries, would undermine empires everywhere.

II.

How, though, could lightness—even absentmindedness—lead to such an outcome? The answer, I think, lies in fitting foundations to the ground on which they rest. A heavy hand and a focused mind

can *appear* to achieve monumentality, but only by smoothing out if not flattening topography, somewhat in the manner of Xerxes and modern highways. You can't do this, though, all the way down, for the earth's irregularities reflect its nature: continents move, slide, collide, and override. Assuming stability is one of the ways ruins get made. Resilience accommodates the unexpected.

There can be reasons, therefore, for resisting uniformity, for respecting topography, even for dithering. Elizabeth ruled in this way, pioneering such innovations as reigning without marrying, tolerating (within limits) religious differences, and letting a language gloriously grow. Each arose in response to circumstances: none reflected grand designs. Joint-stock companies could be similarly flexible. "The absence of close control by the British crown in the early stages of colonization," Elliott points out,

> left considerable latitude for the evolution of those forms of government that seemed most appropriate to the people actively involved in the process of overseas enterprise and settlement—the financial backers of the enterprise and the colonists themselves—as long as they operated within the framework of their royal charter.

In contrast to Spain's "new world" colonies—and to the territories that France, more recently, had claimed (but barely settled) along the banks of the St. Lawrence, the Great Lakes, and the Ohio and Mississippi rivers—British America "was a society whose political and administrative institutions were more likely to evolve from below than to be imposed from above."[10] That made it a hodgepodge, but also a complex adaptive system.

Such systems thrive, theorists tell us, from the need to respond

frequently—but not too frequently—to the unforeseen. Controlled environments encourage complacency, making it hard to cope when controls break down, as they sooner or later must. Constant disruptions, however, prevent recuperation: nothing's ever healthy. There's a balance, then, between integrative and disintegrative processes in the natural world—an edge of chaos, so to speak—where adaptation, especially self-organization, tends to occur.[11] New political worlds work similarly.

III.

British North Americans lived simultaneously on several edges: of a vast but navigable ocean, of a continent claimed by Spain in the south and France to the north and west, of the disruptions unleashed at home by Elizabeth's gyroscopically inept successors. She'd so skillfully charmed, intimidated, cajoled, deferred to, and ignored Parliament that there was never a direct confrontation between them.[12] The first Stuarts, however, went out of their way to pick fights they couldn't win. They also blurred the late queen's distinction between what men believed and what they did, in effect playing with matches as Europe was stumbling into the religiously fueled Thirty Years' War. By 1642 civil war had erupted in England, so confusingly that historians still debate who fought whom for what.[13] Seven years later, however, that conflict cost Charles I his head.

The violence multiplied reasons for emigration, as did the promise, upon arrival in America, of commercial opportunities, the toleration of multiple faiths, and the prospect of lighter-handed rule. Heavy-handed domestic distractions—even, under Oliver Cromwell,

a failed republican experiment—left little choice from London's perspective but to allow a colonial "mosaic of communities." By the time Charles II made lightness his path to "restoration" in 1660, heterogeneity had established itself across the Atlantic.[14]

Charles's "lazy, long, and lascivious"[15] reign ended in 1685 with the accession of his bullheaded brother James II, whose incumbency possessed only the last of these qualities. A staunch Catholic, he set out to return England to Rome while "modernizing" it on the centrally administered model of France's Louis XIV: the colonies were soon to follow.[16] But when, three years later, the birth of a son made a Catholic succession likely, William of Orange, the Protestant Dutch husband of James's Protestant daughter Mary, launched the most successful cross-Channel invasion since that of an earlier William in 1066. James was overthrown, William and Mary replaced him, and the Americans were left to themselves once again. The "revolution" of 1688 ensured, for them, continued *evolution*—even as it justified, by the precedent it set, resistance to future efforts to reverse what had been permitted to evolve.

The lessons of 1688, its chief ideologist John Locke argued, were that "there can be but one supreme power which is the legislative to which all the rest are and must be subordinate," yet "there remains still in the people a supreme power to remove or alter the legislative."[17] The principles seem at odds—how can supremacies share?—but within that puzzle, the modern historian Robert Tombs has suggested, lay the foundations of England's post-Stuart political culture:

> [S]uspicion of Utopias and zealots; trust in common sense and experience; respect for tradition; preference for gradual change; and the view that "compromise" is victory, not betrayal. These

things stem from the failure of both royal absolutism and of godly republicanism: costly failures, and fruitful ones.[18]

Their "odor" (Machiavelli's useful word) was Elizabethan, although Her Majesty wouldn't have welcomed a "constitutional" monarchy. She would have seen benefits, though, in *balancing* opposites: she practiced that art every day. She'd have thought her successors' efforts to *reconcile* opposites dangerously foolish. She understood political horticulture: that things grow best when variety is allowed and roots aren't too closely examined. So she probably would have approved of Edmund Burke.

IV.

Who rose in Parliament, on March 22, 1775, to explain what Britain's Americans had become. They were, Burke noted, a "recent people, . . . not yet hardened into the bone of manhood." They'd shown a "hardy industry" bred from an inheritance of English freedom, homegrown republicanism, diverse faiths, a profitable if uneasy dependence on slavery, a prickly litigiousness spawned by widespread literacy, and the self-reliance demanded by the "[t]hree thousand miles of ocean . . . between you and them." Apart from "a wise and salutary neglect," they "owe little or nothing to any care of ours." In their achievements "I feel all pride of power sink, and all presumption in the wisdom of human contrivances melt. . . . I pardon something to the spirit of Liberty."[19]

"Contrivances" had indeed been few in British North American policy during the first half of the eighteenth century. Indecisively prolonged European wars, together with the rise, under a weakened monarchy, of distinctive political "parties," left little time or energy for ambitious colonial projects. Meanwhile, the insouciance of the Americans, when given instructions, made it easier not to try. "I imagined like most young beginners, that . . . I should be able to make a mighty change in the face of affairs," a chastened colonial governor wrote in 1737, "but a little experience of the people, and reflection on the situation of things at home has absolutely cur'd me of this mistake."[20]

Such looseness, though, could hardly last. The colonies were doubling their population every twenty-five years, Benjamin Franklin pointed out in 1751: in a century, "the greatest Number of Englishmen will be on this Side [of] the Water."[21] That made westward expansion imperative, but the French and their Native American allies blocked the way. When George Washington, then a young colonel, failed to retake a British frontier fort in 1754,[22] a new war broke out. Known for the seven years it took to fight, the struggle soon spread to Europe, India, and the high seas. Its most dramatic event was the French loss of Quebec to the British in 1759, which in turn forced France's withdrawal altogether from North America.

The Peace of Paris of 1763 looked like an Anglo-American triumph, but in fact it drove the victors apart. The war had focused official minds: why then, King George III's ministers asked, should postwar colonial administration again lose its focus? Shouldn't the Americans, by some calculations the least taxed of all people, pay more for the security they'd gained? Could the British, however cleverly financed now by the Bank of England, indefinitely accumulate debt? Shouldn't someone regulate trans-Appalachian settlement, preventing collisions between imported and indigenous

Americans? What good was it even to have an empire if you weren't running it?[23]

For Americans used to a light touch, however, such questions suggested a heavy hand that, once applied, might not be withdrawn.[24] Bewilderment followed, then resentment, and then with the Stamp Act of 1765 active resistance. Possessing few means of enforcement at so great a distance, Parliament backed down, satisfying itself with the Declaratory Act of 1766, which reserved the right to revive what it had just repealed. Burke scathingly mocked the petulance: "After you have made this Law, you must make another to enforce that—and so on in endless rotation of Vain and Impotent Efforts—Every great act you make must be attended with a little act like a Squire to carry his Armour."[25]

The problem lay in Locke's opposed supremacies: the people must obey the government, but the government must reflect the will of the people. He'd meant that tightrope, though, for a small island. When stretched across a great ocean—where distance impeded reflection and empowered disobedience—it was too thin a thread. Burke saw the difficulty as early as 1769:

> The Americans have made a discovery, or think they have made one, that we mean to oppress them: we have made a discovery, or think we have made one, that they intend to rise in rebellion. Our severity has increased their ill behaviour, we know not how to advance, they know not how to retreat.[26]

The only way out was to share dissatisfactions: "All government, indeed every human benefit and enjoyment, every virtue, and every prudent act, is founded on compromise and barter. We balance inconveniences; we give and take; we remit some rights, that we may enjoy others. . . . But in all fair dealings the thing bought must bear some proportion to the purchase paid." Burke concluded his 1775 speech with this peroration: "Deny [the Americans] this participation of freedom, and you break that sole bond, which originally made, and must still preserve, the unity of the empire."[27]

V.

Burke's biographer David Bromwich has observed, with respect to a speech by George Grenville, George III's first minister at the time of the Stamp Act, that the end of its argument didn't "remember its beginning."[28] Grenville sought to show that an empire's center could prize its peripheries' liberties while constraining them. Pericles, in his funeral oration, had attempted something similar: he began by praising the Athenians' respect for their colonies, but ended by extolling the use of force to keep them in line.[29] Both forgot, before finishing, how they'd begun: they lost the proportioning of things bought to prices paid.

The American revolutionaries had longer memories. Steeped as schoolboys in classical texts (if more often recalled in translation), they saw in the failures of Greek democracy and the Roman republic compellingly immediate lessons. They revered what they believed to be Saxon common law, usurped by Normans, clawed back in Magna Carta, endangered by Stuarts, redeemed in 1688, but now at risk from the corruption of kings, parliaments, and colonial administrators. Their Declaration of Independence reinforced even as it reflected the intellectual liberations of 1776: Adam Smith's *The Wealth of Nations,* the first volume of Edward Gibbon's *The Decline and Fall of the Roman Empire,* and most powerfully Thomas Paine's

Common Sense, which found it "repugnant to reason, to the universal order of things, to all examples from former ages, to suppose, that this continent can longer remain subject to any external power."[30]

Monarchies had arisen, Paine insisted, not through merit, but because they'd outlasted memories. The first king had probably been only the "principal ruffian of some restless gang." Certainly the example of William the Conquerer, "a French bastard landing with an armed banditti, and establishing himself king of England against the consent of the natives, . . . hath no divinity in it." If nature respected monarchy, she wouldn't so often "turn it into ridicule by giving mankind an ASS FOR A LION." What sense could it make to have "a youth of twenty-one"—George III had been twenty-two when he took the throne in 1760—"say to several millions of people, older and wiser than himself, I forbid this or that act of yours to be law."[31]

Despite their small size and relative infrequency, republics since Rome's had done better. By encouraging equality, they'd diminished arrogance, and hence the amnesia that pride brings: Holland and Switzerland prospered peacefully in an age of ruinous monarchical rivalries. Americans themselves, as their colonial charters evolved into representative assemblies, had become republicans because left for so long to their own devices. Their lively trade and *absence* of gold and silver could "secure us the peace and friendship of all Europe." So "what have we to do with setting the world at defiance?"[32]

Independence was frightening only because its architecture was incomplete: how could thirteen republics with continental ambitions stay together? Paine, on this point, was unsure, but what he did know was that "[a] government of our own is our natural right," and that the need was urgent. "Freedom hath been hunted round the globe. Asia, and Africa, have long expelled her. Europe regards her like a stranger, and England hath given her warning to depart. O! receive the fugitive, and prepare in time an asylum for mankind."[33] Few ends of arguments have remembered, more ringingly, their beginnings.

VI.

Paine's pamphlet was the literary equivalent of Elizabeth's fireships: an incendiary device meant to unnerve an enemy, rally a defense, and make history pivot. Not all at once, of course. How to *secure* American independence—as opposed to proclaiming it—was not at all clear when *Common Sense* appeared in January 1776. What Paine did, though, was to shift psychologies. The British, like the Spanish in 1588, would retain, for the moment, military superiority. But they'd find it harder now to be confident that God or history, justice or reason, or simply the tilt of the arenas in which they competed, was on their side.[34]

Mr. Jefferson's Declaration, six months later, hammered the point home: "*When* in the Course of human events, it becomes *necessary* for one people . . . to assume among the powers of the earth, the *separate* and *equal* station to which the *Laws of Nature* and of *Nature's God* entitle them, a decent *respect* for the opinions of mankind *requires* that they should declare the causes which *impel* them to the separation."[35] However hastily composed, Jefferson's words left the British tongue-tied, able only to continue what they'd begun at Lexington, Concord, and Bunker Hill the year before: the suppression of freedoms king and Parliament had claimed to respect.

Jefferson was a genius, the historian Joseph Ellis has noted, at concealing contradictions within abstractions. The Virginian who insisted "that all men are created equal" arrived in Philadelphia attended by opulently attired slaves.[36] His declaration coupled universal principles with an implausibly long list of offenses—twenty-seven in all—committed *personally* by George III: that's why the complete document can't be quoted today without sounding a little silly. Nor did Jefferson, any more than Paine, say anything about what *kind* of government might replace that of the British tyrant. Details weren't either patriot's strength.

Had they been, independence might never have been attempted, for details dim the flames fireships require. They disconnect ends of arguments from their beginnings. That's why Paine and Jefferson thought it necessary first to tilt history, and only at that point to begin to make it. Rhetoric, their lever, had to be clearer than truth, even if necessary an inversion of it.[37] George III was no Nero, not even a James II. Jefferson nonetheless struck from his indictments the charge that the king had supported the slave trade, for this would have slandered *slavery's* reputation. And that would have made the vote for freedom less than unanimous.[38]

As through such compromises, it turned out to be. An ideologically consistent declaration would have called forth, unimpressively, "thirteen *disunited* States of America." Nor would a uniform tone have caught the signatories' clashing emotions: patriotic rage, philosophical reflection, a somber sense of the bloodshed ahead, the conviction that eyes everywhere were watching, and an almost adolescent delight at having it "in our power," as Paine put it, "to begin the world over again."[39] John Adams, who usually frowned on combustions beyond those of his own bad temper, was within the spirit of independence when he called for its anniversaries to be "solemnized"—after thanking God—"with Shews, Games, Sports, Guns, Bells, Bonfires and Illuminations from one End of this Continent to the other from this Time forward forever more."[40]

VII.

Adams's pen hadn't slipped when he wrote "Continent," not "Country," for the authors of independence regularly fortified themselves with geography. Paine saw "something very absurd, in supposing a continent to be perpetually governed by an island." Franklin pointed out that the British had spent three million pounds in 1775 to kill only "150 Yankees." During that year, 60,000 Americans had been born. How long would it take and what would it cost "to kill us all?"[41] George Washington, now commanding the Continental army, didn't have limitless space into which to retreat, but he had a lot: he also had an adversary capable of supply only by sea. So he relied on "time, caution, and worrying the enemy," he later explained, "until we could be better provided with arms and other means and had better disciplined troops" to ensure victory.[42]

That could be done only by a government, however, and the Americans were unsure, in 1776, what kind they wanted. So they settled for *governments* grounded in the interests of each state, linked loosely by Articles of Confederation. These established a league but not a nation: there was no chief executive, no judicial review of legislation, and most significant, no authority to tax.[43] It was as if the Americans had made "salutary neglect" their first constitution, but whether the lightness they'd liked in the old British empire could extract them from the new one remained to be seen.

For even on continents, armies could get trapped and forced to surrender. That's what happened to the British at Saratoga in 1777 and at Yorktown in 1781. They carried on after their first defeat but gave up after the second: would the Americans, in such circumstances, have fought on? The Confederation Congress so grudgingly supplied Washington that he'd lost all faith in it by the time peace was made in 1783. "[I]t is only in our united character as an empire," he warned, "that our independence is acknowledged, that our power can be regarded, or our credit supported."[44]

What won the war, for the Americans, was a Machiavellian insight: that a constitutional monarchy's humiliation of an absolute monarchy could cause the latter, years later, to rescue a republican revolutionary upstart. Still bitter over France's loss of North America to the British in 1763, Louis XVI welcomed rebel emissaries to Paris in 1776. The Americans offered trade vaguely but revenge satisfyingly: the French responded with recognition, financing, and a "perpetual" military alliance. Their fleet's timely arrival off Yorktown forced the final British capitulation—whereupon the Americans blithely abandoned their ally to negotiate a settlement with agents of their enemy, extending their boundaries west to the Mississippi River.[45]

The outcome defied categories.[46] Was it a victory for principle or expediency? For the rights of man or the rules of statecraft? For lightness of being or heaviness of hand? For a republic or, as Washington himself put it, an "empire"? To say "all of the above" dodges the question, but usefully. For if Burke was right that governments should balance dissatisfactions, if Elizabeth was right to set precedents rather than be bound by them, if Machiavelli was right to prefer proportionality to consistency, then the Americans weren't just making it up as they went along.[47] Even Augustus might have been impressed by what their leaders did next: they staged a second revolution to correct

failures in the first, but with so skillful a mix of stealth and persuasion that the country didn't grasp, until after it had happened, what
had just happened.[48]

VIII.

Whatever their contradictions, Americans were consistent, before
and after their first revolution, in deeply distrusting government.
Having been left on their own for so long, the colonists saw as sinis-
ter *any* British action affecting them: "[T]he most minor incidents,"
the historian Gordon Wood has shown, "erupted into major constitutional questions involving the basic liberties of the people."[49] Aller-
gies that extreme don't easily disappear, and this one lasted long
after Great Britain accepted the independence of the United States in
1783. The Americans simply turned it upon themselves.

Perhaps victory made forbearance less necessary. Perhaps it exposed an issue they'd so far evaded: had the revolution secured
equality of opportunity—the right to rise to inequality—or of
condition—the obligation not to? Perhaps corruptions in British society had now, like smallpox, infected its American counterpart.
Perhaps legislation, if unchecked, always produced tyranny, whether
in parliaments or confederations. Perhaps the people themselves
weren't to be trusted. Perhaps the British had been right, some
Americans thought but couldn't say, in having tried to replace neglect with a heavier hand.

By outward appearances, the country was flourishing. Despite the
war, population was growing as fast as Franklin had predicted it
would. Peace more than doubled the space available for settlement.
Prosperity was widespread. "If we are undone," one South Carolinian

wrote at the time, "we are the most splendidly ruined of any nation in the universe."[50]

But because expectations were high and the world hadn't begun again, fears gnawed away at self-confidence. Nothing worried the Americans more than the prospect that, having humiliated Great Britain, they wouldn't be taken seriously themselves as a Great Power. If their revolution had established only a league of nations— if authority was shared to the point that it had no center—then how could the new country impress any older one that did? "No treaty can be made with the American states that can be binding on the whole," Lord Sheffield, Gibbon's editor for *The Decline and Fall*, complained in 1784. "We might as reasonably dread the effects of combinations among the German as among the American States, and deprecate the resolves of the Diet, as those of Congress."[51]

An island had shown that it couldn't rule a continent: could a republic? There'd been none on that scale since Rome's, not a happy precedent. The break with Britain had come over taxation without representation, which was hardly possible across a great ocean. But what about an ocean of land?[52] "We have passed the Rubicon," a pamphleteer pointed out, and

> the question now is, whether we shall break up into separate disproportioned clans and hordes, each under petty captains and rulers, who will be as tyrannical as they dare to be, and will keep the whole continent in a constant state of turbulence . . . or whether we will all unite, or the great majority of us, in establishing a general and efficient government, which shall include the whole territory ceded to the United States by the treaty of Paris in 1783.[53]

It was almost as if the British, by granting such boundaries, had planted a time bomb: could a republic become an empire without, as Gibbon seemed to be showing Rome to have done, replacing its liberties with tyrannies?

IX.

The second American revolution began, in the manner of Augustus, with a pyramid scheme of purposefully inconclusive meetings. The first took place at Washington's Mount Vernon in 1785, ostensibly to stop the bickering between Maryland and Virginia over navigation rights on the Potomac. The real issue, the participants concluded, was internal tariffs, and that required a larger conference, at Annapolis, in 1786. But those present saw the need for still larger "adjustments" in the Articles, for which they organized a "constitutional convention" in Philadelphia in 1787. It in turn, in closed sessions, swept the Articles into oblivion.[54] It wasn't a coup d'état: it moved too slowly and politely for that. As a fait accompli, however, it came close.

The Augustus was Washington, whose "reflexive restraint in seeking power," his most recent biographer has suggested, "enabled him to exercise so much of it." He hosted the 1785 meeting while committing himself to nothing. He allowed two young Agrippas— James Madison and Alexander Hamilton—to lead in public, while making it clear privately where he stood: "What stronger evidence can be given of the want of energy in our governments than these disorders?" the great man fumed (sounding a little like George III) when Massachusetts farmers marched on their tax-hungry state government late in 1786.[55] And in 1787, Washington let himself be persuaded—although not easily—to chair the Philadelphia convention. Once there, he said hardly a word. He didn't have to. August presences achieve their purposes, he knew, simply by showing up.[56]

Over the following summer the delegates crafted the world's longest living but least amended constitution[57]—with which few of its signatories were fully satisfied. Which led the Agrippas, with some help from John Jay, to rush into print, as *The Federalist*, a justification for ratification thirty-four times the length of the document it defended.[58] Addressed to "the People of the State of New York," its eighty-five essays, all signed "Publius," didn't determine the outcome. They got little circulation beyond New York, and when that state did finally ratify, in July 1788, ten others—more than enough—had already done so.[59] *The Federalist*'s fame rests elsewhere: as the most enduring work of political grand strategy since Machiavelli's *The Prince*.

The Constitution and *The Federalist* share the qualities of having been *pressed by time* in composition, but *liberated from time* in lasting significance. The paradox gets at the heart of what it means to hold opposing ideas in the mind simultaneously while retaining the ability—here brilliantly—to function. Wherein, then, did the brilliance lie?

X.

It's not enough to chalk it up to Dr. Samuel Johnson's "Depend upon it, Sir, when a man knows he is to be hanged in a fortnight, it concentrates his mind wonderfully."[60] Many men have gone to the gallows with scattered minds, and the American Founders, despite

Dr. Franklin's fondness for gallows humor,[61] were long past literal fears of such a fate. What they did face—as a weak new power in an arena of stronger older ones, as a society unsure of where within itself sovereignty should reside, as idealists disillusioned by human nature, as realists who thought they might reform human nature, as students of history obliged now to make their own—was the need to align incompatible aspirations with limited capabilities. *The Federalist* was meant to do that.

"The subject speaks its own importance," Hamilton announced in the first essay's first paragraph, "comprehending in its consequences nothing less than the existence of the UNION, the safety and welfare of the parts of which it is composed, the fate of an empire in many respects the most interesting in the world." For

> it seems to have been reserved to the people of this country, by their conduct and example, to decide the important question, whether societies of men are really capable or not of establishing good government from *reflection and choice,* or whether they are forever destined to depend for their political constitutions on *accident and force.*

Settling so great an issue would require "a judicious estimate of our true interests, unperplexed and unbiased by considerations not connected with the public good." But—chillingly—"this is a thing more ardently to be wished than seriously to be expected."

> The plan offered to our deliberations affects too many particular interests, innovates upon too many local institutions, not to involve in its discussion a variety of objects foreign to

its merits, and of views, passions and prejudices little favorable to the discovery of truth.[62]

The world, watching, would never forget. The Americans, acting, were inattentive. Means mustered were falling far short of ends envisaged: a crisis was now at hand.

The Federalist was an ambivalent clarion call. For how could submergence within a "UNION"—the capitalization was Hamilton's—not drown its "parts"? Had any "empire" ever functioned without accidents of inheritance and legitimation through force? Could parochial concerns collectively coalesce? Of what use was "a judicious estimate" if "more ardently to be wished than seriously to be expected"? Wise men were so often wrong, Hamilton acknowledged, that they might teach moderation "to those who are ever so much persuaded of their being in the right." That made it foolish to *insist* on consistency: one must remake logic itself. That's why Hamilton began, as had Augustus, by disarming resistance with humility.

XI.

Which somehow made it appropriate that *The Federalist*'s hardest task—showing how a republic could be an empire without becoming a tyranny—fell to Madison, the most easily underestimated of the American Founders.[63] He fulfilled it, triumphantly, by connecting time, space, and scale.

History had shown "instability, injustice, and confusion" always to have extinguished "popular governments," Madison wrote in the tenth Publius essay. Independence had yet to free Americans from these dangers.

> Complaints are everywhere heard . . . that the public good is
> disregarded in the conflicts of rival parties, and that measures
> are too often decided, not according to the rules of justice and
> the rights of the minor party, but by the superior force of an
> interested and overbearing majority.

Revoking liberty would be a remedy "worse than the disease." But
curing it through equality would leave no one safe:

> [D]emocracies have ever been spectacles of turbulence and
> contention; have ever been found incompatible with personal
> security or the rights of property; and have in general been as
> short in their lives as they have been violent in their deaths.

"[Th]e *causes* of faction" were too human to be removed. Relief
could perhaps come, however, from "controlling its *effects*."[64]

Distance had so far kept republics small, because the *representation* upon which they depended required the cooling of passions
that only deliberative assemblies, meeting regularly, could provide.
They couldn't perform that function when territories were widely
dispersed. The American republic now extended across a third of a
continent, and was unlikely to stop there. How then could the British time bomb of generosity—the ocean of land ceded in 1783—fail
to revive familiar protests of "no taxation without representation"?
Where, if that happened, would Hamilton's "UNION" be?

Madison solved these issues of time and space by shifting *scale*.
In doing so he drew, knowingly or not,[65] on Machiavelli. For only in
republics, the Florentine had observed, could the "common good"
be "looked to properly." By expanding the *number* who benefited,
the influence of the few who didn't could be reduced: not *all* parts,

submerged in wholes, need drown.[66] Scale could be the life pre-
server. There were, Madison acknowledged, dangers in this:

> By enlarging too much the number of electors [voters], you
> render the representative too little acquainted with all their
> local circumstances and lesser interests; as by reducing it too
> much, you render him unduly attached to these, and too little
> fit to comprehend and pursue great and national objects.

But surely there existed "a mean, on both sides of which inconveniences will be found to lie." In this way *balancing* factions—a
Burkean enterprise—could put "inconveniences" to good use:

> Extend the sphere, and you take in a greater variety of parties
> and interests; you make it less probable that a majority of the
> whole will have a common motive to invade the rights of
> other citizens; or if such a common motive exists, it will be
> more difficult for all who feel it to discover their own strength,
> and to act in unison with each other.

The proposed Constitution "forms a happy combination in this respect; the great and aggregate interests being referred to the national, the local and particular to the State legislatures."[67]

Madison thus deployed *scale* across *space* to reverse *time:* history
would henceforth strengthen his republic by allowing factions to
compete at all levels, so that as the country grew, its path would
not be that of Rome.[68] *The Federalist*'s arc bent toward a Lincoln, not
a Nero.

XII.

If that's the case, though, why did the Union, under Lincoln, so catastrophically fail? The easy answer might be that no strategy anticipates all contingencies, that every solution creates new problems, and that these can, at times, overwhelm. The harsher one—although I think the more accurate one—lies in the possibility that the Founders left the Union to test itself: knowing the need to *proportion* aspirations to capabilities, recognizing the incompatibilities in good things, they chose to save their new state, and leave to their descendants the saving of its soul.

Augustine and Machiavelli had both seen in proportionality a way to balance the respective claims of souls and states: their differences lay in whether equilibria reached required accountability to God. Augustine said yes and labored mightily to provide it. Machiavelli's God left statecraft to man. Americans, in varieties almost as infinite as those of Elizabeth I, straddled this divide: they could be, like their early leaders, coolly pragmatic, like their revivalists fiercely religious, and like their entrepreneurs anywhere in between. What's clear, though, is that few in the young republic questioned—at least not openly—what so many in the mature republic would give their lives to change: the anomaly that a Constitution promising a "more perfect Union" assumed slavery's legality.[69]

It acknowledged, in doing so, what the Declaration of Independence couldn't say: that all men were *not* created equal. The men of 1776 feared—Jefferson not least among them—that if they freed the slaves along with the country, they'd have no state. The Constitution put the anxiety into legalese by apportioning places in the House of Representatives to "the whole Number of free persons" and to "three fifths of all other Persons," by prohibiting for twenty years any restrictions on the "Migration or Importation of such Persons as any of the States now existing shall think proper to admit," and by requiring that "No Person held to Service or Labour in one State, . . . escaping into another, shall . . . be discharged from such Service or Labour." The word "slavery" was nowhere mentioned.[70]

The evasion left Madison, in *The Federalist,* grasping for straws. "It were doubtless to be wished," he wrote feebly, "that the power of prohibiting the importation of slaves had not been postponed until the year 1808, or rather that it had been suffered to have immediate operation." But that passage of time

> may terminate forever, within these States, a traffic which has
> so long and so loudly upbraided the barbarism of modern
> policy. . . . Happy would it be for the unfortunate Africans, if
> an equal prospect lay before them of being redeemed from
> the oppressions of their European brethren!

Unhappily hypocritical, though, for Madison, who elsewhere defended the three-fifths clause in a long, labored passage that purported to represent the views of American "brethren" who saw slaves as *both* people and property.

> Such is the reasoning which an advocate for the Southern in-
> terests might employ on this subject; and although it may ap-
> pear to be a little strained in some points, yet, on the whole,
> I must confess that it fully reconciles me to the scale of
> representation which the [Constitutional] convention have
> established.[71]

Madison's balancing required a barbarity, so it's no surprise that he found himself straining. The options he faced, however, were irreconcilable: the Founders could have Union or Emancipation but not both, at least not in their generation. And so they chose Union now, postponing Emancipation on the assumption—infrequently expressed—that the *prospects* for it would be better in a single strong state than in several weaker ones.[72] It was a wager: whether with God or the Devil depended on your point of view.

XIII.

The Founders put the reckoning beyond their lifetimes by seeking a republican continental empire. Hamilton, the firmest among them in opposing slavery, nonetheless saw in an expanding Union the opportunity "to become the arbiter of Europe in America, and to be able to incline the balance of European competitions in this part of the world as our interest may dictate." Madison showed how, by balancing internal interests, external expansion could occur.[73] Jefferson, after becoming president, balanced his near-pathological hatred of Hamilton[74] against the windfall of acquiring Louisiana from the French at a bargain price, thereby again doubling the Union's extent. "[T]o lose our country by a scrupulous adherence to written laws," he later rationalized (Hamilton, whether from Heaven or Hell, must have smiled, if thinly), "would be to lose the law itself, . . . thus absurdly sacrificing the end to the means."[75]

And in 1811, John Quincy Adams, then forty-four, took it upon himself to inform his mother that the choice lay between having, on the one hand, "an endless multitude of little insignificant clans and tribes at eternal war with one another for a rock, or a fish pond, the sport and fable of European masters and oppressors," and, on the other, "a nation, coextensive with the North American continent, destined by God and nature to be the most populous and most powerful people ever combined under one social compact."[76] Thus circling back to his father's 1776 anticipation of fireworks from sea to sea.

The younger Adams set off more than his share, mostly at Spain's expense, after becoming James Monroe's secretary of state in 1817. Philip II's empire still sprawled on maps from mid–North America to the Strait of Magellan, but the French Revolution and the rise of Napoleon had infected it with independence, as had the example of the United States.[77] Adams, like a shark, exploited the infirmity. He began with Florida, where he turned a preemptive military attack, launched under questionable authority by Andrew Jackson, into an ultimatum: Spain must secure that territory's borders or "cede to the United States a province . . . which is in fact a derelict, open to the occupancy of every enemy, civilized or savage, of the United States, and serving no other earthly purpose than as a post of annoyance to them."[78]

By 1821 the Spanish had relinquished Florida in return for an American assumption of (American) claims there, an exclusion of Texas (soon to be Mexican anyway) from the United States, and an agreement to make their empire's remaining northern border the 42nd parallel—a line drawn all the way to the Pacific despite the Americans having no clear title to anything on its other side. It was a brash display of audacity in statecraft,[79] unmatched until Adams himself, two years later, exceeded it.

The occasion was Monroe's annual message to Congress, to be delivered in December 1823.[80] The opportunity arose in a quiet offer from the British foreign secretary, George Canning, to work with the United States to prevent Russia, Prussia, Austria, and post–Napoleonic France from any effort to restore Spanish rule—now almost lost—in the "new world." Canning had in mind British commercial interests, which the British navy needed no help in securing: bringing in the Americans might, however, smooth over bitterness still left from the War of 1812 and the British burning of Washington two years later.[81] But Adams saw the chance, through a clever tweak, of a revolutionary pronouncement.

Hence the great "doctrine" for which Monroe is principally remembered: that "the American continents, by the free and independent condition which they have assumed and maintain, are henceforth not to be considered as subjects for future colonization by any European powers." An empty gesture? Given capabilities at the time, certainly—but not in the light of the aspirations Hamilton had invoked in *The Federalist:* to deploy "the natural strength and resources of the country" in the "common interest" of baffling "all the combinations of European jealousy to restrain our growth"—in short, "to become the arbiter of Europe in America."[82]

There could be no such interest, however, had Madison not shown, in *The Federalist,* how first to restrain American jealousies. That was the purpose of the uneasy Missouri Compromise of 1820, which equally apportioned new territories as future free or slave states. Adams went along, convinced that the Constitution's "bargain between freedom and slavery" was "morally and politically vicious, . . . inconsistent with the principles upon which alone our Revolution can be justified"—but also knowing that the bargain was keeping the Union from civil war. The result of which would surely be

the extirpation of slavery from this whole continent; and, calamitous and desolating as this course of events in its progress must be, so glorious would be its final issue that, as God
shall judge me, I dare not say that it is not to be desired.

But—as the young Augustine might have said—not now. Conversion, emancipation, and God Himself would have to wait.[83]

XIV.

How, then, did a young republic, in what still was an age of empires,
get away with proclaiming hegemony over a hemisphere? Perhaps
the British, like weary parents, had learned to indulge the antics of
children: "[T]he principle (if principle it may be called)," Canning
condescended early in 1824, was "new to this government." But
within three years, that particular parent was boasting to the House
of Commons that "I called the New World into existence to redress
the balance of the Old." Having pulled out the plum *and* claimed
credit for the pudding, a furious American historian later complained, Canning had outdone even Little Jack Horner: "What a big
boy am I[!]"[84]

　　Canning, however, had more in mind than that. Convinced that
North America was not about to break up into clans and tribes
quibbling over fishponds, he looked ahead to what the implications
might be. Not yet visible among them was Winston Churchill, born
to an American mother in Blenheim Palace in 1874. The greatest
Englishman since the Great Queen was not one to neglect power
balances or good quotations. He recycled Canning's frequently,
most memorably in his speech to the House of Commons on the

British evacuation from Dunkirk on June 4, 1940. He would never surrender, Churchill vowed, but if

> this Island or a large part of it were subjugated and starving, then our Empire beyond the oceans, armed and guarded by the British Fleet, will carry on the struggle until in God's good time the New World with all its power and might sets forth to the rescue and liberation of the Old.

Both Canning and Churchill sensed a shift in history's tectonics—the foreign minister from afar, the prime minister from beneath his feet—comparable in importance to the one set in motion by the change in the winds a few miles down the coast from Dunkirk on an evening in August 1588.[85]

Which raises a question: why, in the eighteenth and nineteenth centuries, did only one "new world" state build sufficient power to restore balances in the "old"—not once but three times—in the twentieth? How could such strength have emerged from the fractiously disorganized British colonies and not from their larger, richer, and more carefully run Spanish counterparts to the south? Simón Bolívar, their liberator, suggested an answer as early as 1815: there would never be, he acknowledged, a United States of Latin America.[86]

One reason was geography. It might be easier to rule an empire from its seaports than from its interior, but this didn't prepare a nation to rule itself: the internal barriers of climate, topography, habitats, cultures, and communications were too great.[87] "Who is capable [even] of compiling complete statistics of a land like this!" Bolívar complained. The Isthmus of Panama was far from being, "for us, what the Isthmus of Corinth was for the Greeks!"[88]

Why, though, couldn't variety have become strength, as Madison made it in *Federalist #10*? The problem here, Bolívar argued, was political immaturity. Spain had so tightly controlled its territories as to keep them in a "permanent infancy," unable to command self-respect. "[W]e have even been deprived of an active tyranny, since we have not been permitted to exercise its functions."[89] Once the world's greatest empire, Spain was now too weak to prevail, but had trained no one to take its place.

Representative governments, hence, would find it difficult to take root: some form of absolutism—probably disguised as republicanism—was more likely. But not, Bolívar thought, on a continental scale, for authoritarians by their nature resist cooperation. Only under the guidance and protection of a great "liberal" nation could the Latin Americans cultivate "the virtues and talents that lead to glory."[90]

That inspired Adams's contemporary Henry Clay, who ardently advocated United States support not only for Latin American independence movements, but also those of the Greeks, then rebelling against Ottoman rule.[91] Adams himself, though, understood how quickly such help could overstretch resources, material and moral. America "goes not abroad, in search of monsters to destroy," he admonished the House of Representatives in a speech of his own on July 4, 1821:

> She is the well-wisher to the freedom and independence of all.
> She is the champion and vindicator only of her own. . . . She
> well knows that by once enlisting under other banners, . . .
> she would involve herself beyond the power of extrication, in
> all the wars of interest and intrigue, of individual avarice,
> envy, and ambition, which assume the colors and usurp the

standard of freedom. The fundamental maxims of her policy would insensibly change from liberty to force. . . . She might become the dictatress of the world. She would be no longer the ruler of her own spirit.[92]

There, unforgettably, was the compromise characteristic of the age: freedom in principle, perhaps even partially, eventually, in practice. But Union—and its requirement that great ends be kept within available means—came first. Only a state at peace with itself could save its soul. For now.

CHAPTER SEVEN

THE GRANDEST STRATEGISTS

There's a curious moment just prior to Leo Tolstoy's account of the battle of Borodino—page 774 in the Richard Pevear and Larissa Volokhonsky translation of *War and Peace*—when two of its central characters, Pierre Bezukhov and Prince Andrei Bolkonsky, step out of a shed, look up, and see Carl von Clausewitz with another officer riding by. One is saying: "War must be extended in space. I cannot put too high a price on this view." The other agrees: "The aim is to weaken the enemy, so one cannot pay attention to the loss of private persons." This disgusts Andrei, across whose estate this war already has been extended. "[A]ll there is in a German head," he complains bitterly to Pierre, "is reasoning, which isn't worth a tinker's damn. . . . They gave *him* [Napoleon] the whole of Europe and came to teach us. Fine teachers!"[1]

Within the short distance separating the view on horseback from that on the ground, Tolstoy evokes the gap that exists, at all levels, between *theory* and *practice*. It's one of many instances in which his micro-insights have macro-implications, but Clausewitz's writings are full of them too. Few if any others have thought more deeply or written more perceptively about time, space, *and scale* than the horseman who passes and the novelist who portrayed him.

Pierre and Andrei were at Borodino, of course, only in Tolstoy's imagination, but Clausewitz really was there: when the French invaded in 1812, he resigned his commission in the Prussian army, joined the Russians, and fought in the great battle.[2] The meticulous Tolstoy would have known this and could have read *On War,* published posthumously in 1832, before writing *War and Peace* in the 1860s.[3] His Clausewitz prefers abstraction to observation, a charge many critics repeated well into the twentieth century.[4] It's possible, though, that Tolstoy wasn't reproaching Clausewitz, but rather reflecting what Russians thought at the time of their new Prussian allies. For not only do Tolstoy and Clausewitz see the practice of war similarly: they also construct theories, drawn from their own military experiences, *about the limitations of theory itself.*

I.

"Let us accompany a novice to the battlefield," Clausewitz writes in *On War,* leaving not the slightest doubt that he knows his subject:

> As we approach, the rumble of guns grows louder and alternates with the whir of cannonballs, which begin to attract his attention. Shots begin to strike close around us. We hurry up the slope where the commanding general is stationed with his

large staff. Here cannonballs and bursting shells are frequent, and life begins to seem more serious than the young man had imagined. Suddenly someone you know is wounded; then a shell falls among the staff. You notice that some of the officers act a little oddly; you yourself are not as steady and collected as you were: even the bravest can become slightly distracted. Now we enter the battle raging before us, still almost like a spectacle, and join the nearest division commander. Shot is falling like hail, and the thunder of our own guns adds to the din. Forward to the brigadier, a soldier of acknowledged bravery, but he is careful to take cover behind a rise, a house or a clump of trees. A noise is heard that is a certain indication of increasing danger—the rattling of grapeshot on roofs and on the ground. Cannonballs tear past, whizzing in all directions, and musketballs begin to whistle around us. A little further we reach the firing line, where the infantry endures the hammering for hours with incredible steadfastness. The air is filled with hissing bullets that sound like a sharp crack if they pass close to one's head. For a final shock, the sight of men being killed and mutilated moves our pounding hearts to awe and pity.

The novice cannot pass through these layers of increasing intensity of danger without sensing that here ideas are governed by other factors, that *the light of reason is refracted in a manner quite different from that which is normal in academic speculation.*[5]

Now here's Tolstoy—who'd served with the Russian army in the Caucasus, the Balkans, and the Crimean War during the 1850s—on Borodino:

From the battlefield the adjutants he had sent and his marshals' orderlies constantly came galloping to Napoleon with reports on the course of events; but all these reports were false: both because in the heat of battle it is impossible to tell what is going on at a given moment, and because many of the adjutants did not reach the actual place of battle, but told what they had heard from others; and also because, while an adjutant was riding the mile or so that separated him from Napoleon, the circumstances changed, and the news he was bringing became incorrect. . . . On the weight of such unavoidably false reports, Napoleon gave his instructions, which either had been carried out before he ever gave them or were not and could not be carried out.

The marshals and the generals who were closer to the battlefield, but who, like Napoleon, did not take part in the battle itself, but only occasionally rode into the fire, gave their own instructions and orders about where to shoot and from where, and where the cavalry were to ride and the infantry to run, without asking Napoleon. But even their instructions were carried out as rarely and to as small a degree as Napoleon's instructions. For the most part, what came out was the opposite of what they had ordered. Soldiers who were told to advance would come under canister shot and run back; soldiers who were told to stay where they were, suddenly seeing the Russians appear unexpectedly before them, sometimes ran back and sometimes rushed forward, and the cavalry galloped without orders in pursuit of the fleeing Russians. . . . As soon as these men left that space through which the cannonballs and bullets flew, their commanders, who stood in the rear, formed them up, established discipline, and, under the effect of that discipline, again led them into the zone of fire, in which (under the effect of the fear of death) they again lost discipline and rushed about according to the chance mood of the crowd.[6]

These passages are as far from abstraction as it's possible to imagine: indeed you might wonder, from reading them, what the chaos of battle can ever accomplish. And yet Borodino—despite having had no clear winner—accomplished a lot.

The battle weakened both sides, but the Russians had more territory even than the Americans into which to retreat, abandoning Moscow as they did so. The French, far from home, advanced farther when Napoleon couldn't resist taking the city, hoping to shock Tsar Alexander I into making peace. When that didn't happen, the greatest military genius since Julius Caesar assumed the attributes of a dog who'd chased a car and caught it: what do you do next? Meanwhile, as his humblest private could have reminded him, winter was coming on.

Clausewitz called this the "culminating point" of Napoleon's offensive, by which he meant that the French had defeated themselves by exhausting themselves.[7] "[F]lashing [the] sword of vengeance,"[8] the Russians could now drive them from the country. Tolstoy's old, fat, slow-moving commanding general Mikhail Kutuzov makes the point better than Clausewitz did: few figures in history have done more by *appearing* to do less. Napoleon, as a consequence, lost his army and within a year and a half his throne. The Russian tsar triumphantly toured Paris, was received in London respectfully, and even dined at Oxford in the Radcliffe Camera while the dons gawked at him, enthralled, from the balconies.[9]

War's "grammar," Clausewitz writes in *On War*, "may be its own,

but not its logic."[10] With training, discipline, and superior leadership, armies can suspend *temporarily* the all-too-human instinct to
flee from danger: combat, as Clausewitz's novice discovers, defies
common sense. In time, though, logic surrounds, confounds, and
supersedes such grammar. Heroics drain you. Offensives slow as
supply lines lengthen. Retreats invite counterattack. Russia is big
and its winters are cold. Dogs that catch cars never know what to
do with them. Why, then, did Napoleon forget what most fools
remember?

Perhaps because common sense is indeed like oxygen: the higher
you go, the thinner it gets. As each triumph topped its antecedent,
Napoleon's grammar *became* his logic. Like Caesar, he rose so far
above fundamentals as to lose sight of them altogether. Such ascents
can be awe-inspiring: so too, in their day, were hot air balloons. But
gravity is always present.

II.

Clausewitz died in 1831 before finishing *On War,* leaving us with a
huge, unwieldy, and contradictory book, a close reading of which, I
warn my students, risks mental disorientation: you can wind up unsure of what he said and with doubts, even, about who you are. Tolstoy did finish *War and Peace,* in 1868, but with little clearer sense
of what he'd accomplished: "It is not a novel, still less an epic poem,
still less a historical chronicle. *War and Peace* is what the author
wanted and was able to express, in the form in which it is expressed."[11]
Isaiah Berlin detects in Tolstoy's evasiveness "a tormenting inner
conflict"—like the results of too carefully reading Clausewitz?—

between the "delusive experience of free will" and "the reality of in-exorable historical determinism."[12]

But what if Clausewitz and Tolstoy were *wrestling* with contradictions—perhaps even *relishing* the contest—rather than agonizing over them?[13] Both see determinism as laws to which there can be no exceptions: "If even one man out of millions in a thousand-year period of time has had the possibility of acting freely," Tolstoy writes, "then it is obvious that one free act of this man, contrary to the laws, destroys the possibility of the existence of any laws whatever for the whole of mankind."[14] Clausewitz agrees, with the qualification that if laws can't contain "the diversity of the real world," then "the application of *principle* allows for a greater lati-tude of judgment." The proverb speaks of "an exception to every rule," not "to every law," suggesting that as abstractions approach reality, they permit "a more liberal interpretation."[15] That would be consistent with Tolstoy, who seeks at such length to subvert *all* laws.

Too many theories, Clausewitz complains, try too hard to be laws. He cites, as an example, this Prussian fire-extinguishing regulation:

> If a house is on fire, one must above all seek to save the right wall of the house on the left, and on the other hand the left wall of the house on the right. For if, for example, one were to try and protect the left wall of the house on the left, one must remember that the right wall of the house is on the right of its left wall, and thus, since the fire is also to the right of this wall and of the right wall (for we have assumed that the house is on the left of the fire) the right wall is closer to the fire than the left, and the right wall of the house could burn down if it were not protected before the fire would reach the left,

protected wall; consequently something could burn down that was not protected, and sooner than something else, even if this something else was also unprotected; consequently the latter must be left alone and the former must be protected. To fix the point firmly in mind, one need only remember: if the house is to the right of the fire, it is the left wall that matters; and if the house is on the left, it is the right wall.

On War, Clausewitz promises, will avoid such "nonsense," instead presenting "ideas and convictions" gained from "[y]ears of thinking about war, much association with able men who knew war, and a good deal of personal experience with it." These he'll convey "in compressed form, like small nuggets of pure metal."[16]

Which sounds like Machiavelli, whose work Clausewitz knew and admired.[17] But the cholera that killed him at fifty-one denied him the time he'd have needed to shorten *On War* and to make it clearer. So it's not so much nuggets as an immense dripping net of entangled octopi. It therefore benefits, as does Augustine's *City of God,* from fly-over reading: you can't allow yourself to get stranded in what Sir Michael Howard has called Clausewitz's "infuriating incoherence."[18]

It's harder to fly through *War and Peace:* Tolstoy's too captivating a writer. But even he, toward the end, taxes his readers with long, rambling digressions on the ineffectiveness of great men and the pointlessness of history. It helps to let his river of words carry you past these pontifications, and only later revisit them. You'll find Clausewitz reflected and in some ways improved upon. Here, for instance, is Tolstoy's "theory" of recent European history:

Louis XIV was a very proud and presumptuous man; he had such-and-such mistresses and such-and-such ministers, and he ruled France badly. Louis's heirs were also weak men and also ruled France badly. They, too, had such-and-such favorites and such-and-such mistresses. Besides, certain men were writing books at the time. At the end of the eighteenth century, some two dozen men got together in Paris and started talking about all men being equal and free. That led people all over France to start slaughtering and drowning each other. These people killed the king and many others. At the same time there was in France a man of genius—Napoleon. He defeated everybody everywhere—that is, he killed a lot of people—because he was a great genius. And he went off for some reason to kill Africans, and he killed them so well, and was so cunning and clever, that, on coming back to France, he ordered everybody to obey him. And everybody obeyed him. Having become emperor, he again went to kill people in Italy, Austria, and Prussia. And there he killed a lot. In Russia there was the emperor Alexander, who decided to restore order in Europe and therefore made war with Napoleon. But in the year seven, he suddenly made friends with him, then in the year eleven quarreled again, and again they started killing a lot of people. And Napoleon brought six hundred thousand men to Russia and captured Moscow; then he suddenly ran away from Moscow, and then the emperor Alexander . . . united Europe to take up arms against the disturber of its peace. All Napoleon's allies suddenly became his enemies; and this armed force marched against Napoleon, who had gathered new forces. The allies defeated Napoleon, entered Paris, made Napoleon abdicate, and exiled him to the island of Elba, not depriving him of the dignity of emperor and showing him every respect, though five years earlier and one year later everybody considered him a bandit and an outlaw. And so began the reign of Louis XVIII, whom until then both the French and the allies had only laughed at. . . . Then skillful statesmen and diplomats . . . talked in Vienna, and with these talks made people happy or unhappy. Suddenly the diplomats and monarchs nearly quarreled; they were already prepared to order their troops to kill each other again; but at that moment Napoleon arrived in France with a battalion, and the French, who hated him, all submitted to him at once. But the allied monarchs were angered by that and again went to war with the French. And the genius Napoleon was defeated and taken to the island of St. Helena, having suddenly been recognized as a bandit. And there the exile, separated from those dear to his heart and from his beloved France, died a slow death on the rock and bequeathed his great deeds to posterity. But in Europe there was reaction, and the sovereigns all started mistreating their own people again.[19]

We don't normally think of Tolstoy or Clausewitz as laugh riots. But the fact that both could ridicule theories suggests respect for irregularities, not a compulsion to cover them up.

What really obsessed them, I think, was *irony,* which my dictionary defines as "an outcome of events contrary to what was, or might have been, expected."[20] No European could have lived unastonished through or beyond the age of Napoleon. Astonishments haunted Clausewitz and Tolstoy, as did the conviction that they'd arisen from collisions between a universal *law*—that although ends can be infinite, means can never be—and a recurring human peculiarity: that, for characters like Napoleon, Hellesponts are there to be crossed.

III.

Napoleon had crossed so many by June 24, 1812, that the river Niemen, then the boundary between the Russian empire and the French-controlled Duchy of Warsaw, didn't much worry him: his *Grande Armée* had over six hundred thousand men and—surpassing Xerxes—three pontoon bridges. It still took five days to get everyone across, but when they returned in December, only ninety thousand were left.[21] This rate of attrition couldn't help but revive a question asked of the Persians in Greece, the Athenians in Sicily, the Romans in the Teutoburg forest, the Spanish in the English Channel, and the British in America: what were they thinking? Or, to put it another way, what had Napoleon forgotten?

Clausewitz answers this question with acute insights that, like Augustine's on just war, require recovery from where he's hidden them. The opening page of *On War,* for example, could be Patton's harangue to his troops in the eponymous movie's opening scene:

> *War is . . . an act of force to compel our enemy to do our will. . . .*
> Attached to force are certain self-imposed, imperceptible
> limitations hardly worth mentioning, known as international
> law and custom, but they scarcely weaken it. Force—that is,
> physical force, for moral force has no existence save as expressed in the state and the law—is thus the means of war; to
> impose our will on the enemy is its object.

But then you get this qualification: "that, *in theory,* is the true aim of warfare." So what should its *practice* be? "The maximum use of force is in no way incompatible with the simultaneous use of the intellect," Clausewitz assures us. For if "civilized nations do not put their prisoners to death or devastate cities and countries, it is because intelligence plays a larger part in their methods of warfare and has taught them more effective ways of using force than the crude expression of instinct."[22] Our heads are spinning now, and we're only two pages into a very big book. Whatever else you might say about Patton, he was at least clear.

In telling his troops *what* to think. Clausewitz, however, is trying to teach us *how* to think. You can't know anything, he's sure, without first grasping its purest form. The idea is Plato's, but its most influential recent advocate was Clausewitz's near contemporary Immanuel Kant, who sought to reconcile opposites by first starkly posing them. Gradations, qualifications, and mitigations could then follow.[23] Or, as Clausewitz himself explained:

> Where two ideas form a true logical antithesis, . . . then fundamentally each is implied in the other. If the limitations of our mind do not allow us to comprehend both simultaneously, and discover by antithesis the whole of one in the whole of the other, each will nevertheless shed enough light on the other to clarify many of its details.[24]

The method isn't for the literal-minded, whom it will confuse, or for the faint-hearted, who'll find it shocking. If Clausewitz's purpose is however, like Virgil's in Dante, to guide us through an inferno, then it's grimly appropriate.

IV.

For war, in Clausewitz's time, had become an inferno, approaching what "civilized" nations were no longer supposed to do. The campaigns of the French Revolution and Napoleon killed millions of people, ruined vast territories, and snuffed out sovereignties throughout Europe. Technology alone can't explain these upheavals, for as Michael Howard has pointed out, arms hadn't improved for a hundred years and transport for over a thousand. But *politics* had turned upside down, and this in turn inflamed war.

The Americans, unintentionally, set the process in motion. They'd welcomed Louis XVI's assistance in their war for independence—a Machiavellian calculation on his part and theirs—but rewarded him with un-Machiavellian claims about universal rights of man, which they took less literally than did the king's combustible subjects. As a consequence, Louis lost his head and the French lost all restraint, but through their revolution in politics they acquired mass armies, "the terrible instrument," Howard writes,[25] with which Napoleon—the emperor who acquired France—conquered Europe.

Which led Clausewitz to his first and most urgent finding: that if war, in this sense, reflects politics, it must be *subordinate* to politics and therefore to *policy,* the product of politics.[26] Otherwise it's senseless violence, a Kantian abstraction that shouldn't exist but which, Clausewitz feared, now was nearer.[27] War required redefinition, therefore, as "a true political instrument, a continuation of political intercourse, carried on with other means. . . . The political object is the goal, war is the means of reaching it, and means can never be considered in isolation from their purpose."[28]

Napoleon had a political aim when he crossed the Niemen. It

was to secure Alexander I's compliance with the Continental System, the embargo on trade with Great Britain that the French were trying to impose on Europe after the British navy blockaded their ports. He'd do this by defeating the Russians quickly, accepting capitulation graciously, and then crossing the Niemen in the opposite direction before leaves began to fall. He'd keep his ends within means, thereby achieving proportionality. And why wouldn't this work? Napoleon was, after all, a genius.[29]

Far from standing, fighting, and losing, however, as most of Napoleon's previous foes had done,[30] the Russians retreated, scorching the earth through which they passed—of which, unlike most Europeans, they had no shortage. That's what Tolstoy's Clausewitz meant by extending the war in space to weaken the enemy: no army strengthens itself by outrunning its supply lines. Retreat in turn extended the war in time: the farther the French advanced, the longer it would take for them to get back. Napoleon might have stopped at this point, admitted his miscalculation, and ordered a withdrawal. But, Xerxes-like, he refused: that would be "never [to] finish anything." And so Napoleon forgot the strategy with which he'd begun: "[M]y campaign plan is a battle, and all my politics is success."[31]

He got the battle in early September at Borodino, but not success, for despite heavy losses, Alexander refused to negotiate. And when Kutuzov decided that he couldn't defend Moscow, Napoleon took what turned out to be bait, finding only a burned-out husk.[32] Only then did the genius start doubting himself, long after his army had begun to. That shifted the psychological balance, which at such moments, Clausewitz reminds us, *becomes* the military balance.[33] The war did in fact take place, therefore, across space, time, and scale, this last being the fears and hopes of each Russian and French soldier as well as the only French emperor: "The same confidence that led [Napoleon] to Moscow in 1812," Clausewitz concludes, "left him there."[34]

V.

Tolstoy captures the moment on page 993 of *War and Peace* by having a hungry Cossack kill a hare and wound another, chasing it into a forest—where he encounters, instead, a large but unguarded French army encampment. Kutuzov, expecting little, orders an attack, but his troops surprise him by winning a complete victory, their first since Napoleon invaded. "With the least strain, with the greatest confusion, and with the most insignificant losses," Tolstoy writes, "the greatest results of the whole campaign were achieved." The battle of Tarutino, fought on October 18, provided "the push [for] which Napoleon's army was only waiting . . . to begin its flight."[35]

So did history pivot, here, on a hare? Probably not, just as Clausewitz didn't really ride into a novel on a horse. Turning points do often originate, however, below historians' radars. That only imagination evokes them doesn't diminish their significance, for what documents could show a great army losing its confidence overnight? Tarutino was a far less bloody fight than Borodino, but it came just as Napoleon no longer knew what to do. By the time he'd decided on a retreat, he'd lost the authority to prevent confusion, then panic, and then an epic rout.[36]

"The Fabian system of warfare which succeeded in our Revolutionary War," John Quincy Adams wrote his father from St. Petersburg, where he was serving as the first American minister to Russia, "probably was never brought to a severer test; but the modern Alexander may . . . be destined like his predecessor to be arrested in his career of domination by the Scythians." Adams family correspondence was often this kind of classical crossword puzzle: Fabius Maximus Cunctator had exhausted Hannibal by allowing him to invade Italy in the Second Punic War, the "modern Alexander" was Napoleon, and the "Scythians" were Russians, not the nomads the ancient Alexander had once vanquished. Soon, though, John Quincy was sparing his mother nothing:

> Of the immense host with which six months since [Napoleon] invaded Russia, nine-tenths at least are prisoners or food for worms. . . . From Moscow to Prussia, eight hundred miles of road have been strewed with his artillery, baggage wagons, ammunition chests, dead and dying men, whom he has been forced to abandon to their fate—pursued all the time by three large regular armies of a most embittered and exasperated enemy, and by an almost numberless militia of peasants, stung by the destruction of their harvests and cottages . . . and spurred to revenge at once [by] themselves, their country, and their religion.

Two Russian generals—"Famine" and "Frost"—had completed the destruction, so that "[i]n all human probability the career of Napoleon's conquests is at an end. France can no longer give law to the continent. . . . A new era is dawning upon Europe."[37]

VI.

"Genius," Clausewitz writes, "does not consist in a single appropriate gift—courage, for example—while other qualities of mind or temperament . . . are not suited to war." Instead it requires "a harmonious combination of elements, in which one or the other ability may predominate, but none may be in conflict with the rest." It demands, in short, an *ecological* sensibility. "The man responsible for evaluating the whole must bring to the task the quality of intuition that perceives the truth at every point. Otherwise a chaos of opinions . . . would arise, and fatally entangle judgment."[38]

How, though, can anyone perceive "truth at every point"? Clausewitz answers by linking strategy to imagination.[39] Artists approach truth, he observes, with "a quick recognition" of what "the mind would ordinarily miss or would perceive only after long study and reflection." His term for this is *coup d'oeil,* or an "inward eye."[40] It's what Machiavelli meant by "sketching"—conveying complexity usably.[41] Complexity fully rendered would take too long and contain too much, thereby entangling judgment. Complexity as what you want or expect would only confirm what you think you know. You need something in between.

So when your troops get sick, or their horses begin to starve, or tsars don't follow the scripts you've written for them, you sketch what you know and *imagine*—informed by the sketch—what you don't: this allows recovering from surprises and moving on. Strategists and artists are, therefore, on the same page in Clausewitz, or, more accurately, pages, given the hundreds he left behind.

But how can *planning* anticipate *surprises*? Only by living with contradictions, Clausewitz maintains: "Everything in war is very simple, but the simplest thing is difficult." He elaborates in a passage Tolstoy could have written:

Imagine a traveler who late in the day decides to cover two more stages before nightfall. Only four or five hours more, on a paved highway with relays of horses: it should be an easy trip. But at the next station he finds no fresh horses, or only poor ones; the country grows hilly, the road bad, night falls, and finally after many difficulties he is only too glad to reach a resting place with any kind of primitive accommodation. It is much the same in war.

The military grammar of discipline can in theory overcome such problems, and in practice—for a time—it does. In the end, though, a larger logic of *friction* sets in, degrading the functioning of the multiple parts on which armies depend. "[O]nce conditions become difficult, as they must when much is at stake, things no longer run like a well-oiled machine."

> The machine itself begins to resist, and the commander needs tremendous willpower to overcome this resistance. [It] need not consist of disobedience and argument, though this occurs often enough in individual soldiers. It is the impact of the ebbing of moral and physical strength, of the heart-rending spectacle of the dead and wounded, that the commander has to withstand—first in himself, and then in all those who . . . have entrusted him with their thoughts and feelings, hopes and fears. As each man's strength . . . no longer responds to his will, the inertia of the whole gradually comes to rest on the commander's will alone. The ardor of his spirit must rekindle the flame of purpose in all others; his inward fire must revive their hope. Only to the extent that he can do this will he retain his hold on his men and keep control.

Something or someone will sooner or later break, but you can't know how, where, or when. What you can know is that, owing to friction, "one always falls far short of the intended goal."[42]

VII.

Clausewitz, in one sense, says nothing new here. Asymmetries in aspirations and capabilities have always constrained strategies, which is one of the reasons they're needed in the first place. He's highly original, though, in specifying friction as the cause, while showing that it can occur at any level: the passage of time and extension across space make it more probable.[43] Perhaps he knew that Napoleon's carriage, on the advance to Moscow, required having water poured onto its wheels to prevent overheating.[44]

Just as *coup d'oeil* links strategy to imagination, so Clausewitz's concept of friction ties theory to experience. These "must never disdain or exclude each other," he writes: "[O]n the contrary, they support each other."[45] That places uncertainty within a universal framework. Or, to put it another way, Clausewitz anticipates, by more than a century, Murphy's Law: that what can go wrong will. Or, still more succinctly, shit happens.[46]

Napoleon, in theory, knew this. That's why, despite his limited objectives, he crossed the Niemen with such an enormous force: Xerxes at the Hellespont did the same. Both sought to overcome friction by intimidating their enemies. Neither saw, though, that the retreat of a foe can become resistance, owing to the ascending costs of protracted pursuits. Both, for this reason, wore out their military machines, to the point that further advances emboldened adversaries, not themselves. Thermopylae and Borodino showed that Greeks and Russians weren't afraid. Salamis and Tarutino revealed that Persians and French now were.

Where, then, did Xerxes and Napoleon go wrong? They failed, Clausewitz would probably say, to perceive "truth at every point," which in these instances meant landscapes, logistics, climates, the morale of their troops, and the strategies of their enemies. They missed what their own soldiers understood: that Greece and Russia were traps, just as the English Channel was for the Spanish Armada. "The good general," Clausewitz concludes, "must know friction in order to overcome it whenever possible, and in order not to expect a standard of achievement in his operations which this very friction makes impossible."[47]

But why did Xerxes and Napoleon so limit peripheral vision, as if they were carriage horses wearing blinders? There are many examples, Clausewitz tells us,

> of men who show great determination as junior officers, but lose it as they rise in rank. Conscious of the need to be decisive, they also recognize the risks entailed by a wrong decision; since they are unfamiliar with the problems now facing them, their mind loses its former incisiveness. The more used they had been to instant action, the more their timidity increases as they realize the dangers of the vacillation that ensnares them.[48]

And so they stare straight ahead, listening to no one, fearing distractions, clinging to command even as it leads them into disaster. Thereby confirming the high-altitude rarity of common sense.

Where, in an Alice-in-Wonderland world of weary "genius," a horse can become a hedgehog, then a bewildered dog, scuttling home.

VIII.

"If we then ask," Clausewitz writes, "what sort of mind is likeliest to display . . . military genius, experience and observation will both tell us that it is the inquiring rather than the creative mind, the comprehensive rather than the specialized approach, the calm rather than the excitable head to which in war we would choose to entrust the fate of our brothers and children."[49] He elaborates no further in *On War,* but Tolstoy does, in *War and Peace,* in the contrast he draws between Napoleon and Kutuzov.

Napoleon appears most memorably in the novel's portrayal of a real event: his meeting with General Alexander Balashov, the tsar's aide-de-camp, in Vilnius on July 1, a week after the French crossed the Niemen. The emperor expects an offer of negotiations, but when Balashov insists that Alexander won't extend one as long as a single French soldier remains on Russian soil, Napoleon's face starts twitching and his left calf trembling: "[H]e began to speak in a higher and more hurried voice than before." The more he speaks the less he controls himself, quickly reaching "that state of irritation in which a man has to talk and talk and talk, only so as to prove his rightness to himself."

> Know that if you stir up Prussia against me, . . . I will wipe her off the map of Europe. . . . I'll hurl you back beyond the Dvina, beyond the Dnieper, and rebuild that barrier against

you which Europe was criminal . . . to have allowed to be destroyed. Yes, that's what will happen to you, that's what you've
gained by distancing yourselves from me.

The emperor stalks angrily around the room, sniffing from his
snuffbox. Suddenly he stops, looks into Balashov's eyes, and says,
menacingly but also wistfully: "[W]hat a fine reign your master
might have had!"

After which Napoleon invites his guest to a friendly dinner,
where he says nothing at all about what's occurred. Mistakes, Tolstoy notes, are no longer possible for him: "[T]o his mind everything he did was good, not because it agreed with any notion of
what was good and bad, but because he did it." And so Napoleon
winds up "exalt[ing] himself and insult[ing] Alexander, . . . the
thing he had least wanted to do at the beginning of the meeting."[50]

Tolstoy shows Kutuzov, in a fictional scene, arriving at his head-
quarters, dismounting with difficulty, and wheezing up steps. There
he embraces Prince Andrei, whose father has just died. The old
commander then asks for the report he's come to hear, while taking
more interest in the sounds his mistress is making in the next room.
"[H]e could not be surprised [by] anything the general on duty
could tell him," Tolstoy explains, for "he knew beforehand everything he was being told and listened to it only because he had to
listen, as one has to listen to the singing of a prayer service."

But when he learns that the French—maybe even the retreating
Russians—have sacked Andrei's family estate, Kutuzov bursts out
indignantly: "See . . . see what they've brought us to!" He adds,
though, that "it's hard to win a campaign." For that one needs "patience and time." These, he promises Andrei, will force the French

to "eat horseflesh for me!" At which point his only eye—the other having been lost long ago in combat—glistens with tears.

Andrei returns to his regiment "relieved with regard to the general course of things and . . . to the man to whom it had been entrusted." Kutuzov, he knows, will never invent anything,

> but he'll listen to everything, remember everything, put every-thing in its place, won't hinder anything useful or allow any-thing harmful. He understands that there is something stronger and more significant than his will—the inevitable course of events—and he's able to see them, able to understand their significance, and, in view of that significance, is able to renounce . . . his personal will and direct it elsewhere. And the main reason why one believes him . . . [is] that his voice trem-bled when he said, "See what they've brought us to!" and had a catch in it when he said he'd "make them eat horseflesh."

Kutuzov leads from a lower altitude than Napoleon: that keeps his head out of his own clouds. He may doze off, but he never forgets what he's set out to do. And so, Tolstoy writes, despite the tsar's doubts, "widespread approval . . . accompanied the people's election of Kutuzov as commander in chief."[51]

IX.

Long before Virgil took Dante through Hell, he was tutoring Octa-vian on the fundamentals of beekeeping, cattle breeding, crop rota-tion, and vine cultivation.[52] Leaders, he seemed to be saying, must keep their feet on the ground. Clausewitz thinks similarly. He'd avoided no logical conclusions in his writings, he explains, "but whenever the thread became too thin I have preferred to break it off. . . . Just as some plants bear fruit only if they don't shoot up too high, so in the practical arts the leaves and flowers of theory must be pruned and the plant kept close to its proper soil—experience."[53]

How, though, do you "prune" theory? By not asking too much of it, Clausewitz replies. "[I]t would indeed be rash" to deduce, from any particular reality, "universal laws governing every single case, regardless of all haphazard influences." But those who never rise "above anecdote"—those indefatigable repeaters of pointless stories—are equally useless, for they "would construct all history of individual cases, . . . digging only as deep as suits them, never get[ting] down to the general factors that govern the matter."

> Theory exists so that one need not start afresh each time sorting out the material and plowing through it, but will find it ready to hand and in good order. It is meant to educate the mind of the future commander, or, more accurately, to guide him in his self-education, not to accompany him to the battlefield; just as a wise teacher guides and stimulates a young man's intellectual development, but is careful not to lead him by the hand for the rest of his life.

Clausewitz sees theory, then, as *training*. It's what "hardens the body for great exertions, strengthens the heart in great peril, and fortifies judgment against first impressions." It's the "lubricant" that reduces friction. It "breeds that priceless quality, calm, which, passing from hussar and rifleman up to the general himself, will lighten the commander's task."[54]

Troubles come not from embracing theory as a beginner, but from clutching it too closely while rising, a practice that "defies common sense." Theory then becomes an excuse through which "limited and ignorant minds . . . justify their congenital incompetence."[55] Clausewitz especially despises the "*jargon, technicalities, and metaphors*" that "swarm" at high altitudes, a "lawless rabble of camp followers" torn from context and enlisted as principles. "The light of day usually reveals them to be mere trash," making theory "the very opposite of practice, and not infrequently the laughing stock of men whose military competence is beyond dispute."[56]

An example was Clausewitz's former instructor in the Prussian War School, General Karl Ludwig von Pfuel, who by 1812 had become a top military adviser to Tsar Alexander. Pfuel, Clausewitz wrote confidentially at the time, was a man "without a knowledge of actual things"—among them how best to deploy the Russian army against Napoleon.[57] It's unlikely that Tolstoy ever saw that comment, but he conveys clearly, in *War and Peace,* what Clausewitz thought:

> Pfuel was one of those theorists who so love their theory that they forget the purpose of the theory—its application in practice; in his love for theory, he hated everything practical and did not want to know about it. He was even glad of failure, because failure, proceeding from departures from theory in practice, only proved to him the correctness of his theory.

Tolstoy ends his scene by having Pfuel acknowledge the respectful but skeptical Andrei—an eerie stand-in for Clausewitz—with the disdain "of a man who knows beforehand that it will all go badly and who is not even displeased by that."[58]

It's one of many points at which Tolstoy seems to be finishing

Clausewitz's book, like close couples who finish each other's sentences.[59] Nowhere is this clearer than in what each says about the role of chance in war—and in life.

X.

"No other human activity is so continuously or universally bound up with chance," Clausewitz writes of war in *On War*. It's a "paradoxical trinity," composed of the passions that cause combatants to risk their lives, the skill of their commanders, and the coherence of the political objectives for which the war is being fought. Only the last is fully governed by reason: the others inhabit the murky realms of emotion, "where all the usual landmarks seem to have disappeared."[60] What's needed, then, is "a theory that maintains a balance between these three tendencies, like an object suspended between three magnets."[61]

But anyone who's experimented with magnets will know—Clausewitz surely did—that the difference between two and three, when a pendulum swings freely above them, *looks like* that between order and chaos: the third magnet shifts the oscillation from regularity to apparent randomness, or, in mathematical terms, from linearity to nonlinearity.[62] Clausewitz's magnets force us to ask, therefore, how a theory can balance behaviors that seem themselves to be, in their relation to one another, unbalanced.

Not by promising certainty, Clausewitz replies. He places theory within the category of rules to which there can be exceptions, not laws that allow none. He values theory as an antidote to anecdotes: as a compression of the past transmitting experience, while making minimal claims about the future. He relies on theory for training, not as a navigational chart for the unforeseen. He trusts *coup d'oeil* more than quantification: any reduction of war to numbers "would not [stand] up for a moment against the realities of life." And he distrusts novices who, without theory, will lack judgment, which must work "like a ship's compass," recording "the slightest variations" from courses set, "however rough the sea."[63]

Roughness originates, Clausewitz tells us, in sources known, if at all, only "to those who were on the spot."[64] Like the movements of a pendulum above three magnets, it can be as difficult to anticipate as auroras, blizzards, and earthquakes were to the first Kennan's remote Siberians.[65] War, for Clausewitz, is like that: three-quarters of it is "wrapped in a fog." Comprehension requires "a sensitive and discriminating judgment . . . , a skilled intelligence to scent out the truth." Which won't come from theories built only on what theorists, through their blinders, think they can measure.

Such simplifiers, Tolstoy adds—completing the argument—are like workmen assigned to plaster a church wall "who, taking advantage of the foreman's absence, in a fit of zeal smear their plaster all over the windows, the icons, [and] the scaffolding," delighted with how, "from their plastering point of view, everything comes out flat and smooth."[66] Tolstoy is the least plasterer-like of novelists, as is Clausewitz among theorists of war: there's nothing flat or smooth about either of them. They seek out irregularities at the edge of chaos,[67] which is, or appears to be, the realm of chance.

XI.

Where Clausewitz is content to leave it. But not the pit bull Tolstoy, who's so determined on further attack that he abandons his characters well short of the end of *War and Peace,* devoting its final pages instead to a relentlessly ponderous search for chance within the polarity of determinism versus freedom. Here's his conclusion:

> [T]he new methods of thinking which history should adopt for itself are being worked out simultaneously with the self-destruction towards which, ever subdividing and subdividing the causes of phenomena, the old history is moving.
>
> All of mankind's sciences have followed this path. Having arrived at the infinitely small, mathematics, the most exact of sciences, abandons the process of subdividing and starts on a new process of summing up the unknown infinitesimals. Renouncing the concept of cause, mathematics seeks laws, that is, properties common to all unknown infinitely small elements.
>
> Other sciences, though in a different form, have followed this same path of thinking. When Newton formulated the law of gravity, he did not say that the sun or the earth has the property of attraction; he said that all bodies, from the largest to the smallest, have this property of attracting each other. . . . History stands on the same path. And if history has for its subject of study the movements of peoples and of mankind, and not the description of episodes from people's lives, it should set aside the notion of causes and seek for the laws common to all the equal and inseparably bound together infinitely small elements of freedom.[68]

What Tolstoy means here—I think—is: (a) that because everything connects with everything else, there's an inescapable *interdependency* across time, space, and scale—forget about distinguishing independent from dependent variables; (b) that, as a consequence, there'll always be things that can't be known—breaking them into components won't help because there'll always be smaller components; (c) that owing to what we can't know, we'll always retain an illusion of agency, however infinitesimal; (d) that while laws may govern these infinitesimals, they make no difference to us because we can't feel their effects; therefore (e) our perception of freedom is, in practice, freedom itself.

If I've got this right, then Tolstoy has used scale to solve an ancient problem: how, if God is omnipotent, can man have free will? Being Tolstoy, though, his answer didn't satisfy him, and he soon reverted to the belief in God he'd once derided as the habit of primitives. He even tried, not very successfully, to become primitive himself.[69] But if considered, alongside Clausewitz, as a commentary, in advance, on F. Scott Fitzgerald—on how to hold opposing ideas in mind at the same time while retaining the ability to function—then Tolstoy's reasoning has significant implications for strategy in the largest sense.

XII.

Begin with theory and practice, both of which Clausewitz and Tolstoy respect without enslaving themselves to either. It's as if, in their thinking, abstraction and specificity reinforce each other, but never in predetermined proportions. Each situation requires a *balancing* derived from judgment and arising from experience, skills acquired by learning from the past and training for the future.

Theory reduces history's complexity to teachable moments. It's not the reductionism of Tolstoy's plasterers, who smooth over irregularities in search of predictability. Instead theory functions, with respect to the past, as Clausewitz's *coups d'oeil* do in the present: it extracts lessons from infinite variety. It sketches, informed by what you need to know, without trying to tell you too much. For in classrooms as on battlefields, you don't have unlimited time to listen. Theory, then, *serves* practice. And when practice corrects theory—when it removes theorists' horse blinders—it returns the favor, preventing stumbles off cliffs, into swamps, and toward Moscow.

An artist, when sketching, looks at a landscape and then a sketch pad, repeating the process until an image appears, depicting, but not duplicating, what's there. Landscape *and* sketch pad guide the artist's hand, but no two artists will sketch the scene in just the same way. It's a dependent yet distinctive reciprocity, without which no balancing of reality and representation can occur.[70]

The modern term for sketching in strategy is "net assessment,"[71] an evocation—never simply a list—of the elements, in environments, most likely to determine outcomes. If done well it will include "knowns"—geography, topography, climate, your own capabilities, the objectives you're seeking; "probabilities"—the goals of adversaries, the reliability of allies, the constraints of cultures, your country's capacity to endure adversity; and, finally, a respectful acknowledgment of the "unknowns" that will lurk in the intersections of the first two.

Like Clausewitz's magnets, the configuration is triangular, although in two ways. For as you balance knowns, probabilities, and unknowns, you're also doing so across time, space, and scale. "[I]n war, as in life generally," Clausewitz explains, "all parts of a whole are interconnected and thus the effects produced, however small their cause, must influence all . . . operations and modify their final outcome to some degree, however slight."[72] And so he anticipates Tolstoy on infinitesimals.

Not, however, because Clausewitz sees the future: it's rather because he and Tolstoy have seen, in the past, the face of battle.[73] From which they know that ends, potentially infinite, can never be means, which are poignantly finite. That's why war—explicitly in Clausewitz, implicitly in Tolstoy—must *reflect* policy. For when policy reflects war, it's because some high-level hedgehog—a Xerxes, or a Napoleon—has fallen in love with war, making it an end in itself. They'll stop only when they've bled themselves bloodless. And so the culminating points of *their* offensives are self-defeat.

Overstretch—the enfeeblement that comes with confusing ends and means—allows enemies to apply *leverage:* small maneuvers that have big consequences. Themistocles wouldn't have won at Salamis without spinning a Delphic oracle. Elizabeth trusted her admirals to trust the winds. And Kutuzov could safely slumber after Borodino, certain that geography, topography, and climate—the "knowns" Napoleon had ignored—would drive the French out even if the Russians did nothing. The border would be the "golden bridge" the enemy would *want* to cross to get home.[74]

Kutuzov's bridge could serve as grand strategy's gold standard. For if ends are to fit within available means, then solvency and morality—practicality and principle—demand that they do so with the least possible expenditure of resources and lives. "The means to be employed must be proportioned to the extent of the mischief," Hamilton writes in *The Federalist*,[75] and however much the astonishments of their age may have haunted Clausewitz and Tolstoy, both saw their books as paths back to proportionality. *On War* and *War and Peace* incessantly and at epic length balance opposites. That's where proportionality—the simultaneous comprehension of contradictions[76]—comes from.

Theory versus practice. Training versus improvisation. Planning versus friction. Force versus policy. Situations versus sketches. Specialization versus generalization. Action versus inaction. Victory versus defeat. Love versus hate. Life versus death. Leading from within clouds versus keeping the ground in view. But no "versus" whatever between art and science. It's not too much to suggest, therefore, that Clausewitz and Tolstoy together are, in the amplitude, imagination, and honesty with which they approached these great issues, the grandest of strategists.

CHAPTER EIGHT

THE GREATEST
PRESIDENT

John Quincy Adams doesn't appear in *War and Peace,* despite having spent more time in Alexander I's Russia than Clausewitz and Napoleon together.[1] But as the American presidential election of 1824 approached, three Shakespeare specters appeared to Adams. One was Macbeth, whose "unhallowed ambition" had won a king his crown but lost his soul. Another was Hamlet, for whom death in dark moments was "a consummation devoutly to be wished." The third was Bolingbroke, in *Richard II:* "Oh, who can hold a fire in his hand / By thinking on the frosty Caucasus?" Adams tried hard, but he'd begun fearing his own hopes. "We know so little of . . . which is best for ourselves," he wrote in his diary, "that whether I ought to *wish* for success is among the greatest uncertainties of the election." And yet, "I have more at stake . . . than any other individual in the Union."[2]

What he meant was what he owed his parents. His mother had seen to it that John Quincy, not yet eight, witnessed the bloodletting at Bunker Hill. His father had him reading the classics in Greek and Latin—and speaking French—as a preteen: he'd later add Spanish, German, and Dutch (though never Russian) to his fluencies. The younger Adams was minister to the Netherlands at twenty-six, to Prussia at thirty, and a United States senator at thirty-six: while still in the Senate, he took a Harvard professorship in rhetoric and oratory. Following his years in Russia he co-negotiated the Treaty of Ghent ending the Anglo-American War of 1812, stayed on as minister to Great Britain, and in 1817 became secretary of state, arguably the most influential occupant ever of that position.[3] Madison and Monroe had made it their path to the presidency, but because Adams's family expected no less, he'd been preparing his own path since childhood.

By 1824, though, the deference that allowed American dynasties—whether of Virginians[4] or Adamses—was giving way to a boisterous irreverence. Elites didn't wear well on an expanding frontier, in cutthroat competitive newspapers, or among freshly enfranchised voters. Gentlemen shouldn't scramble for anything, Adams believed, but not becoming president would be a "censure by the Nation upon my past service."[5] As well as, by implication, that of his father, so far the only one-term chief executive, still living and, from Massachusetts, closely watching. Seeking but not suggesting—balancing fire and frost—had worked for Washington in the late 1780s. It wasn't likely to for Adams, however, in the early 1820s.

So when Andrew Jackson, the next major military hero,[6] won the 1824 popular vote but only a plurality—not a majority—in the electoral college, Adams gave up on frost altogether. The Constitution required the House of Representatives to decide such elections, and there Adams's supporters joined with those of a runner-up, Henry Clay, to make Adams president. He, in turn, made

Clay secretary of state. Whether there'd been a deal didn't matter: it looked, tasted, and smelled enough like one for Jackson and his followers to denounce, furiously, the "corrupt bargain." Adams and Clay, therefore, began their administration, historian Sean Wilentz has observed, with "a complete failure of political intelligence and imagination."[7]

Which President Adams tried to repair by marching to Moscow. Not literally, of course, but his first annual message to Congress, submitted against his cabinet's advice in December 1825, mismatched aspirations and capabilities on a Napoleonic scale. From a mandate so minuscule that only he could detect it, Adams asked for everything: a national university, federally financed roads and canals, uniform weights and measures, a stronger navy and a naval academy, the promotion of global commerce, and vigorous diplomacy to bolster the Monroe Doctrine. Indulging his fascination with astronomy, Adams even called for a national observatory—an American version of Europe's "lighthouses of the skies"—thus opening himself to allegations that his head wasn't just in clouds but in the stars.

To neglect these priorities, he insisted, would be "to hide in the earth the talent committed to our charge." For "liberty is power," and "the nation blessed with the largest portion of liberty must in proportion to its numbers be the most powerful nation upon earth." A slumbering indolence "palsied by the will of our constituents" could only "doom" the country to "perpetual inferiority."[8] Adams's message palsied what little support he had left, however, winning him, after less than a year in office, the certainty of his own single term.

Perhaps, having abandoned his principles to gain the presidency, Adams hoped to regain them by giving it up. Perhaps he'd always self-doubted: his parents made ambition a duty but kept reassurance rare. Perhaps he was behind the times: the near future of American politics lay with Jacksonian devolution, not Hamiltonian consolidation. Perhaps he was ahead of his times: a more distant future would resurrect federalism to win a civil war. Probably he saw that slavery would start it and hoped to postpone, with distractions, the evil day: knowing the fragility of the Missouri Compromise, Adams like most of his contemporaries hardly dared speak slavery's name.[9] Whatever the explanation, he left office in 1829 much as Napoleon had left Russia in 1812: exhausted, bereft of allies, chased out by his own miscalculations.

But Adams regrouped in a way that wouldn't have occurred to Napoleon: he demoted himself. He agreed to run from his Massachusetts district for the House of Representatives, the only former president ever to seek service there. Winning easily, he took his seat in December 1831, and over the next decade and a half asked for only one thing: a debate on the thousands of anti-slavery petitions he'd put before his colleagues. Although he was often alone in defying the "gag rule" the House had placed on that subject, Adams prevailed in the end. For just as the Constitution protected slavery, he argued, so its First Amendment guaranteed free speech and the right to petition "for a redress of grievances." With persistence, logic, and a principled purpose, he boxed in his opponents.

Then, in March 1841, at the age of seventy-four, Adams did the same to the Supreme Court. After speaking for eight hours on behalf of the *Amistad* captives—Africans sold for slavery in Spanish Cuba who'd freed themselves at sea, been seized by the American navy, and through sympathetic lawyers appealed their forced return—Adams reminded the justices that framed copies of the Declaration of Independence flanked them on adjoining walls. How, sitting between these, could they *not* free the captives? Moved by this invocation of morality, original intent, and interior design, the court unexpectedly agreed. In time, if at tragic cost, the country would too.

More than any other American before Lincoln, therefore, it was Adams who placed the Constitution *within the frame* of the Declaration—*all* men were created equal—where he knew that the Constitution, as it then stood, couldn't comfortably sit.

I.

On February 21, 1848, the House of Representatives was debating a resolution of thanks to military officers who'd served in the recent war against Mexico: the Treaty of Guadalupe Hidalgo, concluding that conflict, had gone to the Senate earlier that day. It expanded the United States from Texas—annexed in 1845 before the war—to the Pacific, but despite his earlier transcontinental ambitions Adams would have *opposed* the settlement if he'd had the opportunity. President James K. Polk, he believed, had provoked the conflict to bring new slave territories into the Union. The House, however, didn't vote on treaties, and Adams, on its floor that afternoon, suffered the stroke that killed him two days later. Abraham Lincoln, a first-term Illinois congressman and fellow war critic, probably witnessed the dramatic event.[10]

It was, the stricken Adams managed to say, his "end of earth," but also that of the last generation who'd known the Founders. Lincoln was born in a ramshackle cabin on the Kentucky frontier in 1809, the year Madison sent Adams to Russia. The death of Abe's mother and his father's neglect left the boy and his sister near starvation at nine and twelve, their clothes in tatters, their hair infested with lice:

Adams, as Monroe's secretary of state, was at the time acquiring Spanish Florida. And when Abe, rescued by a stepmother, felt the need still to escape his father, who thought only a year of schooling quite enough, the teenager and a friend poled a flatboat they'd built down the Mississippi without ever having heard of Huck Finn: the year was 1828 and Adams was still president. When asked, years later, to specify his education, Lincoln wrote a single word: "defective."[11]

That would have been true at the time, though, of most Americans, so what set Lincoln apart? First his looks or, as he'd have put it, his lack of them. At an adult height of six feet four inches, he loomed over almost everyone else. His hands were enormous, his arms too long, and his pants usually too short. He thought his face ugly, failed to tame his disobedient hair, and moved with an alarmingly gangly gawkiness, as if about to run into things and knock them over. But Lincoln seems rarely to have regretted his appearance, taking refuge instead in self-deprecation while reserving, for infrequent use, his intimidating strength. Having found it impossible not to be noticed, he decided early on that he might as well be liked.[12]

So he perfected *performance:* no one used humor more readily, more aptly, or with less recycling. His anecdotes, often scatological, flowed as easily as the paper the shaky banks of his day issued as currency, but the stories never lacked point or purpose: it was said of Lincoln that he could "make a cat laugh."[13] Behind the mask, though, was an enduring fatalism, as if something or someone else—probably not God[14]—were directing him. It could have been the shadow of a desperate childhood, or the death of Ann Rutledge, whom he'd hoped to marry, or the exasperations of life with Mary Todd, whom he did marry, or the loss of two of their four children—who knows? But maybe also Shakespearian complexities, for Lincoln lived the

parts, not only of Adams's specters Macbeth, Hamlet, and Boling-
broke, but also of Falstaff *and* Henry V *and* Bottom *and* Lear *and*
Prospero *and* later of course, in the eyes of his enemies, Julius
Caesar.[15]

The young Lincoln loved lolling on a riverbank reciting Shakespeare. The stream was the Sangamon, near New Salem, the first
Illinois town in which he settled. To the west lay emptiness filled
with possibilities. To the east lay property, roads and bridges, the
rule of law, the spirit of enterprise, the right of all whatever their
origins to rise. Lincoln straddled these geographies without committing to either: he tried boatbuilding, river navigation, surveying,
military service, rail-splitting, co-managing a general store, even
serving briefly as village postmaster—but never farming—before
finally taking up the practice of law and the vocation of politics to
which that led.[16]

In both of which he educated himself. He read voraciously,
remembered pragmatically, and applied lessons ingeniously. Oratorical skills smoothed his path from law to politics: not being
ponderous helped. Defeated for the state legislature in 1832, he ran
again and won two years later. After that, he never lost an election.[17]
With Jackson in his second presidential term, political parties had
begun organizing across the country.[18] Lincoln chose Whigs over
Democrats out of respect for Clay, who'd tactfully repackaged
Adams's proposals for "internal improvements." The young legisla-
tor's more immediate priority, though, was to improve Springfield,
where he'd moved, by making it the state capital. With that accomplished in 1839, and with the Whigs having won the presidency in
1840,[19] Lincoln could seek wider opportunities.

Wisely, he took his time. Winning elections required assembling
coalitions, and in Illinois that meant waiting your turn: that's why

Lincoln didn't seek the Whigs' nomination for the national House of Representatives until 1846. It's also why, having secured the seat, he promised to fill it for only a single term. He arrived in Washington in December 1847, eager to make his mark. So he demanded that Polk specify the "spot" on which, a year and a half earlier, Mexicans had shed American blood. If, as the president claimed, the war started in self-defense, then who, exactly, had been defending themselves? But Polk ignored him and Lincoln gained only the nickname "Spotty." Uncharacteristically, he'd moved too soon, a mistake he'd avoided in the past and would in the future.[20]

Lincoln returned to Springfield in 1849, having failed to snag a patronage plum—commissioner of the General Land Office—that would have kept him in Washington. His congressional service, apart from the "spot" resolution, had been unmemorable. Despite its use, throughout his absence, by his partner, William Herndon, Lincoln found his law office so dirty that the seeds he'd sent constituents had spilled on the floor and sprouted: he was forty and not far himself, it seemed, from going to seed.[21]

II.

Within five years, though, Lincoln had embraced a cause, acquired a compass, and set a course. It was that of the old man whose last days he'd seen in the House of Representatives: reminding Americans of the uncomfortable position in which, in order to form their Union, they'd been obliged by its Founders to sit. "Necessity" was their only excuse for slavery, Lincoln insisted in 1854, and "so far only as it carried them, did they ever go." They'd inherited the institution from the British, knew they'd have no nation without it, but hoped it would disappear on its own. So they wrote slavery into the Constitution without naming it, "just as an afflicted man hides away a wen or a cancer, which he dares not cut out at once, lest he bleed to death. . . . Less than this our fathers COULD not do; and MORE they WOULD not do."[22]

Slavery, however, was *not* disappearing. It was becoming more profitable where it was legal. The three-fifths rule for apportioning congressional seats and electoral votes privileged its position in national politics. It could well spread, by invitation or imposition, into the new territories—soon to be states—won from Mexico: the "compromise of 1850," meant to settle slavery's status in those regions, was already less stable than that of 1820, itself never robust.[23] And even where slavery was illegal, federal laws allowed owners to recapture fugitive slaves. "The Fourth of July has not quite dwindled away," Lincoln wrote witheringly in 1855: "[I]t is still a great day—*for burning fire-crackers!!!*"[24]

No one fanned more flames over slavery than the man who tried, too cleverly, to extinguish them. Stephen A. Douglas, the senior senator from Illinois, was a fellow Springfield lawyer and frequent Lincoln debating partner who, although a Democrat, shared the Whigs' enthusiasm for economic development. Both sought to position their region between eastern innovation and western opportunity. Both favored, as the first step, an Illinois-based transcontinental railroad. Both knew it would need federal subsidies, land grants, and military protection. Both expected southerners, wanting their own route, to demand compensation. But only "Judge Douglas," as Lincoln called him, thought he knew what it should be.

Why not in the vast Kansas-Nebraska territory—extending west to the Rocky Mountains and north to the Canadian border—repeal *all* congressional restrictions on slavery and let settlers themselves decide its future? Self-determination, after all, had been enshrined in the Declaration of Independence, but topography and climate ensured that slavery, in the new territories, would never thrive. Douglas could have it both ways: the Kansas-Nebraska Act, which he proposed and Congress passed in May 1854, would be *simultaneously* principled and expedient.[25]

Instead it exploded, sending "red hot nails," Harriet Beecher Stowe later wrote, "in every direction."[26] The compromises of 1820 and 1850 had balanced *known interests*. Douglas, however, was juggling *unknown processes*—settlement patterns, election outcomes, the uncertainties of transplantation in unfamiliar terrain—in an era of extreme political anxiety. Nor was that the worst, Lincoln pointed out, for Douglas's "popular sovereignty" doctrine challenged the legacy of the Founders themselves.

They'd seen slavery as a necessary evil, to be tolerated within existing limits until it went away. Douglas, however, professed neutrality: if the inhabitants of new territories wanted slavery, then they should have it, perhaps even indefinitely. Lincoln, normally even-tempered, could scarcely contain his fury when the two shared a platform at Springfield in October:

> This *declared* indifference, but, as I must think, covert *real* zeal for the spread of slavery, I cannot but hate. I hate it because of the monstrous injustice of slavery itself. I hate it because it deprives our republican example of its just influence in the world—enables the enemies of free institutions, with plausibility, to taunt us as hypocrites—causes the real friends of freedom to doubt our sincerity, and especially because it forces so many really good men amongst ourselves into an open

war with the very fundamental principles of civil liberty—criticizing the Declaration of Independence, and insisting that there is no right principle of action but *self-interest*.[27]

Why, though, should Douglas, or anyone else, care what Lincoln hated? He'd gone nowhere after his single congressional term. He came across in public as a beanpole with a high squeaky voice. He was up against a powerful senator: the "Little Giant," as Douglas liked to be called, was short, sleek, resonant, and consequential. Lincoln, if not quite nobody, had done little as yet to become somebody.

III.

But Illinois politics tended to smooth out asymmetries. It wasn't enough for politicians to publish speeches in newspapers: oratory was lengthy, print was microscopic, and not everybody could read. Anyone could, however, attend performances—there wasn't much else to do in small towns. So the court circuit, which sent lawyers and judges around the state trying cases, became a road show for rhetorical acrobatics.[28] It was no great step from this to outdoor political rallies, with audiences standing transfixed for hours. And from those to debates, through which Judge Douglas, again too cleverly, made Lincoln famous.

Lincoln started his speeches slowly, appearing at first to search for thoughts, words, even the more distant parts of his own anatomy. But as he warmed up, his gestures became purposeful, his voice began to carry, and his arguments laid lethal traps—so

effectively that reporters, fascinated, could forget to take notes.[29] Like John Quincy Adams, Lincoln had studied Euclid—Adams at Harvard, Lincoln on his own[30]—and both drew from him a relentless geometrical logic. Here, for example, is Lincoln, in a note probably prepared for his Springfield speech:

> If A. can prove, however conclusively, that he may of right enslave B.—why may not B. snatch the same argument, and prove equally, that he may enslave A?—You say A. is white, and B. is black. It is *color,* then; the lighter, having the right to enslave the darker? Take care. By this rule you are to be slave to the first man you meet, with a fairer skin than your own. You do not mean *color* exactly?—You mean the whites are *intellectually* the superiors of the blacks, and, therefore have the right to enslave them? Take care again. By this rule, you are to be slave to the first man you meet, with an intellect superior to your own. But, say you, it is a question of *interest;* and if you can make it your *interest* you have the right to enslave another. Very well. And if he can make it his interest, he has the right to enslave you.[31]

Then, in that speech, Lincoln quoted the Declaration of Independence: "[A]*ll* men are created equal." Did Judge Douglas consider slaves to be men? If not, what were they? Certainly not hogs, who hadn't three-fifths representation in the national Congress. But if slaves were men, didn't "popular sovereignty" guarantee them the right to self-determination? And how could any man *choose* to be a slave? Men fled *from* slavery *to* freedom, not the other way around. Douglas's views, Lincoln concluded mildly, "seem not to rest on a very firm basis even in his own mind."[32]

But logic also required picking some fights and postponing others. Lincoln refrained from questioning constitutional safeguards for slavery where they existed, or the three-fifths rule itself, or even fugitive slave laws. He did, though, deploy Jefferson,[33] a slave owner, Declaration drafter, and founder of Douglas's Democratic Party, who'd also written the Ordinance of 1787 *prohibiting* slavery in the territories that became Ohio, Indiana, Illinois, and Wisconsin: why now *lift* such restrictions in Kansas-Nebraska? Nor did asking this question make Lincoln an abolitionist: that claim was "very silly."

> Stand with anybody that stands RIGHT . . . and PART with him when he goes wrong. Stand WITH the abolitionist in restoring the Missouri Compromise; and stand AGAINST him when he attempts to repeal the fugitive slave law. . . . What of that? You are still right. . . . In both cases you oppose the dangerous extremes.

The point was to deny slavery moral neutrality, to return it to the legality reluctantly granted it by the Founders, and thereby—like them—to preserve the Union. For which "succeeding millions of free happy people, the world over, shall rise up, and call us blessed."[34]

IV.

Douglas squirmed under Lincoln's linkages of pragmatism with principle, reason with passion, and respect for the nation's past with a vision of the world's future. The senator preferred to split differences, not to explore polarities. Lincoln, in contrast, drew strength from contradictions, maybe because he contained so many. They gave him an *amplitude*[35]—physically, intellectually, morally—absent in his rival. Douglas couldn't refuse to debate Lincoln without losing political credibility, but with each encounter the beanpole's reputation rose and the Little Giant's fell. By 1858 Lincoln was seeking Douglas's Senate seat as the candidate of a new anti-slavery Republican Party—for which Douglas, in yet another miscalculation, had paved the way.

The "*avowed* object" and "*confident* promise" of the Kansas-Nebraska Act, Lincoln reminded the state convention that nominated him in June, had been to end "slavery agitation." Over the past four years, however, the opposite had occurred.[36] Pro-slavery settlers streamed into Kansas, setting up sovereignties intensely *unpopular* there and throughout the free states. That split national Democrats and Whigs into northern and southern factions, opening opportunities for Republicans. Then, in 1857, the Supreme Court widened divisions by ruling, in *Dred Scott v. Sandford,* that Congress lacked the authority to regulate slavery in *any* of the new territories: the Declaration of Independence, it gratuitously added, couldn't have meant to include "Africans," slave or free, when it proclaimed "all men" to be created equal.[37] Douglas, his schemes shattered, had failed to foresee any of this.

"If we could first know *where* we are, and *whither* we are tending," Lincoln told the Illinois Republicans in 1858, "we could then better judge *what* to do, and *how* to do it."[38] That required a compass, but Douglas's aligned itself only with his own maneuvering.[39] Too often looking back to cover his tracks, he fell too frequently into the thickets, swamps, and sinkholes that lay ahead. Lincoln also maneuvered—he *was* a politician—but his compass aligned with timeless principles. Such as: "a house divided against itself cannot stand."[40]

It followed, then, that "this government cannot endure, permanently half *slave* and half *free*." The Founders had allowed a *temporary* contradiction—which lasted longer than they'd have liked—but their trajectory for slavery was always one of decline. Douglas was ratifying a slavery ascendency: as Burke might have put it, the end of his argument didn't remember the country's beginning. Between these paths, there could be no compromise. "I do not expect the Union to be *dissolved*," Lincoln emphasized. "I do not expect the house to *fall*—but I *do* expect it will cease to be divided."

> It will become *all* one thing, or *all* the other. Either the *opponents* of slavery, will arrest the further spread of it, and place it . . . in [the] course of ultimate extinction; or its *advocates* will push it forward, till it shall become alike lawful in *all* the States, *old* as well as *new*—*North* as well as *South*.[41]

The seven Lincoln-Douglas debates of 1858—memorable for their length, substance, and oratorical pyrotechnics[42]—nonetheless crept cautiously around this polarity: the possibility that the Union *might* dissolve, as an alternative to becoming all one thing or all the other, was still too explosive to make explicit.

Lincoln concentrated instead on showing how little the Supreme Court had left of "popular sovereignty": it was now only a soup made from "the shadow of a pigeon that starved to death." Was there any way, he asked Douglas, in which the settlers of a territory could legally keep slavery out? Boxed in, the judge had to admit that they could do so only by withholding protection for slave owners and their property, a right hitherto sacrosanct in fugitive slave laws. Feigning astonishment, the beanpole pounced: had his *rival* become an *abolitionist*?[43]

Douglas's reply satisfied no one, including himself, but the Democratic majority in the Illinois legislature nonetheless voted to keep him in the Senate.[44] Lincoln was thought to have won the debates, though, and that won him national prominence: he'd emerged as a plausible candidate, if not yet the leading one, for the 1860 Republican presidential nomination.

What Lincoln had shown was the practicality, in politics, of a moral standard. I mean by this an external frame of reference that *shapes* interests and actions, not—like Douglas's—an internal one that only *reflects* them. Lincoln's didn't arise from faith, or formal ethics, or even the law, a profession necessarily pragmatic in its pursuit of justice. It emerged instead from what experience had taught, from the self-education that widened it, and from the logic in which Lincoln grounded his oratorical lightning. Judge Douglas's *amorality,* therefore, was not just wrong: it violated the most basic requirements of common sense.

V.

Despite the "rail-splitter" nickname with which Lincoln's supporters saddled him, he now had to be a political "lumper." Party-splitting he left to Douglas.[45] The Republicans had first competed for the presidency in 1856: they lost, but unlike the fractious Democrats or the nearly extinct Whigs, they agreed in opposing slavery's expansion.[46] Their problem in 1860 was too many hopefuls: *Harper's Weekly* identified eleven, the front-runner being the longtime senator from New York, William H. Seward.[47] Lincoln had to win their allegiance without weakening the party's resolve. "My name is new in the field," he wrote in March, "and I suppose I am not the

first choice of a very great many. Our policy, then, is to give no of-
fence to others—[to] leave them in a mood to come to us, if they
shall be compelled to give up their first love."[48]

So he made himself the party's center of gravity. He started by
speaking, with unexpected success, as far afield as Wisconsin, Ohio,
New York, and New England.[49] He then brought the nominating
convention to Chicago, so that rivals would have to circle him, not
he them. He watched the orbiting quietly from Springfield, carefully avoiding the *appearance* of any deals.[50] After securing the
nomination on the third ballot he campaigned, as was customary,
only from his office and trampled front yard—not, however, without authorizing complimentary biographies, posing for photographs, and keeping in touch by mail and telegraph with party
organizers in the states he hoped to carry: he was, for his day, tech-
savvy.[51] Because the other parties remained split, he won a clear
electoral college majority in November, if by no means that in the
popular vote.[52]

As president-elect he recruited a cabinet of frustrated first lovers
or, as the historian Doris Kearns Goodwin has called it, a "team of
rivals." They included his major competitors at Chicago—the indignantly disappointed Seward as secretary of state, the transparently
ambitious Salmon P. Chase of Ohio as treasury secretary, the corrupt but politically necessary Simon Cameron of Pennsylvania as
secretary of war, the reliably steady Edward Bates of Missouri as
attorney general—and a stalwart noncompetitor, Gideon Welles of
Connecticut, as secretary of the navy. Perhaps they'd devour one
another, Lincoln told his young aide John Nicolay, but he needed
the best men he could get. So he'd "risk the dangers of faction to
overcome the dangers of rebellion."[53]

The outgoing president, James Buchanan, had refused to risk

anything: hence his terrifying passivity as seven slave states seceded after Lincoln's election, seizing federal facilities as they did so. Anxious senators—among them Seward, Douglas, and John Crittenden of Kentucky—tried stitching together compromises, but after briefly considering a few, Lincoln returned to the fundamentals:

> I am for no compromise which *assists* or *permits* the extension of [slavery] on soil owned by the nation. And any trick by which the nation is to acquire territory, and then allow some local authority to spread slavery over it, is as obnoxious as any other.[54]

Lincoln does appear to have underestimated the South's determination: "I cannot see that more than two or three regiments will be required to execute all the United States laws in disaffected States," he assured a skeptical visitor in January 1861. "This, however, I will do, no matter how much force may be required."[55]

For the moment, though, Lincoln allowed logic a last chance. His inaugural address, delivered on March 4, took the secessionists at their word when they claimed to be defending the Constitution: what rights specifically had been denied? Not the ownership of slaves where that was legal, or their recovery anywhere when they escaped. Not respect for the Supreme Court, whose specific rulings could never require general subjugation to "that eminent tribunal." Surely not the responsibility of each duly elected president to enforce federal laws faithfully in every state. The only real point at issue was that "[o]ne section of our country believes slavery is *right*, and ought to be extended, while the other believes it is *wrong*, and ought not to be extended."

But was that worth separation, given its geographic improbability, given the illogic of a union legislating its own extinction, given all the other unknowns sure to attend so unprecedented an enterprise?

> Before entering upon so grave a matter as the destruction of our national fabric, . . . would it not be wise to ascertain precisely why we do it? Will you hazard so desperate a step, while there is any possibility that any portion of the ills you fly from, have no real existence? Will you, while the certain ills you fly to, are greater than all the real ones you fly from?

Nothing valuable could be lost, he insisted, by "taking time."[56] Yet no secessionist should doubt where he stood: "You can have no conflict, without being yourselves the aggressors. *You* have no oath registered in Heaven to destroy the government, while *I* shall have the most solemn one to 'preserve, protect and defend' it." And so he'd wait for "the chorus of the Union"—frustrated first lovers?—again to be touched, "as surely they will be, by the better angels of our nature."[57]

VI.

Angels, however, don't always respond to logic, and the secessionists didn't either. The Confederate States of America fired on Fort Sumter in Charleston harbor—which Lincoln had announced he was resupplying, not reinforcing—on April 12, 1861, and from that moment war was under way, with the South bearing the stigma of having started it.[58] Lincoln's unvarying objective over the next four years was to restore the Union, thereby saving his state for what he foresaw as a future of *global* greatness. But that wouldn't be possible, he also believed, without expunging the originally necessary sin of slavery.[59] As far as I know, Lincoln never read Augustine or Machiavelli on the competing demands of souls and states. Yet few who came after them more skillfully navigated the polarity.

The eleven states comprising the Confederacy—four more seceded after Fort Sumter—had the benefits of interior lines, but the disadvantages of a slave-based agrarian economy ill-suited to modern war. Geography therefore allowed, even as scarcity required, a strategy of mobility, ingenuity, and surprise, all present in the military genius of Robert E. Lee.[60] The Union had superior manpower, industry, and logistics, but its exterior lines befuddled its generals, making them sluggish and risk-averse. Offensives launched from such positions would fail, General Henry Halleck warned Lincoln in January 1862, "in ninety-nine cases out of a hundred." They were "condemned by every military authority I have ever read."[61]

Lincoln knew, though, that you can't fight only wars that fit textbooks. And so he proposed a "general idea"—he wasn't ready yet to make it an order—of how to deploy the Union's power against the Confederacy's skills. It was

> that we have the *greater* numbers, and the enemy has the *greater* facility of concentrating forces upon points of collision; that we must fail, unless we can find some way of making *our* advantage an over-match for *his;* and that this can only be done by menacing him with superior forces at *different* points, at the *same* time; so that we can safely attack, one, or both, if he makes no change; and if he *weakens* one to *strengthen* the other, forbear to attack the strengthened one, but seize, and hold the weakened one, gaining so much.[62]

Could the Union not counter Confederate concentrations of forces at single moments and points with multiple simultaneous concentrations? Could it not balance "greater numbers" against "greater facility"? Could *it* not think and act within time, space, and scale?[63]

It's fortunate that Lincoln never studied at West Point, because these queries might have got him expelled. They violated the professional orthodoxy of an army still focused on the occupation, fortification, and defense of fixed positions. Although intrigued by Napoleon's wars of maneuver, the pre–Civil War American military was better prepared for engineering than for combat: it had no experience of a *nation* in arms. Its dominant authority was the Swiss strategist Antoine-Henri Jomini, best known for treating war as geometry. Clausewitz wasn't available in English until 1873.[64]

Lincoln, nevertheless, *intuited* Clausewitz—although it would take him three years to find, in the unprepossessingly lethal Ulysses S. Grant, a general who also did.[65] The president's strategy was to destroy enemy forces, wherever they were, whenever opportunities arose to do so: in short, and above all else, to *fight*.[66] The Union's human, territorial, and technological reserves would in time exceed the Confederacy's: bloodshed would compel its armies' surrender, and that would kill the rebellious state. War was, then, for Lincoln— despite his never having seen this sentence—"*an act of force to compel our enemy to do our will*."[67]

VII.

It comes, of course, from the first page of *On War,* after which things get more complicated. As did military command for Lincoln, who knew without having to read Clausewitz that wars, however ferocious, must serve, not consume, the states waging them. War could never be an end in itself, but it could be the means by which an endangered state saved itself. And Lincoln saw that a *civil* war—which he'd allowed to be forced upon him—might also permit the *American* state, tainted by slavery, to save its soul.

Saving the state, however, came first: giving souls that priority was for prophets, not politicians. Lincoln had to hold his truncated Union together in the face of the sacrifices it would now have to make. That meant retaining the allegiance of Missouri, Kentucky, Maryland, and Delaware, four loyal states where slavery was legal. Lose them, the president acknowledged, and "[w]e would as well consent to separation at once, including the surrender of this capitol." Or, as he's said to have added: he "*wanted* God on his side, but he *must* have Kentucky."[68]

So Lincoln ordered his commanders *not* to declare, on their own authority, that slaves their troops captured were free: only the president could do that, and he wasn't yet ready. He signed a congressional Confiscation Act authorizing the seizure of rebel property including slaves, but refrained from enforcing it: he'd hold it for what he later might choose to do. But when Northern pro-slavery partisans tried to impede the recruitment and transportation of troops to the front, Lincoln immediately crushed them: he arrested the troublemakers, denied them habeas corpus, and, when the Supreme Court objected, defied it.[69]

Lincoln's goal, in each of these instances, was to balance law against military necessity, in the expectation that the passage of time and the success of his armies would stabilize the equilibria. "If slavery is not wrong, nothing is wrong," he wrote in 1864. "I cannot remember when I did not so think, and feel. And yet, I have never understood that the Presidency conferred upon me an unrestricted right to act officially upon this judgment and feeling." It did, though, give him the duty, even by desperate means, to preserve the Union.

> By general law life *and* limb must be protected; yet often a limb must be amputated to save a life; but a life is never wisely given to save a limb. I felt that measures, otherwise unconstitutional, might become lawful, by becoming indispensable to the preservation of the nation. Right or wrong, I assumed this ground, and now avow it.[70]

Lincoln here stated, more clearly than Clausewitz, a Clausewitzian fundamental: that it made *no* sense to save a part while losing the whole. Hence it was only *common* sense to conclude that "the political object is the goal, war is the means of reaching it, and means can never be considered in isolation from their purpose."[71]

VIII.

In his history of the Emancipation Proclamation, Allen C. Guelzo suggests that "the gift of *coup d'oeil*" allowed Lincoln to "take in the whole of a situation at once and know almost automatically how to proceed." Guelzo doesn't cite Clausewitz's use of that term, but he does evoke, with a precision Tolstoy might have envied, the nature of the proficiency:

> It is an ironic rather than a tragic attitude, in which the calculation of costs is critical rather than crucial or incidental. It prefers incremental progress to categorical solutions . . . [y]et, unlike mere moderation, it has a sense of purposeful motion

and declines to be paralyzed by a preoccupation with process, even while it remains aware that there is no goal so easily attained . . . that it rationalizes dispensing with process altogether.

Lincoln critically assessed costs, neither brushing them aside—like Napoleon in Russia—nor dreading them to the point of immobility—like Union army generals before Grant. He relied on experience, incrementally accumulated, to show what worked, not on categories, professorially taught, to say what should. He respected processes—and in the legal sense due process—but knew the risks of respect when much was at stake. He committed himself purposefully to union throughout the war and to emancipation by its end, although with exquisite timing: no one more artfully stuck to nonnegotiables while selectively stating them. And Lincoln fully grasped at all times Clausewitz's great paradox: that "everything in war is very simple, but the simplest thing is difficult."[72]

General George B. McClellan, Lincoln's longest-serving commander during the first half of the war, saw only the last half of the paradox and made it a principle. The self-styled "Young Napoleon"—so posed in his photographs—built a great army but underemployed it: he was, the historian James McPherson has written, "perpetually *almost* but not *quite* ready to move."[73] That frustrated Lincoln's strategy of multiple simultaneous concentrations. "[I]f General McClellan did not want to use the army," the president fumed at one point, he "would like to borrow it."[74] He knew, though, that he couldn't do that and run the country, so while trying out a string of similarly static generals, Lincoln began seeking alternative ways to win the war. One was to become, at last, an abolitionist.[75]

To have done so too early might have lost the war, but the

experience of fighting it, Lincoln saw, was shifting its purpose: this meant that policy, embedded in purpose, could also shift. The president forbade his commanders from freeing captured slaves, but he didn't object when they put slaves to work supplying the army. It then seemed reasonable to arm some and, once this had been done, to recruit them into the army, where many in any event wanted to go. That augmented Northern manpower while unnerving the South, always fearful of slave revolts. And once former slaves had fought for the Union, no Northerner could credibly support re-enslavement: *practicality* was freeing slaves, if not yet a presidential decree.[76]

Lincoln knew what was happening, didn't try to prevent it, and yet retained a careful detachment from it. He publicly assured the hyperbolic abolitionist Horace Greeley as late as August of 1862:

> My paramount objective in this struggle *is* to save the Union, and is *not* either to save or destroy slavery. If I could save the Union without freeing *any* slave I would do it, and if I could save it by freeing *all* the slaves I would do it; and if I could do it by freeing some and leaving others alone I would also do that. . . . I shall do *less* whenever I shall believe what I am doing hurts the cause, and I shall do *more* whenever I shall believe doing more will help the cause. I shall try to correct errors when shown to be errors; and I shall adopt new views so fast as they shall appear to be true views.

Leaving these options open was his "*official*" duty, Lincoln added, but "I intend no modification of my oft-expressed *personal* wish that all men every where could be free." So what had he really said? "[T]hat he was preparing for a dramatic step," his biographer

Richard Carwardine has concluded, *and* "that he had no such intention."[77]

But Lincoln had already found a way to make his wish his duty: he'd declare abolition a military necessity. This was, he'd quietly told Seward and Welles in July, "absolutely essential to the salvation of the nation." He proposed to act, not under congressional confiscation legislation, but through "war powers" *implied* in his constitutional designation as "commander in chief." No one had yet established what those were, but Adams, in the House of Representatives two decades earlier, had claimed their inclusion of authority "to order the universal emancipation of the slaves." His opinion—a ghostly whisper?—reached Lincoln soon after the Civil War began, but this president, unlike Adams, had the gift of *coup d'oeil*. So he waited for just the right moment.[78]

It came when McClellan at last delivered, at Antietam on September 17, a plausible military victory. The battle, like Borodino, was a bloody draw, but the fact that McClellan attacked and Lee retreated—even if, to Lincoln's disgust, with his army intact—was a psychological triumph. It allowed the president five days later to proclaim, not from desperation, but from strength:

> That on the first day of January in the year of our Lord, one thousand, eight hundred and sixty-three, all persons held as slaves within any state, or designated part of a state, the people whereof shall then be in rebellion against the United States shall be then, thenceforward, and forever free.[79]

Lincoln said nothing of slaves held in states remaining loyal: he could hardly have claimed war powers if not at war with them.[80] He also knew, though, that he didn't have to: the more blood the

Union shed the more just—and, therefore, the more legitimate—emancipation would become. The proclamation, in this sense, was Lincoln's Tarutino: with no more *apparent* effort than the strokes of his pen, the North seized the initiative and the South, if not yet on the run like Napoleon fleeing Russia, was from this moment on the defensive.

IX.

On December 1, 1862, President Lincoln sent the third session of the Thirty-Seventh Congress his second annual message. Like most such communications, it compiled trivialities. It proposed reimbursing Norwegians for a ship illegally seized off the blockaded port of Charleston, welcomed a new commercial treaty with the Turkish sultan, and commended the improved financial condition of the post office. But it also called for a constitutional amendment legalizing for all time the wartime abolition of slavery. And it ended with this ringing *coup d'oeil*:

> We *say* we are for the Union. The world will not forget that we say this. We know how to save the Union. The world knows we do know how to save it. . . . In *giving* freedom to the *slave,* we *assure* freedom to the *free*—honorable alike in what we give, and what we preserve. We shall nobly save, or meanly lose, the last best, hope of earth.[81]

This wasn't, for Lincoln, a new epiphany. "[T]he world's best hope depend[s] on the continued Union of these States," he'd claimed as early as 1852 in a eulogy for Henry Clay.[82] He'd often invoked a world watching while debating Douglas across Illinois.[83] And in 1861, having attained the position Clay and Douglas hoped for but never got, Lincoln defined his nation's responsibility as one of

> maintaining in the world, that form and substance of government, whose leading object is, to elevate the condition of men—to lift artificial weights from all shoulders; to clear the paths of laudable pursuit for all; to afford all, an unfettered start, and a fair chance, in the race of life.[84]

Thereby proving, Lincoln added privately at the time, "that popular government is not an absurdity."[85]

What would be absurd, he argued in his 1862 message, would be a broken-up Union, for "[o]ur abundant room—our broad national homestead—is our ample resource." Its ports assured access, for all Americans, to all oceans. Their numbers, by 1925, could well exceed those of Europe. Emancipation would ensure growth by shortening the current war even as it expanded correspondingly "the wealth of the country." But secession's success would spawn further secessions, the results of which would be "great and injurious."[86] It's not clear whether Lincoln recalled, or even had read, Adams's message to Congress in 1825. Both shared, though, this central point: that "liberty is power," and that "the nation blessed with the largest portion of liberty must in proportion to its numbers be the most powerful nation upon earth."[87]

To that end, Lincoln seized the opportunities secession provided when it removed, from Washington, Southern opponents of national economic development. He'd been a Whig before he was a Republican. Had he lived earlier, he could have been a Hamiltonian Federalist. And so Lincoln asked for and got what Adams and Clay would have envied: internal improvements including a railroad to the Pacific, the cheap sale for settlement of western public lands, subsidized state universities, a protective tariff, a centralized banking system, and even, while the war lasted, a federal income tax. Only the banks and taxes had current military utility. The rest laid foundations for the power without which, in the twentieth century, the "new world" couldn't repeatedly have rescued liberty in the "old."[88]

X.

It's not clear either whether Lincoln read Marx. But he could have: the author of *The Communist Manifesto* was, until 1861, the London correspondent for Greeley's nationally circulated *New-York Tribune*. Historian Kevin Peraino imagines Lincoln unfolding himself on the dusty couch in his Springfield office, picking up the paper, and annoying his partner, Billy Herndon, with revolutionary quotations. So he might have seen Marx's forecast that the North would, although not easily, win a civil war, owing to its material assets but also the possibility of igniting, in the South, a slave revolt.[89]

Material *interests,* however, could thwart this outcome. The Founders had sought to deter any return of European great powers to North America, but now the global capitalism of cotton was raising the stakes: could industrial revolutions permit their primary supplier of that commodity—the self-styled Confederacy—to be cut off by a Union blockade? Might the means meant to suppress secession earn it international legitimacy?[90] "I don't know anything about diplomacy," Lincoln admitted. "I will be very apt to make blunders."[91]

In fact, he made very few. Still desperate to forestall disunion, Secretary of State Seward went so far as to suggest, just prior to the firing on Fort Sumter, a diversionary provocation of crises with Spain, France, Great Britain, and Russia: if the president didn't feel up to this task, then some other cabinet member, not excluding Seward himself, might take it on.[92] Lincoln never said what he thought of this improbable scheme, but he did let Seward know that if anything was to be done "*I* must do it."[93] That pulled Seward back from the multiple brinks onto which *he'd* blundered, and the two worked harmoniously from then on.

Most valuably in November 1861, when Captain Charles Wilkes of the USS *San Jacinto,* on his own authority and in international waters, seized and removed as "contraband" from a British vessel, the RMS *Trent,* two Confederate diplomats, James Mason and John Slidell: their mission had been to seek diplomatic recognition in London and Paris. At first pleased, Lincoln backed down as the prospect loomed of an Anglo-American war. Seward helped him save face by placing Wilkes's initiative within the legal definition of "impressment," the British practice Americans had gone to war to protest in 1812. Now that *both* had protested it, Lincoln smoothly and successfully argued, there could be no grounds for another such conflict. Or, as he explained to his cabinet: "one war at a time."[94]

Meanwhile, the French emperor Napoleon III—the vainglorious nephew of a greater uncle—had set out to exploit American weakness by invading Mexico and installing an even shakier emperor, the Austrian archduke Maximilian, on a throne that didn't yet exist. Lincoln and Seward limited themselves to diplomatic protests despite pressures, some from their own supporters, to settle the Civil War, invoke the Monroe Doctrine, and send a combined Union-Confederate army south of the Rio Grande. Union victories *over the Confederacy*, they understood, would more quickly deflate French and Austrian pretensions, while preserving the purpose of the one war worth fighting. And with Vicksburg and Gettysburg in July 1863, victories had begun to come.[95]

Lincoln proclaimed emancipation chiefly for military reasons, but as its moral implications became evident, they simplified his diplomacy. They gave the Union the high ground of conscience:[96] just as no Northerner would re-enslave former slaves who'd served in its army, so no foreign state could afford, by the middle of 1864, to recognize the Confederate slavocracy, much less to intervene on its behalf.[97] Behind this shield the world's largest population of cotton cultivators staged what the historian Sven Beckert has called an "agrarian insurrection," unequaled in its speed and scope. That hastened the Union's victory while securing the single integrated economy it would need to give hope to the world—and, in his expectation of an eventual *proletarian* revolution—even to Marx.[98]

XI.

War powers, Lincoln insisted, could make the unconstitutional constitutional: emancipation was the greatest uncompensated confiscation of private property in American history.[99] But Lincoln seems never to have considered canceling or postponing the constitutionally mandated election that could, he acknowledged, replace him with a Democratic Party candidate he himself had at last replaced—*former* General George B. McClellan. In which case, the president informed his cabinet in August of 1864, "it will be my duty to so cooperate with the President-elect, as to save the Union between the election and the inauguration." For, Lincoln added, "he will have secured his election on such grounds that he can not possibly save it afterwards."[100]

The danger of military defeat had long since passed, but that of a stalemate hadn't. Lincoln's fighting generals—Grant in Virginia, William Tecumseh Sherman in Tennessee and northern Georgia, and Philip Sheridan in the Shenandoah Valley—were wearing down the Confederacy: with no end in sight, though, the human, material, and political costs would be unsustainable. That prospect sustained McClellan's presidential campaign, along with Lincoln's anxieties that a negotiated peace could save slavery while sacrificing the Union.[101]

But then, on September 2, Sherman took Atlanta. This wasn't Tarutino or Borodino, but an ignition on land of Elizabethan fireships, with flames spreading through the Confederacy all the way to the sea. Lincoln's confidence rose with the smoke, and two months later he won reelection triumphantly, losing only three of the twenty-two states voting. "The election having passed off quietly," Grant wrote, "is a victory worth more to the country than a battle won. Rebeldom and Europe will so construe it."[102] Marx emphatically did: "[T]he triumphant war cry of your re-election is Death to Slavery," he wrote the president from London. "The workingmen of Europe . . . consider it an earnest of the epoch to come that it fell to the lot of Abraham Lincoln, the single-minded son of the working class, to lead his country through the matchless struggle for the rescue of an enchained race and the reconstruction of a social world."[103]

John Quincy Adams had seen, while Lincoln was still a child, that a civil war could remove slavery "from this whole continent," a result "so glorious" that even at "calamitous and desolating" costs, "I dare not say that it is not to be desired."[104] What costs would have been too much for Adams we can never know, but it's clear enough what Lincoln endured: more than 3 million men, North and South, under arms, and at least 750,000 dead.[105] His 1861 estimate that "two or three" regiments could snuff out secession—it took over three thousand—seems stunningly naïve. Except that he coupled it with a determination to use "no matter how much force may be required."[106]

That stretched Lincoln's options from simply spooking an adversary to as much destruction as his era could inflict. He kept them all within the physical, emotional, and moral tolerances of the moment: that allowed expanding war aims to include abolition, but only after he'd convinced himself that this would aid the war's conduct. Lincoln's sensitivity to evolving contexts—his ability to let even lethal things grow—kept the war Clausewitzian: saving the state remained his compass, despite the startling expansion of means he employed.[107] Over the next century, American militaries would shrink when possible but snowball when necessary. No one in Lincoln's time could know the circumstances in which they'd do this. What he showed, though, was that it *could* be done.[108]

Lincoln saw himself, not so much as a son of the working class, but of the Founders: "Four score and seven years ago our fathers . . ." Who, strangely, had no sons of their own as distinguished as they—except for John Adams. Which makes it seem right that Lincoln was with John Quincy on his last public day, and that this Adams then posthumously guided Lincoln toward the constitutional rationale for emancipation. Which led the republic toward "a new birth of freedom," so that "government of the people, by the people, for the people, shall not perish from the earth."[109]

XII.

"Somehow he managed," Lincoln's most thorough modern biographer has concluded, "to be strong-willed without being willful, righteous without being self-righteous, and moral without being moralistic," thus yielding a "psychological maturity unmatched in the history of American public life."[110] Which is simply to say that he managed polarities: they didn't manage him. But how, with so "defective" an education? The answer lies, I think, in the common sense Lincoln extracted from an uncommon mastery of scale, space, and time.[111]

Scale sets the *ranges* within which experience accrues. If, in evolution, edges of chaos reward adaptation; if, in history, adaptation fortifies resilience; and if, in individuals, resilience accommodates unknowns more readily than rigidity, then it stands to reason that a *gradual expansion* of edges better equips leaders for the unexpected than those that shock, leaving little time to adapt, or those inherited, which breed entitlement and arrogance, its companion.

To see the difference, compare Lincoln's life with that of John Quincy Adams. Great expectations inspired, pursued, and haunted Adams, depriving him, at critical moments, of common sense. Overestimations by others—which he then magnified—placed objectives beyond his reach: only self-demotion brought late-life satisfaction. No expectations lured Lincoln apart from those he set for himself: he started small, rose slowly, and only when ready reached for the top. His ambitions grew as his opportunities expanded, but he kept both within his circumstances. He *sought* to be underestimated.

Space is where expectations and circumstances intersect. Lincoln and Adams both saw, in westward expansion, the power to secure liberty, but they also feared its dangers. Madison had shown, in *Federalist #10,* that a republic balancing interests could become an empire; the interests he had in mind, however, were multiple and regional, even parochial. The Founders' sons had to balance a *single* interest—whether to expand slavery into new territories—on which *national* unity had come to depend. Resilience had gone rigid: any choice would, for someone, carry unacceptable costs.[112] Demotion and death spared Adams the need to choose, but Lincoln seems to have welcomed it.

He, therefore, used space, in war, to restore the Union. He ignored orthodoxies, pored over maps, and calculated capacities. These showed Northern strengths to be the *exterior* lines along which new technologies—telegraphs, railroads, industrially produced weaponry—could combine with new thinking to allow mobility *and* concentrated force. All Lincoln needed were generals who'd fight, and the time it would take them to exhaust the Confederacy. After which the country would control the continent, as the Founders intended.

Finally, then, *time.* Lincoln kept it on his side: he knew how to wait, when to act, and where to seek reassurance. He'd come close to agnosticism before assuming responsibilities: as these grew, however, his faith did also, but not conventionally.[113] Instead it resembled a dialogue between a man and—Lincoln's term—his "Maker." Why, the president once asked a group of self-certain ministers, if God had revealed His will to *them,* had He not "directly to me"?[114]

Lincoln came to believe that God was doing this through the course of events, not divine revelation. McClellan's Antietam victory, the president told his cabinet, had been a sign to proceed with emancipation.[115] But he worried still over the war's prolongation: each side "claims to act in accordance with the will of God," he wrote in a note to himself, but "[b]oth *may* be, and one *must* be wrong. God can not be *for* and *against* the same thing at the same time." Quickly, though, he caught the impiety, for God, even more than His angels, was above earthly logic. "[I]t is quite possible that God's purpose is something different from the purpose of either party." Perhaps "God wills this contest, and wills that it shall not end yet."[116]

Yet when Lincoln told the world at his second inaugural on March 4, 1865, that if God wanted the war to continue "until all the wealth piled by the bond-man's two hundred and fifty years of unrequited toil shall be sunk, and until every drop of blood drawn with the lash, shall be paid by another drawn with the sword, as was said three thousand years ago, so still it must be said 'the judgements of the Lord, are true and righteous altogether,'"[117] he knew perfectly well that this was *not* God's will: thanks to Him, to Lincoln, and to his fighting generals, the war would be over within five weeks.[118] So who was in charge? Lincoln would have said, I'm sure, that we don't need to know.

Tolstoy suggests, in the last pages of *War and Peace,* that the interdependence of time, space, and scale simultaneously reflects choice and necessity: the *illusion* of agency causes us to *believe* in free will even as inexorable laws deny the possibility. Lincoln never read this, just as he never read so much else, including *On War.* But as he *intuited* Clausewitz, so he may have anticipated Tolstoy. For Lincoln found, or thought he'd found, in the direction of history the will of God. That's no great distance from Tolstoy, for whom history, in his greatest novel, reflects laws beyond our capacity to detect. And in the crisis of faith he underwent soon after finishing it, Tolstoy went well beyond Lincoln in attributing earthly phenomena to divine oversight.[119]

For Lincoln it was enough to say, in a letter to a friend in 1864: "I claim not to have controlled events, but confess plainly that events have controlled me."[120] The Tolstoy of *War and Peace* would have been satisfied with that. Probably we should be too.

CHAPTER NINE

LAST BEST HOPE

One night during the Civil War, Georgina Cecil awoke to find her husband standing, asleep but agitated, before an open second-floor window. He seemed to be expecting invaders, "presumably Federal soldiers or revolutionary mob leaders." Strangely, though, this happened in England, and the sleepwalker was Lord Robert Talbot Gascoyne-Cecil, a descendant of Queen Elizabeth's trusted counselor Lord Burghley. As the 3rd Marquess of Salisbury, this Cecil would go on to serve his own queen, Victoria, three times as prime minister. Never though, his wife recalled, did he suffer "such extremes of depression and nervous misery as at that time."

For the United States terrified Salisbury, his biographer Andrew Roberts has explained. He'd never been there and disapproved of slavery, but he *despised* democracy—so deeply that he sympathized with secession, favored the Confederacy, and regarded Lincoln's assassination as a legitimate last act of resistance. Most of all, Salisbury worried that the Union's pursuit of ideological ends through vast military means would revive Napoleonic ambitions in Europe. Salisbury died in 1903, not before nightmares, however, anticipating the trenches, tanks, killing fields, and even aerial bombardments of the 1914–18 Great War. "If we had interfered," he'd written of the Civil War in the last year of his life, it might have been possible "to reduce the power of the United States to manageable proportions. But *two* such chances are not given to a nation in the course of its career."[1]

Americans through most of Salisbury's life, however, had been anything but Napoleonic. Eager to heal their wounds of war—even if that meant weakening emancipations for which the Union had fought—they'd returned to the states most of the power Lincoln centralized, dismantled their world-class military, and concentrated on populating, developing, and exploiting a continental republic, swollen after 1867 by Seward's purchase, from the Russians, of what became Alaska.[2] National security receded as a concern: the United States, historian Robert Kagan writes, was now "too large, too rich, and too heavily populated to be an inviting target for invasion even by the world's strongest powers."[3]

That in itself alarmed Salisbury the sleepwalker, for where did it leave the British Dominion of Canada, with its long, indefensible southern border? He could hardly rely indefinitely on American self-restraint. Salisbury the strategist, however, distinguished between predation—what strong countries do to weak ones—and baiting—what adolescents do to parents. Putting up with the second might forestall the first. "[O]ur best chance of ordinary civility," he concluded while foreign minister in 1888, "is to have a thoroughly anti-British Administration in Washington."[4]

But even Salisbury, as prime minister, thought it excessive when, in 1895, Grover Cleveland's secretary of state, Richard Olney, turned an old Venezuelan boundary dispute with British Guiana into a brash reassertion of the Monroe Doctrine. "Europe as a whole is monarchical," he superfluously announced. "America, on the other hand, is devoted to the exactly opposite principle—to the idea that every people has an inalienable right of self-government. . . . Today the United States is practically sovereign on this continent."[5] Despite its erratic targeting—Confederate rights? Venezuela's geography?—Olney's "twenty-inch gun" (Cleveland's gloat) caught Salisbury at a bad time.

Five years earlier Germany's inexperienced kaiser, William II, had dismissed his legendary chancellor, Otto von Bismarck, who'd unified the country by provoking wars but then secured peace by balancing resentments.[6] William lacked such dexterity: "There is a danger," Salisbury warned as the Venezuela crisis escalated, "of him going completely off his head."[7] At which point, while Salisbury was trying to calm the Americans, the kaiser congratulated South African Boers for thwarting a raid the British may (or may not) have authorized. Suddenly, it seemed, a nearer gun with Napoleonic pretensions—*and* a military-industrial potential not seen since the American Civil War—was firing randomly.[8]

Baited now on two fronts, Salisbury yielded on one. "There is no such thing as a fixed policy," he observed, "because policy like all organic entities is always in the making."[9] And so he and his successors began methodically and unilaterally eliminating all sources of friction with the United States. They not only gave in on Venezuela (where the Americans promptly lost interest and accepted arbitration), but subsequently and more significantly on the Spanish-American War (Britain stayed neutral), on the Philippines (Salisbury supported American, not German, annexation), on a future Panama Canal (Britain relinquished long-held rights in the region), and on Alaska's boundary (Canada sacrificed for the greater good).[10] It may not have been appeasement,[11] but it was lubrication: like Mikhail Gorbachev almost a century later, Salisbury set out to deprive an enemy of its enemy.[12]

As a careful student of history,[13] he'd have known of George Canning's claim, from 1826, to have "called the New World into existence to redress the balance of the Old."[14] Self-congratulation wasn't Salisbury's style, but he could more credibly own the accomplishment. Which he tactfully did in 1897 by congratulating his queen—his ancestor Burghley would have approved—as she celebrated her sixtieth year on the throne:

> The impulse of democracy, which began in another country
> in other lands, has made itself felt in our time, and vast
> changes in the centre of power and incidence of responsibility
> have been made almost imperceptibly without any distur-
> bance or hindrance in the progress of the prosperous devel-
> opment of the nation.[15]

The sleepwalker still regretted the Confederacy's defeat, and the consequent loss of a balance of power in North America. The strategist, however, never forgot that "[w]e are fish," and "alone can do nothing to remedy an inland tyranny."[16] So Great Britain learned to live with a democracy dominating a continent. For that, with whatever ambivalence, Salisbury had Lincoln to thank.

I.

On the evening of January 25, 1904, five months after Salisbury's death, Halford Mackinder, recently appointed director of the London

School of Economics and Political Science, read a paper on "The Geographical Pivot of History" before the Royal Geographical Society. Future historians, he suggested, would regard the past four centuries as "the Columbian epoch," and conclude that it ended "soon after the year 1900." The age of maritime exploration was over—there being little left to discover—but that of continental development was only beginning. The technology driving it wasn't ships but railroads, operating with far greater speed and efficiency. Lincoln's transcontinental had been completed in 1869, its Canadian counterpart in 1885, and the trans-Siberian line from Moscow to Vladivostok opened over its full six thousand miles in the year Mackinder spoke. Eurasia would soon be "covered with railways," he predicted, making its vast spaces with their "incalculably great" potential, as in the days of Asiatic hordes, "the pivot region of the world's politics."[17]

England's maritime superiority had relied, since the Tudors, on *rivalries within continents* to prevent projections of power beyond their shores. But now, Mackinder was arguing, *consolidations of continents* were taking place that, if used to build fleets, could empower an "empire of the world." Probably Russia would run it. Or maybe Germany allied with Russia. Or perhaps a China organized by Japan to overthrow Russia by bringing "the yellow peril to the world's freedom" through the addition of "an oceanic frontage to the resources of the great continent, an advantage as yet denied to the Russian tenant of the pivot region."[18]

With this sudden swerve into racism and real estate, Mackinder ended his presentation, the vagueness of which heightened the anxieties it induced. It didn't matter that hordes in the past had caused little to pivot beyond their horses. Or that Alfred Thayer Mahan had recently and more systematically shown the importance of sea power in history. Or that Mackinder neglected altogether the potential of air power, precariously demonstrated only a month earlier when, in North Carolina, the Wright brothers first flew. Or that he assumed a Prussian-like purposefulness in a Russia drifting toward military and naval defeats at the hands of Japan and, as a result, a dangerous if inconclusive revolution: St. Petersburg's "Bloody Sunday" lay just short of a year ahead.

Mackinder's paper was a professorial equivalent of Olney's "twenty-inch gun," aimed badly, argued illogically, but startling enough to expose what few had yet seen: that railroads, over the past half century, had made Europe and Asia a single continent; that Britain, over the next half century, might lose control of the sea; and that from these patterns of rise and fall a new struggle for the world could emerge between distinctively different forms of government, and potentially incompatible ways of life.[19]

II.

How, though, and why? It fell to Eyre Crowe, a Foreign Office mandarin, to cut through Mackinder's murk in a report to King Edward VII in 1907, quickly circulated and discussed at the highest levels. Like George F. Kennan's "long telegram" from Moscow at the beginning of the Cold War, the "Crowe memorandum" became famous before it became public. Both shook scales from official eyes.[20]

Crowe began where Mackinder left off. Great Britain was an island off the coast of a continent, but with "vast overseas colonies and dependencies."[21] Its survival required the "preponderant sea power" it had long maintained. This had made it "the neighbour of every [other] country accessible by sea," a status that could have provoked "jealousy and fear"—Crowe knew his Thucydides—had

Britain not "harmonize[d]" its interests with "desires and ideals common to all mankind."

> Now, the first interest of all countries is the preservation of national independence. It follows that England, more than any other non-insular Power, has a direct and positive interest in the maintenance of the independence of nations, and therefore must be the natural enemy of any country threatening the independence of others, and the natural protector of the weaker communities.

Maritime supremacy, then, demanded not just the *balancing* of power on continents that Mackinder had emphasized, but also the *reassurance* of states bordering seas that the single dominant power at sea respected their interests, as well as its own.

The British had accomplished this, Crowe argued, by promoting "the right of free intercourse and trade in the world's markets." That served their interests, given the rejection of mercantilism that had accompanied industrialization. But it also strengthened Britain's "hold on the interested friendship of other nations" by making them "less apprehensive" of its naval preeminence. For if these states couldn't themselves rule the sea, they preferred having "a free trade England" do it instead of "a predominant protectionist Power." Crowe, like Pericles, saw no contradiction in *securing,* as well as *earning,* overseas friendships.[22]

Why, though, would a continental state projecting *its* power at sea *not* nurture such relationships? Because, Crowe maintained, it could have gained that capability only by consolidating a continent: what gave Salisbury his nightmares and Mackinder his artillery. And it couldn't have done that without absorbing, or at least terrifying, its neighbors.[23] Very few states, lacking the power themselves to control a continent, would wish to have someone else do it through blood, iron, and intimidation.

Which the younger Bismarck had memorably promised.[24] Crowe had been born in Prussia, knew German well, and saw in the emergence of a modern Teutonic empire in Europe a pattern of "systemic territorial aggrandizement achieved mainly at the point of a sword." To borrow a phrase from the future, Germany's had hardly been a "peaceful rise." Knowing this, Bismarck sought to assure surviving neighbors that, having achieved hegemony, his new great power would harmonize its interests with theirs. But appetites turned on weren't as easily turned off.[25]

Bismarck's solution had been to scavenge for colonies other great powers hadn't wanted: could an empire really content itself, though, as do vultures, with leftovers? Now he was gone, and his successors were still hungry. Crowe voiced their views:

> We *must* have real Colonies, where German emigrants can settle and spread the national ideals of the Fatherland, and we *must* have a fleet and coaling stations to keep together the Colonies which we are bound to acquire. . . . A healthy and powerful State like Germany, with its 60,000,000 inhabitants, must expand, it cannot stand still, and it must have territories to which its overflowing population can emigrate without giving up its nationality.

Unsure—perhaps not wanting to be sure—of where to stop, Germany under William II seemed willfully to be welcoming "a world set at defiance." For "*the union of the greatest military with the greatest*

*naval Power in one State would compel the world to combine for the
riddance of such an incubus."*[26]

III.

Or so the *theory* in Crowe's thinking suggested. What happened in
history, however, neither he nor anyone else in authority foresaw.
Bismarck's reassurances—a web of shifting political alliances with
him at the center—hardened after his death into two competing
military alliances, so unreassuringly tied to mobilization and transportation timetables that, once activated, they disconnected the
causes of war from its conduct.[27] That's how the killing of two royals
in Sarajevo on June 28, 1914, led to the slaughter, by November 11,
1918, of between eight and ten million combatants and another
seven to eight million civilians.[28] Crowe's world united against an
"incubus" became a Europe divided, devastatingly, against itself.

The Great War saw instances at all levels of intentions projected
beyond capabilities, a frequent cause of past military calamities. But
capabilities, this time, also outran intentions. Those in command,
Henry Kissinger has explained, grossly underestimated the lethality
they commanded.

> They seemed oblivious to the huge casualties of the still rela-
> tively recent American Civil War, and expected a short, deci-
> sive conflict. It never occurred to them that the failure to
> make their alliances correspond to rational political objec-
> tives would lead to the destruction of civilization as they
> knew it. . . . Instead the Great Powers managed to construct a

diplomatic doomsday machine, though they were unaware of what they had done.[29]

Americans had at least known, in their Civil War, what they were fighting for. This new war's participants had to find purposes for which to die as it was killing them.

Great Britain's progression from Salisbury's "we are fish" through Mackinder's "Eurasian hordes" to Crowe's "world set at defiance" suggests why. For if war must reflect policy, as Clausewitz had insisted, with what policy had Britain entered this one? Retaining supremacy at sea? Balancing power on land? Removing incubi everywhere? The 1907 "triple entente" with France and Russia carried no clear obligation, when the fighting began in July 1914, to enter a war against Germany.[30] And yet, the Germans' invasion of Belgium on August 4—their plan for war against France having ignored long-standing international guarantees of Belgian neutrality—caused the British not only to declare war, but to abandon a centuries-old aversion to combat on the continent. Where Britain would lose, over the next four years, more men killed than the Union and the Confederacy *together* in 1861–65.[31]

This "continental commitment" seems almost to have been made, as was once said of the British empire, "in a fit of absence of mind."[32] But if one *links* the concerns of Crowe, Mackinder, and Salisbury, then a larger logic emerges. Crowe's claim of a connection between sea power and self-determination on the one hand, and between land power and authoritarianism on the other, would mean that the continental consolidation of which Mackinder had warned could endanger more than just control of the sea: the future of freedom itself might be at stake.[33] Which gets to what Salisbury may have meant when he said that Britain couldn't *alone* "remedy an inland tyranny."

Perhaps that the old British distrust of alliances must end: Salisbury's final diplomatic accomplishment had been the first departure from that tradition, the Anglo-Japanese treaty of 1902.[34] Or that some similar European alignment, like what became the "triple entente," might become necessary. Or that Britain could no longer afford its "splendid isolation," an epithet from the Venezuelan crisis of 1895–96.[35] Certainly that despotism on continents, in an interconnected world, required containment. And this, for those who remembered him, circled back to Canning.

For if Salisbury could balance a democracy's domination of North America against an autocracy that might control Europe, then he was, in effect, relying on a "new world" to redress the balance of power in the "old." If Mackinder could alarm audiences with images of hordes trading horses for trans-Eurasian trains while seeing no such danger in their American equivalents, then he was in a different way doing the same. And if Crowe could foresee a coalition of satisfied states countering a voracious one—a prospect an American president would soon make more explicit—then it would rest on foundations Mackinder, Salisbury, and Canning had prepared. All were speculating in futures as yet ill-defined.

IV.

Which at some point, they all assumed, the United States would significantly shape. Its manufacturing output, by 1914, exceeded that of Britain and Germany together. Its steel production was almost twice Germany's, which was itself twice that of Britain, France, and Russia. Its technological innovations were unrivaled; its food surpluses fed much of Europe; its favorable trade balances had earned it a third of the world's gold reserves. And although their navy was still smaller than those of Britain and Germany, the Americans had, in the month Europe went to war, opened the Panama Canal, allowing quicker transits between the two largest oceans than were available to anyone else. The United States had become a great power, the historian Paul Kennedy has observed—but it wasn't yet part of the great power system.[36]

The continental hegemony Americans won in the 1840s and retained in the 1860s left them, as the twentieth century began, with little apparent need for wider responsibilities. External threats were still neither clear nor present. Colonialism, they'd found in the Philippines, was more trouble than it was worth. Diplomacy allowed posturing without commitments, as in the 1899–1900 "Open Door" notes on China. The United States could even make peace— Theodore Roosevelt's Treaty of Portsmouth (New Hampshire) did that for the Russo-Japanese War in 1905—while maintaining an army no larger than Bulgaria's or Serbia's.[37] All of which absolved the Americans of any responsibility whatever for the outbreak, in 1914, of the European Great War.

It, however, had more than they'd anticipated to do with them. The nine decades following Monroe's proclamation and Canning's paternity claim fell within the century of Europe's freedom from great wars extending from 1815 to 1914. But in three previous instances—the Seven Years' War, the wars of the French Revolution, and those of Napoleon—Americans had been drawn in: through the French and Indian War of 1754–63, the Quasi-War with France of 1798–1800, and the War of 1812 with Great Britain, which ended in 1815. The same would happen in 1917–18 and in 1941–45. The Cold War, which never became a hot war, brought the longest of all American overseas involvements—which may be why it, unlike the Great War, never had to be renamed.

Like fish who fail to notice the expansion and contraction of oceans, the Americans weren't so much outside a great power system between 1823 and 1914 as oblivious to it—and even that generalization needs qualification for Lincoln and Seward.[38] The system was this: that from the age of Elizabeth, England had planted its culture more widely in the world than in Europe.[39] That made it necessary to balance potentially hostile Europeans—and hence to fear what Crowe called "systemic" sword-based "territorial aggrandizement." Which, when it did occur, also alarmed British transoceanic offspring, for where might they be without the protection provided by the world's largest navy? However rudely Americans might mock their aged parent, they could no more reject what they'd inherited of its language, institutions, religions, enterprise, and security than they could unwind and re-entwine their own DNA. So when Britain made its "continental commitment," it was also, for better or for worse, committing them.

V.

Woodrow Wilson's first response was to call, redundantly, for neutrality "in fact as well as in name," impartiality "in thought as well as in action," and "a curb upon our sentiments."[40] But if Germany won, he warned his confidential adviser, "Colonel" Edward M. House, "it would change the course of our civilization and make the United States a military nation." It had been Germans, after all—not the

British or French—who'd violated *Belgian* neutrality, sacking cities, universities, and even ancient irreplaceable libraries. That kind of brutality, the former president of Princeton feared, could "throw the world back three or four centuries."[41]

As president of the United States, however, Wilson saw no immediate need to take sides. There was no national consensus for doing so. Food and war matériel exports to Britain and France were booming, so much so that when the importers could no longer pay, Wilson rescinded the ban he'd initially imposed on extending credit. With the British navy denying Germany equal opportunities, he could profess neutrality in public while privately welcoming its absence.[42] Delaying entry would also allow Wilson to choose the moment: if he did this carefully, House assured him, then he'd be in a position to determine the war's outcome, not just through military deployments, but by designing a new international system to replace the one that had failed by allowing war.[43]

With House's guidance, Wilson set up an overhang of presumptions under which the belligerents would have to fight. One was that if the United States did enter the war, it would do so decisively: the scale of its Civil War more than hinted at the military capabilities it could now deploy. Another was that the likelihood of American entry would increase the longer the war lasted, because stalemates on battlefields would bring progressively more provocative maritime blockades. A third was that submarines were proving as disruptive to older methods of war at sea as railroads had been to the previous deterrence of continental consolidations.[44]

Germany saw U-boats as a legitimate response to British surface superiority: the problem was that they couldn't easily search ships, take prizes, or determine passengers' nationality, all standard practices in earlier blockades. They thus endangered the right of neutrals to trade with belligerents, a privilege staunchly defended (even belatedly by Lincoln) in previous American wars. They threatened profits from wartime exports to Britain and France, and from anticipated postwar repayments of loans extended. Worst of all, they killed noncombatants: Wilson almost went to war when 128 Americans perished, in May 1915, on the torpedoed British liner *Lusitania*.[45]

When Wilson finally did ask for a declaration of war, on April 2, 1917, he was chiefly responding to the Germans' removal of restrictions they'd imposed on U-boats after the *Lusitania* crisis: this would, they'd gambled, force Britain and France to make peace before the United States could get an army to Europe. Wilson doubted, though, that public opinion would support going to war "no matter how many Americans were lost at sea."[46] Something more would be necessary, and in the weeks preceding his war message, the Germans provided it.

They'd accompanied their resumption of all-out submarine warfare with a secret proposal to Mexico that if, as expected, the Americans entered the European war, it seize the opportunity to retake lost territories in Texas, New Mexico, and Arizona—with German and perhaps Japanese assistance. British code breakers intercepted the cable, leaked it to Washington, and Wilson made it public. That put Germany at odds not only with neutral rights, but with the territorial integrity of the United States, a far more inflammatory sensitivity.[47]

Then, in March, an unexpected revolution in Russia, the third member of the Anglo-French coalition, toppled the Romanov dynasty, appearing to end autocracy in a nation about to become an American ally. That freed Wilson, in his war message, to embrace the still loftier mission of making the world "safe for democracy."

He wasn't suggesting that the United States alone could accomplish this task.[48] But he was now claiming, for a nation that had seen no need to behave as a great power when the Great War broke out, a *determining* influence over its conduct, outcome, and aftermath. As Wilson had announced in his second inaugural address: "We are provincials no longer."[49]

VI.

So far, he'd managed well. By portraying preparedness as avoiding war, Wilson had begun building an army without provoking the antiwar opposition that might have denied him reelection in 1916. He waited for the Germans' military priorities again to subvert, as with Belgian neutrality, their political interests: unleashing U-boats and ill-advisedly courting Mexico did that. He transformed a revolution in Russia into a war aim for America, leaving allies no chance to object. Wilson then got his army to France in time to turn Germany's failed spring 1918 offensive into the collapse that brought victory that fall. And after securing an armistice in November, the president himself crossed the Atlantic—the first to do so while in office—where he accepted triumphs worthy of ancient Romans in Paris, London, and (fittingly) Rome itself.[50]

House had warned Wilson, though, that his influence would peak as the war was ending. The negotiation of peace, in which he planned to participate, would require more diplomacy than management, and for that Wilson was less prepared. The long absence of the United States from the international system had left it few foreign policy professionals: Wilson had no Bismarck, Salisbury, or even an Eyre Crowe on whose expertise he could draw. Instead he had House, who'd sharpened his skills only in Texas politics but now found himself, alongside the president, "remaking the map of the world, as we would have it."[51]

They did have help from "The Inquiry," academic consultants they'd recruited to suggest *principles* for a postwar settlement: Wilson distilled these into his "Fourteen Points" address to Congress on January 8, 1918. But neither he nor they gave sufficient thought to how "points," however well-intentioned, might align with histories, cultures, and precedents. "Unversed in European politics," a French diplomat recalled, Wilson devoted himself "to the pursuit of theories which had little relation to the emergencies of the hour."[52]

What would it mean, for example, to conduct diplomacy "always frankly and in the public view"? Or to secure "[a]bsolute freedom of navigation," except as seas "may be closed in whole or in part by international action"? Or to reduce arms "to the lowest point consistent with domestic safety"? Or to give "equal weight," in colonial disputes, to "the interests of the populations concerned" and "the equitable claims of the government whose title is to be determined"? Wilson's ends floated too freely above means, nowhere more so than in his claim that the resolution of Balkan rivalries—like the one, presumably, that had ignited the Great War—required only "friendly counsel along historically determined lines of allegiance and nationality." In such "rectifications of wrong and assertions of right," he grandly concluded, "we feel ourselves to be intimate partners of all the governments and peoples associated together against the imperialists. . . . We stand together until the end."[53]

There was more than a whiff of expediency here, for Wilson's speech—like an earlier one by British prime minister David Lloyd George—came two months after another Russian revolutionary surprise: the Bolshevik coup of November 1917, which threatened withdrawal from the Anglo-American-French "imperialist" war, while urging "proletarians" everywhere to overthrow their capitalist masters.[54] Wilson responded with a fog bank, through which he called for

> [t]he evacuation of all Russian territory and such a settlement of all questions affecting Russia as will secure the best and freest cooperation of the other nations of the world in obtaining for her an unhampered and unembarrassed opportunity for the independent determination of her own political development and national policy and assure her of a sincere welcome into the society of free nations under institutions of her own choosing; and, more than a welcome, assistance also of every kind that she may need and may herself desire.

Who, one might wonder, did he think "the imperialists" were? Lenin and Trotsky, at least, said what they really thought.

Whereupon Wilson confused matters further by sending American troops into Siberia and northern Russia as part of a multinational effort aimed ostensibly at keeping Russia in the war, but in fact at deposing the Bolsheviks.[55] After which he saved the Bolsheviks by defeating the Germans in France, thereby undoing their victory on the eastern front and the Carthaginian peace they'd imposed in the Treaty of Brest-Litovsk.[56] The skills with which Wilson brought America into the war eluded him totally when Russia left it. That foreshadowed a larger problem, which was that Wilson's principles for peace, which he meant to be timeless, turned out not only to have been time-bound, but bowled over by times so quickly changing around them. For as Wilson was trying to make the world safe for democracy, democracy was making war unsafe for the world.[57]

VII.

When Clausewitz insisted that war reflect policy, he set a standard from which exceptions like the Thirty Years' War or the wars of Napoleon—wars detached from discernible purposes—weren't supposed to recur. None did for eight decades after *On War* appeared: interstate wars took place, but with specific objectives and on limited scales. The bloodiest post-Napoleonic conflicts were *inside* the United States and, with the Taiping Rebellion, in China.[58] The Great War, however, was a pre-Clausewitzian regression: would *any* of its original participants have entered it if they'd foreseen its costs?[59]

And yet crowds throughout Europe welcomed war, in August 1914, with all the democratic spontaneity of the Athenian assembly: when Pericles tried to rekindle that spirit in his funeral address, it wasn't for the purpose of making peace. We can't know what losses he'd have been prepared to accept—the plague took him before he could learn what Lincoln knew in 1865. But we do know that Athens, the model for all subsequent democracies, defeated itself in the end because it bore deaths more easily than questions about the purposes of its wars.[60]

Wilson's "Peace Without Victory" speech to Congress, made three months before he entered his war,[61] raised several such questions. Weren't wars supposed to *secure* states, not exhaust or extinguish them? Might compromises recover that role? Was the killing accomplishing anything? His and other mediation efforts failed, though, because no leader dared tell his "democracy"[62] that its war had achieved so little. Each hoped that one more new weapon, one more offensive, one more lunge "over the top" from one more trench, would provide the meaning so evidently lacking.

After the United States went to war, Wilson gave up on mediation: the nation wouldn't fight, he was sure, for anything other than total victory. But it wouldn't support either an unjust peace. So he tried writing victory *and* justice into the "Fourteen Points," at the cost of making most of them contradictory. His last point, however, proposed an instrument of adjudication: a "general association of nations," formed "under specific covenants for the purpose of affording mutual guarantees of political independence and territorial integrity to great and small states alike."[63]

The idea had multiple roots,[64] one of which was Eyre Crowe's 1907 vision of a "world" combining against an "incubus." Sir Edward Grey, then foreign secretary, had endorsed Crowe's memorandum when it first appeared. Still in that position in 1915, he'd offered Wilson, through House, a postwar league of nations instead of mediation: only entry into the current war, he maintained, could prevent wars in the future.[65] "Grey knew his man," Kissinger has observed. "From the days of his youth, Wilson had believed that American federal institutions should serve as a model for an eventual 'parliament of man.'"[66]

If so, though, Wilson overlooked an ambivalence in *American* democracy that went back to its English Whig origins: was the purpose of such institutions to wield power, or to guard against its abuses?[67] Americans convinced themselves willingly enough, in April of 1917, that only war could *restore* their security—even their honor and self-respect. That didn't mean, though, that after winning the war they'd commit to *guaranteeing* security for everyone else. Democracy in America sought power, but also deeply distrusted it.

Anglo-French democracy had its own contradictions. Haunted by sacrifices the war had required, it insisted that the Germans admit "guilt" and pay reparations—even if this precluded the peace through reconciliation the Congress of Vienna had achieved, under undemocratic circumstances, in 1815. Nor was self-determination reconcilable, in all respects, with the boundary "rectifications" Wilson had specified in the "Fourteen Points"—or with the perpetuation of British and French colonial empires.[68] Nor was anyone, including Wilson, prepared to admit Germany or Soviet Russia as founding members of the new League of Nations, despite his reliance on it to correct the Versailles treaty's inequities.[69]

Wilson had again aroused expectations, this time without ways to meet them. Maybe, like the Athenians after Pericles, he confused strengths with hopes.[70] Or he was too inclined to postpone what he couldn't resolve. Or he missed the irony of trying to turn democracies against their elected representatives. Or his increasing infirmity deadened his political sensitivity: he fell ill while barnstorming America in support of the League in the fall of 1919, and never recovered. Or he didn't understand democracy in the first place, despite years spent at Princeton studying and teaching it. Or perhaps he just lost, with his rise to greatness, the gravitational tether of common sense.

Whatever the explanation, the Senate's refusal to approve the Versailles treaty—and thus to authorize United States membership in the League of Nations—not only broke Wilson: it also broke off the enlargement of hopes, running from Canning through Lincoln, Salisbury, Mackinder, Crowe, Grey, House, and Wilson himself, that the "new world" might one day correct imbalances in the "old." Contrary to what the Athenians told the Melians,[71] "the strong" this time didn't do what they could have, which freed "the weak" to do what they wanted—even, in Russia and Germany, to reshape reality to fit theory, and from this to construct tyrannies.

VIII.

Vladimir Ilich Lenin had been an exile in Zurich when the Russian Revolution started without him in March 1917, but that was its mistake, not his. For Lenin's specialty was transforming the unexpected into the predetermined.[72] His certainty came from Marx, who'd claimed that capitalism carried within itself the seeds of its own destruction: the Great War, begun, fought, and sure to be won by capitalists, confirmed the conclusion. The surprise came in Russia, where Marx and most subsequent Marxists had expected the revolution *not* to occur. Lenin alone saw opportunity in the anomaly. "So long as we have not won the entire world," he later explained,

> so long as, from the economic and military point of view, we remain weaker than the rest of the capitalist world, we must know how to exploit the contradictions and antagonisms among the imperialists. If we had not kept to that rule, we should long ago have all been hanging from the lamp-posts.[73]

Instead of a lamppost Lenin got his own train, on which the Germans sent him back to St. Petersburg, recently renamed Petrograd. From there, as they'd intended, he overthrew the Provisional Government and took Russia out of the war. But he'd also predicted, while on the way, that "[t]he Bolshevik leadership of the revolution [will be] much more dangerous for German imperialist power and capitalism than the leadership of Kerensky and Miliukov."[74]

Lenin understood more clearly even than Marx that the capitalists' addiction to immediate gains diverted them from more distant destinations. As Lincoln might have put it—at least in Spielberg's movie[75]—they focused so compulsively on compasses that they sank into swamps and fell off cliffs. That's how American, British, and French pressure on Russia not to leave the war discredited its new leaders, opening, for Lenin, his revolutionary path. Nor did capitalists learn from mistakes: why otherwise would the Americans have saved the Bolsheviks by undoing the Germans' eviscerations, at Brest-Litovsk, of the new Soviet state?

The same thing happened again when famine threatened Russia in 1921–22: the American arch-capitalist Herbert Hoover admitted that the international relief effort, which he'd led, had wound up strengthening the Bolshevik regime. And when Lenin's New Economic Policy, meant to plant the revolution more robustly in Russia, dangled concessions before American entrepreneurs, they eagerly snapped them up. "[N]o country in the world is better fitted to help Russia," Stalin concluded after Lenin's death in 1924. "The unsurpassed technology of America and the needs and tremendous population of Russia would yield large profits for Americans, if they cooperated."[76]

Which some of them continued to do on a grand scale. Stalin's first Five-Year Plan imported entire factories from the United States, along with the appropriate mass-production techniques—Henry Ford himself led the way. American exports to the Soviet Union exceeded those of any other country by the end of the 1920s, and the Russians were becoming the largest foreign purchaser of American agricultural and industrial equipment.[77] But the Harding and Coolidge administrations surprised Stalin by retaining Wilson's policy of diplomatic non-recognition, warning—with no evident irony—of international communism's subversive objectives. Material interests didn't *always* determine capitalist behavior.

The United States was, in one sense, more powerful than ever: its industrial output now exceeded that of Britain, Germany, France, Russia, Italy, and Japan *combined*. But the distrust of power written into its Constitution deprived its leaders of the authority—at least in peacetime—to deploy that power. Lenin would have seen this as another of democracy's failures: without a dictatorship there could be no vanguard, whether of proletarians or of anyone else. As if to confirm this, most Americans at the time saw little need for foreign policies of any kind.[78]

The world, though, wouldn't indefinitely allow them that luxury: the *potential* power of the United States was already shaping events in unexpected ways.[79] One was a cross-fertilization, in a single strange place, of old German ambitions with new German resentments. Unlike Lenin, Adolf Hitler had experienced the Great War in the trenches. The combination of British sea power with American land power, he was sure—under the direction of an international Jewish conspiracy, he was even surer—had brought about Germany's defeat. Convinced that the United States would again seek, from North America, to crowd out all rivals, Hitler saw its post-Wilsonian withdrawal from Europe as Germany's last chance to secure the space and resources it would need to compete, survive, and prevail. "War was inevitable," historian Adam Tooze says Hitler believed. "The question was not if, but when."[80]

None of this would have mattered if Hitler had stuck to amateur putsches, like the one he staged at Munich in 1923. But after an easy imprisonment, he settled into a steady political rise within the increasingly strained democracy of Weimar Germany. Its problems worsened when the New York stock market crashed in October 1929, dragging the American economy and those of other industrial capitalisms into a catastrophic depression. The Hoover administration, in office less than a year with at least three to go, was, like leadership in most democracies, clueless as to what to do.[81]

"[T]he capitalist system of economy is bankrupt and unstable," Stalin assured the Communist Party of the Soviet Union on January 7, 1933, reporting on the success—over just four years—of his first Five-Year Plan. Capitalism had "outlived its day and must give way to another, a higher, Soviet, socialist system of economy," which "has no fear of crises and is able to overcome the difficulties which capitalism cannot solve."[82] Three weeks later and by constitutional means, Hitler became chancellor of Germany—whereupon he set about dismantling that constitution. Five weeks after that, Franklin D. Roosevelt took the oath of office as president of the United States, having trounced Hoover in the 1932 election. The long shadow of Lincoln loomed over them all, for they would now test his greatest gamble—that liberty and power could coexist—as it had never been tested before.

IX.

"If one was young in the 1930s, and lived in a democracy," Isaiah Berlin later recalled, "then, whatever one's politics, if one had human feelings at all, the faintest spark of social idealism, or any love of life whatever, one must have felt . . . that all was dark and quiet, a great reaction was abroad: and little stirred, and nothing resisted." The choices seemed to be narrowing to "bleak extremes, Communism and Fascism—the red or the black" with the only light left Roosevelt's New Deal. It didn't matter that he ran it "with an isolationist disregard of the outside world," for that was America's tradition, and probably its strength. What counted was that he "had all the character and energy and skill of the dictators, and he was on our side."[83]

FDR wasn't really an isolationist. As Theodore Roosevelt's simultaneous fifth cousin and nephew-in-law, Wilson's assistant secretary of the navy, and the Democratic Party's vice presidential candidate on a pro–League of Nations platform in 1920, that would have been unlikely. After becoming president in 1933, however, this Roosevelt did insist on putting America first. With its banks collapsing, a fourth of its workforce unemployed, and its self-confidence badly shaken, recovery took precedence over everything else. Despite Hitler's descent into authoritarianism in Germany—and Japan's conquest of Manchuria two years earlier, and Italy's invasion of Ethiopia two years later—the United States remained, through FDR's first term, if anything *more* reluctant to take on international responsibilities than it had been under Hoover.[84]

Except—that in November 1933, Roosevelt extended diplomatic recognition to what had been, for over a decade, the Union of Soviet Socialist Republics. Non-recognition, he pointed out, had failed to overthrow or isolate the Bolsheviks. American investments and exports had flourished under them, and Stalin had now promised to rein in the activities—mostly ineffective anyway—of the minuscule Communist Party of the United States. That was all the new president said publicly, but he had one other quieter objective: normalizing relations with the Soviet Union might one day allow alignment with it against the aggressions of Nazi Germany and imperial Japan.[85]

Ideological purity was less important to FDR than geography, balances of power, and the requirements of navies: he'd worked for Wilson but his model had always been TR. Both Roosevelts read Mahan, and the younger one delighted in inspecting—as often as possible—the Panama Canal.[86] Through British wartime contacts, he'd have absorbed the substance, if not the provenance, of Mackinder's and Crowe's warnings about Eurasian continental consolidations. One of FDR's first actions as president was to upgrade the United States Navy—but as a job-creating public works project, he thought it prudent to claim.[87] For Roosevelt also doubted his country's willingness again to make overseas commitments. That, he knew, had been Wilson's unintended legacy: an overhang of American *incapacity* under which the weakened European democracies would, for the foreseeable future, be on their own.

If, as seemed likely, Germany and Japan rearmed—both left the League of Nations in 1933[88]—then they could be in a position soon to dominate most of Europe, much of China, and even to challenge American naval supremacy in the Western Hemisphere.[89] Because the Soviet Union, like the old Russian empire, lacked easy access to oceans, the possibility that it might control Eurasia seemed less alarming to Roosevelt: he'd even approved a proposal from Stalin in 1936—eventually torpedoed by the United States Navy—to build a Soviet battleship in an American shipyard.[90] An authoritarian ally wedged massively between the resource-hungry Germans and Japanese, therefore, might not be a bad thing. If they moved outward, the Red Army could wear them down from the rear. If they moved inward, it would, like Kutuzov, wear them out. Either way, democracies on both sides of the Atlantic would benefit.

Roosevelt never explained this: he cloaked his intentions more expertly even than Lincoln. But if that president, whose prior military experience had been limited to the Black Hawk War of 1832, could outdo his West Point generals in devising Civil War strategy,[91] then it's not implausible to credit FDR, who'd mostly run the American navy during the Great War,[92] with comparable skills.

Lenin, I'm sure, would have done so. For he'd have recognized, as soon as he saw it, an exploitation of "contradictions and antagonisms" *among authoritarians*. Dictators, to be sure, would still be "vanguards." But Roosevelt saw how infrequent and impermanent their agreements would be.

X.

He wasn't running a dictatorship, so he couldn't fit his country to his ideology, as Stalin had done and as Hitler was doing: given how little FDR's economists knew about the Great Depression's causes, they wouldn't have agreed on a five-year plan if he'd asked them for one.[93] Instead he improvised, edging forward where possible, falling back when necessary, always appearing to do something, never giving in to despair, and in everything remembering what Wilson forgot—that nothing would succeed without widespread *continuing* public support. "It is a terrible thing," Roosevelt once admitted, "to look over your shoulder when you are trying to lead—and to find no one there."[94]

His caution carried over into foreign policy. Despite concerns about Germany and Japan, FDR didn't try to thwart congressional efforts to legislate the neutrality Wilson had only professed: he knew he'd lose the battle. He'd speak firmly on one day of the need to "quarantine" aggressors, but on the next retract what he'd just said. His flexibility exhausted his credibility in London and Paris, limiting his ability to oppose the Anglo-French appeasement of Hitler. And in 1937, he sent Joseph E. Davies, the campaign-contributing trophy spouse of a breakfast-food heiress, to Moscow as his second ambassador, provoking a near revolt among foreign service officers who under the first, William C. Bullitt, had begun meticulously documenting Stalin's increasingly arbitrary purges of his alleged internal enemies.[95]

So was Roosevelt an appeaser? Certainly he thought himself weak: he could hardly be stronger than the country was, and its power seemed not to extend beyond his ingenuity. Capabilities might, at some point, catch up with interests: that couldn't happen, though, until Americans again perceived dangers, revived their economy, and regained faith in themselves. Meanwhile, he'd position the geopolitics as best he could. That's why he appointed Davies.

Roosevelt didn't so much distrust experts as lament their limited horizons. It irked him that his own agents—the diplomats and military attachés in the Moscow embassy, the Washington officials who read their reports, even his beloved navy—were close to considering Stalin worse than Hitler: they failed to see the larger possibilities that came with a wider view. If the Soviet autocracy was to help the American democracy reduce dangers to them both, then Roosevelt would need deal makers like Davies with more breadth than depth, not specialists who knew too much to make deals.[96]

Not even Davies, though, could deflect Stalin from *his* geopolitical trajectory. Seeing little on offer from any democracy, he cut his own deal with Hitler on August 23, 1939, setting off what immediately became World War II. The Nazi-Soviet "nonaggression" pact didn't surprise Roosevelt: Davies, before leaving Moscow, had seen it coming, and the embassy, after his departure, had tracked its approach through a well-placed spy.[97] It was hard now, however, not to regard the Soviet Union, the president admitted early in 1940, as "a dictatorship as absolute as any other dictatorship in the world."[98]

And when, in the spring of that year, Hitler's *Blitzkrieg* accomplished in three months what the kaiser's armies hadn't in four years—conquering Denmark, Norway, the Netherlands, Belgium, and France—it looked as though the ultimate Mackinder-Crowe nightmare had arrived: a single "incubus" controlling a super continent. Hitler and Stalin ruled now "from Manchuria to the Rhine," one distraught aide warned FDR, "much as Genghis Khan once ruled and nothing to stop the combined Russo-German force at any point, with the possible exception of the Himalayan Mountains."[99]

Roosevelt, though, remained calm. He knew that Stalin had long seen Hitler as a capitalist-imperialist, and that Hitler had long seen Stalin as an agent of the global Jewish conspiracy. Germany's military successes in the west, FDR suspected, had surprised the Soviet dictator, who could readily imagine where they might be sought next. The authoritarians' respect for each other, therefore, couldn't be deep and wouldn't be durable: they'd sooner or later devour each other. And so Roosevelt left a door open for Stalin whenever he was ready to walk through it.[100] Somewhat as Salisbury had done, four decades earlier, for the Americans.

XI.

Roosevelt's anticipation of an autocratic ally, I think, helps to explain why his self-confidence rose as one European democracy after another fell in the spring of 1940. He'd promised, when the war broke out, to *try* to keep the United States out of it, but he hadn't asked for Wilson's neutrality in fact, impartiality in thought, and a curb upon sentiments. He'd already set up secret military contacts with the British and, until their collapse, the French. He'd started a rearmament program that seemed at last to be creating jobs. He let the Democrats "draft" him that summer—the charade showed but didn't matter—for an unprecedented third term. He welcomed the Republicans' nomination of the dark-horse internationalist Wendell Willkie, against whom he nonetheless vigorously campaigned in the fall. And on the day before his third inauguration in January 1941, Roosevelt received his defeated rival, whom he was sending to London on a special mission, at the White House.

There he wrote out by hand, and apparently from memory, this passage from Henry Wadsworth Longfellow's 1849 poem "The Building of the Ship":

> Sail on, O Ship of State!
> Sail on, O Union, strong and great!
> Humanity with all its fears,
> With all the hope of future years
> Is hanging breathless on thy fate!

It was a "wonderful gift," Lincoln remarked when he read those lines early in the Civil War, "to be able to stir men like that."[101] They were FDR's gift, by way of Willkie, for Winston Churchill.[102]

Who'd become prime minister eight months earlier with France about to fall, Britain about to be bombed, and the English language about to be enriched on a Shakespearian scale over the recently perfected technology of shortwave radio. "What is the answer that I shall give in your name," Churchill asked his country after reading the poem aloud with the Americans listening in, "to this great man, the thrice-chosen head of a nation of a hundred and thirty million?" And then, in a slow, snarled, spine-chilling crescendo: "*Give us the tools and we will finish the job!*"[103]

The most important tool, he and Roosevelt agreed, would be "Lend-Lease," which Congress approved in March 1941. The legislation authorized military assistance to *any* country whose defense the president deemed vital to that of the United States. Great Britain would be the principal beneficiary, but FDR insisted on not specifying recipients. This could, critics complained, allow aid even to the Soviet Union: that seemed so unlikely, however, that the objection hardly registered. But Roosevelt was already getting reports—this time through the American embassy in Berlin—that Hitler would invade the USSR in the spring. After checking with Churchill, FDR had Stalin's ambassador in Washington alerted, but if he or his master were grateful, they didn't show it. Instead Stalin himself, still wishfully thinking, signed yet another nonaggression pact, this time with Japan.

That's how, at great cost and wholly unnecessarily, he let himself be surprised when Germany attacked the Soviet Union on June 22, 1941. Roosevelt and Churchill, unsurprised, began contemplating the ultimate ideological impurity: a deal with the devil—perhaps recalling how Wilson and Lloyd George must have come to regret abandoning a lesser demon, Nicholas II, after March 1917. At first immobilized by the shock, Stalin soon rallied sufficiently to demand what his ideology told him should be his due: help from *his* devils, the capitalist democracies, as if the Nazi-Soviet pact had never happened.

Brushing aside still more diplomatic and military misgivings, Roosevelt dispatched two deal makers to Moscow: Harry Hopkins, who'd become his Colonel House, and W. Averell Harriman, the railroad magnate who'd run manganese concessions in the Caucasus in the 1920s. Meanwhile, Davies, at the president's request, rushed into print *Mission to Moscow,* a sanitized but widely read account of his 1937–38 ambassadorship. After satisfying himself, from these and other sources, that Stalin wasn't about to surrender, Roosevelt on November 7, 1941—twenty-four years to the day *after* the Bolsheviks' coup and one month to the day *before* Japan's attack on Pearl Harbor—proclaimed the security of the Union of Soviet Socialist Republics vital to that of the United States. Enough had happened by then that hardly anyone noticed.[104]

XII.

"So we had won after all!" Churchill remembered exulting on getting the news from Hawaii. "[T]he United States was in the war, up to the neck and in to the death." "[S]illy people" had thought Americans too soft, too talkative, too paralyzed by their politics to be anything more than "a vague blur on the horizon to friend or foe."

> But I had studied the American Civil War, fought out to the last desperate inch. American blood flowed in my veins. I thought of a remark which Edward Grey had made to me more than thirty years before—that the United States is like "a gigantic boiler. Once the fire is lighted under it there is no limit to the power it can generate."

And so, "[b]eing satiated with emotion and sensation, I went to bed and slept the sleep of the saved and thankful."[105]

Churchill was too tactful to mention the fire lit, in Grey's time, that after winning a war unexpectedly had gone out. Re-ignition required a quarter century, a more dangerous crisis than that of 1917, and a more careful coordination of means with ends than

Wilson had achieved. So Roosevelt took his time. Churchill could only wait—however magnificently—for twenty-seven of the sixty-eight months in which Britain was at war.

Roosevelt was waiting for three things: First, an American rearmament that would restore prosperity, allow selective support to selected allies, and still hold out the hope—never the promise—of not going to war. Second, assurance that the Soviet Union would survive, and hence serve as a continental ally between the larger threats posed by smaller peripheries, Germany and Japan: left, by Stalin's bad choices, with no choice at all, his autocracy would do most of the fighting needed to save the American and British democracies. Finally, FDR wanted his own Fort Sumter, the moral high ground of having been attacked, which would at once silence all domestic demands to remain at peace. In the end he got two: the Japanese attack on Pearl Harbor and Hitler's declaration of war four days later.

Over the next four years, it was Roosevelt, more than anyone else, who rescued democracy and capitalism—not everywhere and in all respects, but sufficiently to stabilize both so that the setbacks they'd suffered in the first half of the twentieth century could reverse themselves in the second. He brought two great wars fought on opposite sides of the earth to almost simultaneous victories at a cost in American lives of less than 2 *percent* of the total for all the participants in those wars.[106] His country emerged from them with half the world's manufacturing capability, two-thirds of its gold reserves, three-fourths of its invested capital, its largest navy and air force, and its first atomic bombs.[107] There were, to be sure, pacts with devils in all of these: strategies, like politics, are never pure. But as historians Hal Brands and Patrick Porter have pointed out, "If this wasn't a successful grand strategy," then "nothing would be."[108]

XIII.

Franklin D. Roosevelt, Isaiah Berlin wrote ten years after the president's death, had been "a handsome, charming, gay, very intelligent, very delightful, very audacious man" accused, by his critics, of many weaknesses. He was, they claimed, "ignorant, unscrupulous, irresponsible," and had "betrayed his class." Surrounded by "adventurers, slick opportunists, [and] intriguers," he'd been "ruthless in playing with . . . lives and careers." He made "conflicting promises, cynically and brazenly." He used his "vast and irresistible public charm" to make up for his irresponsibility. "All of this was said and some of it may indeed have been just." But Roosevelt had "countervailing qualities of a rare and inspiring order."

> [H]e was large-hearted and possessed wide political horizons, imaginative sweep, understanding of the time in which he lived and of the direction of the great new forces at work in the twentieth century—technological, racial, imperialist, anti-imperialist; he was in favour of life and movement, the promotion of the most generous possible fulfillment of the largest possible number of human wishes, and not in favour of caution and retrenchment and sitting still. Above all, he was absolutely fearless.

As a result—and unusually for leaders of his or any other country—he seemed to have "no fear at all of the future."

Wilson, at his postwar triumphs in Paris, London, and Rome, had conveyed something like this, but only briefly: "[I]t disappeared quickly and left a terrible feeling of disenchantment." He'd been the kind of leader who, possessed by a "bright, coherent dream, . . . understands neither people nor events," and hence is able "to ignore a good deal of what goes on outside him." The weak and the vacillating may find "relief and peace and strength" in following such a person, "to whom all issues are clear, whose universe consists entirely of primary colors, mostly black and white, and who marches toward his goal looking neither to right nor to left." But there are also, within this category, "fearful evildoers, like Hitler."

Roosevelt, in striking contrast, was one of those politicians equipped with "antennae of the greatest possible delicacy, which convey to them . . . the perpetually changing contours of events and feelings and human activities." Gifted with the capacity "to take in minute impressions," they absorb and extract purpose from—as do artists—vast multitudes of "small evanescent unseizable detail."

> Statesmen of this type know what to do and when to do it, if they are to achieve their ends, which themselves are usually not born within some private world of inner thought, or introverted feeling, but are the crystallisation, the raising to great intensity and clarity, of what a large number of their fellow citizens are thinking and feeling in some dim, inarticulate but nevertheless persistent fashion.

Which allows such leaders then to convey, to those citizens, "a sense of understanding their inner needs, of responding to their own deepest impulses, above all of being alone capable of organising the world along lines [for] which [they] are instinctively groping." In this way, Berlin concluded, Roosevelt made Americans "prouder to be Americans than they had been before. He raised their status in their own eyes—[and] immensely in those of the rest of the world."

For he showed "that power and order are not . . . a straitjacket of doctrine, . . . that it is possible to reconcile individual liberty—a loose texture of society—with the indispensable minimum of organising and authority." In which coexistence of opposites resides "what Roosevelt's greatest predecessor once described as 'the last best hope of earth.'"[109]

XIV.

The date is May 26, 1940. The place is just outside Trinidad, Colorado, on the route of the old Santa Fe Trail. The time is dusk, and the sun is setting behind the mountains. A car has pulled over, and in it sit two men, tuning a radio. One is thirty-nine, the other twenty-two, and they're driving across America.[110] A few locals approach, asking if they can listen too: for the men in the car they're "Mexicans"—even though their ancestors may once have owned everything in sight. All light cigarettes as the voice they know breaks through the static: "My friends . . ."

The men are Bernard DeVoto, a Harvard English lecturer who'd prospered as a bootlegger, failed as a novelist, and would soon succeed as a historian: with him is his assistant and driver, Arthur Schlesinger, Jr. Having grown up in Utah, DeVoto is reacquainting himself with the American West prior to finishing his epic *The Year of Decision: 1846,* which will appear in 1943. But on this evening they, like the "Mexicans," have much else on their minds.

For France is about to fall, England may be next, and as Schlesinger writes to his parents a few days later: "[T]he kind of world I have been preparing to live in is gone." DeVoto, who'd served in the Great War, has seen it all before: "We were the war generation and then some called us the lost generation and then we were the depression generation and now we regress to our first estate." Both have read, and discussed, an article in the June issue of *Harper's Magazine*—for which DeVoto writes a column—entitled "Enter Atomic Power."[111] It mentions no military applications, but the men in the car can't help but wonder "whether a cupful . . . could be used to run a tank."

And yet, the country has reassured as they've crossed it. There've been two thousand miles of sturdy houses, well-kept lawns, and bright flowers—"a windbreak . . . against the erosion of the times; each one a place where roots go down to hold the soil." The schools look better than ever before. The people, "habituated to peace," are unfailingly kind. And never again, DeVoto vows, "would I speak condescendingly of the radio." For suddenly, "out of advertisements for cereals and shaving lotions, you get an instrument of democracy." No one this time will be able to say "that the Americans did not know what they were in for, or why."

Roosevelt's address isn't one of his best. There're too many statistics on rearmament achieved so far, soon to be eclipsed exponentially by what the country will achieve when it does go to war. What the president most wants Americans to know, though, is that their security can't come any longer solely from ocean distances. The new technologies of "ships"—the kind that move under and above water as well as on its surface—have made isolation impossible. But from within its boundaries, the country will make whatever it will take to keep it safe.

For more than three centuries we Americans have been building on this continent a free society, a society in which the promise of the human spirit may find fulfillment. . . . We have built well.[112]

When he finishes, the car is filled with cigarette smoke and a brief silence, after which one of the "Mexicans" says: "I guess maybe America declare war pretty soon now." "I guess maybe," DeVoto acknowledges. Then "[w]e waved good-by and drove on to Trinidad."

CHAPTER TEN

ISAIAH

I hate discontinuities of all kinds," Isaiah Berlin wrote his friend the novelist and poet Stephen Spender in 1936. "[W]hich is only another way of saying that I am a slow starter & hate to be uprooted . . . , consequently I passionately defend all small societies, fixed disciplines etc. which merely rationalizes my love of the womb I expect (a womb with a view, a womb of one's own etc.)"[1] When the war broke out three years later, though, Berlin's Oxford became claustrophobic even for him. Unfit for military service owing to an arm injured at birth, excluded from intelligence work by his Latvian and Russian origins, he admitted after the fall of France that "the private world has cracked in numerous places. I should terribly like to help in the great historical process in some way."[2]

That letter went to Marion Frankfurter, the wife of Felix, the former Harvard law professor and continuing close adviser to Franklin D. Roosevelt, who'd recently appointed him to the Supreme Court:

Berlin knew the Frankfurters from a year they'd spent at Oxford.[3] But his habitual rootedness—perhaps also his finances—had so far kept him from seeing America. When he finally got there, in the summer of 1940 and at the age of thirty-two, it was, like Columbus, by way of a perilous voyage and a miscalculated landfall.

Yet another acquaintance, Guy Burgess of the Foreign Office, claimed to have found Berlin a job at the British embassy in Moscow. Fluent in Russian, desperate to be of use, he'd seized the opportunity, and by mid-July the two were on a ship, zigzagging across the Atlantic to avoid U-boats, bound for Quebec: after a brief stop in New York, they'd planned to proceed by way of Japan and Siberia. But the unreliable Burgess, known then to be a drunkard and exposed later as a Soviet spy,[4] hadn't cleared Berlin's position with Sir Stafford Cripps, the British ambassador to the USSR. When told they were on their way, he refused to accept either of them. Burgess's superiors ordered him back to London, leaving Berlin, "who is not in the employ of His Majesty's Government," stranded in America, free to do "what he thinks best."[5]

"I must obviously create my own job," he wrote a friend. "I can't say how bad at this I probably am."[6] So he began networking, at which he was very good. He started with the Frankfurters, where he coaxed a houseguest, the theologian Reinhold Niebuhr, into writing Cripps to ask him to change his mind. Berlin then secured Washington lodging through Oxford friends, and soon talked his way into lunch with the Soviet ambassador: why, he asked his host, had Stalin recently annexed Latvia? "New Deal" for Baltics, that dignitary mumbled, while authorizing the visa Berlin had come for.[7] Which he turned out not to need because Cripps didn't budge—and because a job Berlin hadn't sought found him.

"I had never met, nor . . . even heard of Isaiah before," John Wheeler-Bennett of the British embassy staff later admitted. But "as we sat on the garden-patio with our drinks, I fell at once under the spell of his brilliant intellect." Despite having been in the United States for only a few days, Berlin conveyed the sense of "a lifetime of acquaintance with that country."

> [H]e never seemed to stop talking, though he never bored us, even if we did sometimes have difficulty in understanding him. . . . He sparkled and scintillated, yet not one of us who listened to him felt that we were being overwhelmed or left out. One of Isaiah's most priceless attributes is that he evokes genius in others . . . , giving them the impression that they are really more coruscating and witty than they would otherwise believe themselves to be.

Knowing that their new prime minister had, after Dunkirk, revived an old prophecy—that "in God's good time the New World with all its power and might" would seek "the rescue and liberation of the Old"[8]—Wheeler-Bennett and his colleagues conspired to keep Berlin on their side of the ocean: he was, for them, an "answer to prayer."[9]

His job, they decided, would be explaining the "new world" to the "old." By the time of Pearl Harbor, Berlin was preparing "weekly political summaries," each hundreds of words in length, focusing on, but not limited to, what was happening in Washington. Pouched to London and when necessary cabled, these confidential reports filled the gap between top-secret communications and open news.[10] They provided much-needed context, while making the most of

Berlin's social skills. For he could now, in good conscience and as his contribution to victory, go to as many parties as he liked.

I.

"We must . . . always base ourselves on the assumption that Americans are foreigners to us and we to them," Berlin wrote in one of his first reports, early in 1942. Whereas Britain had suspended politics—it held no general election between 1935 and 1945—the United States "to a considerable degree continued as before." Roosevelt still appointed multiple people to similar jobs. Congress busied itself, as always, with logrolling. Local issues and machine loyalties influenced elections at least as much as the outside world: even after Pearl Harbor it was no disgrace to have been an isolationist, because "half [of those voting] have done same or worse and other half have never heard of such a thing."[11]

Meanwhile, "the sheer productive effort of this continent is still gathering strength and speed and effects of this can be felt in the sense of its own power on the part of the American people." Who now acknowledged that "to get into one war may have been bad luck but to have got into two looks like something wrong with the system." How to fix it, though, wasn't yet clear. Would Americans follow "country-bred liberal reformers" like their vice president, Henry A. Wallace, toward a global New Deal without boundaries of nationality, race, and class? Or would they embrace the "economic imperialism" of the publisher Henry Luce, who'd already proclaimed the century to be "American"? Either way, Roosevelt would lead "with infinitely greater political skill, though less compelling moral force, than Mr Wilson."[12]

Not least because he, unlike Wilson, would have to deal with the Soviet Union. "Stalin might well be the devil of the coming peace," Berlin reported, but "the United States thought it possessed a long enough spoon to sup with him." It would, of course, try to avoid extremes: that the Russians "sweep all before them in Europe and establish Communism everywhere," or that they "stop at their own frontiers and make a peace with Germans." But neither these nor compromises between them would leave much room "for small nations upon whom Russia's demands may fall heavily."[13]

The price of victory, therefore, would be the denial of justice, because the price of justice could be the denial of victory. Berlin confirmed this with chilling gossip:

> The Greek ambassador is reliably reported to have said that at his last interview with the President the latter had told him that no fuss would be made by the United States Government about the incorporation of the Baltic States by Soviet Russia. . . . The Greek Ambassador then inquired about Poland. According to our informant, the President made gestures of mock despair and said that he was thoroughly tired of the Polish problem, and had told the Polish Ambassador so in clear language, and warned him personally about the effects of continued Polish agitation.

> [The] general sentiment, discernible in the press and in conversation of young 'tough-minded' Washington and other executives . . . , is that Russia is doing [the] only sensible thing for a rising great continental power, that America's resources enable her to act likewise, [and] that on a hard and

unsentimental basis the two countries will be able to agree after some hard pokerplay without [the] intermediary of Britain or any other 'old' power whose day is passing. They do not deny that . . . Wilsonian ideals are going by the board but since Russians wish it so, this is perhaps way world is inevitably going and it would be a foolish luxury to continue to wag a warning figure at Russia in name of ideals which United States knows it does not propose to implement by force.

Governor [Alf] Landon [defeated Republican candidate for president in 1936] is said to have telephoned [Secretary of State Cordell] Hull recently to enquire why no guarantees for Poland were obtained at the [October 1943] Moscow Conference. Hull is said to have suggested that [Landon] go to Moscow himself and plead the Poles' cause with Marshal Stalin in the name of the great Middle West; Landon asked whether Hull really thought this might save the Poles. Hull begged him on no account to forget to take a specific commitment from the Republican Party to go to immediate war for the integrity of Poland, should the Russians prove obdurate, and a clear promise from the United States Army and Navy to lend them assistance in that event. Landon, who began by taking Hull's words seriously, is said to be much wounded by this irony and to be sulking in Kansas.[14]

Lest his reports seem too depressing, Berlin did what he could to brighten them:

A Democrat departing from the Washington [birthday] din-
ner was heard to observe [that] 'on Lincoln's birthday he
[Roosevelt] thought he was Lincoln. Today he thought he was
Washington. What will he say on Christmas Day?'

Colonel [Robert] McCormick [isolationist publisher of the
Chicago Tribune] . . . intends to [urge] incorporation [into] the
United States of Australia, New Zealand, Canada, Scotland,
Wales, etc. Entertainment value of this campaign should be
considerable since we are assured that Colonel is in deadly
earnest.

[Wallace's] passionate desire to secure renomination for the
Vice-Presidency [in 1944] is unique in United States history:
this odd spectacle is observed with pain or enjoyment according to the sympathies of the observer.

Senator [Hiram] Johnson [of California] was obliquely supported in milder terms by Senator [Walter] George [of Geor-
gia] speaking in his native Georgian.

His [Roosevelt's] light touch, so often a method of getting out
of a tight corner, sometimes seems to put too great a strain
upon the earnestness of his own followers.[15]

But not Berlin's on that of his London readers, for whom his lightness provided relief, if only momentary, from the somber realities of
rescue and liberation.

One reader's gratitude occasioned the war's most famous case of confused identity. On February 9, 1944, Winston Churchill invited the author of the weekly summaries, "I. Berlin," to lunch at 10 Downing Street. Where the prime minister found himself seated, baffled, next to an equally bewildered guest of honor, the composer of "White Christmas." The story spread, making Isaiah Berlin, in the words of his biographer Michael Ignatieff, "a minor celebrity by mistake."[16]

II.

Berlin's summaries catapulted him from the cramped conversations of Oxford into the far more capacious ones of a vast republic fighting a total war, with his eagle eye and fluid tongue facilitating the leap. "Who would have thought," he wrote his parents, that "I should become avidly interested in American politics?" Perhaps America *was* Oxford on an enormous scale: in both, institutions meant less than individual relationships, "the pattern of which . . . has, of course, always fascinated me." Whatever the explanation, Berlin would remember his years in Washington as a "last oasis . . . after which youth is finally over & ordinary life begins."[17]

He finally made it to Moscow in September 1945, having secured Foreign Office approval, this time, for the trip: it hoped, Berlin told friends, for a "lapidary" dispatch from him that would "guide British policy for ever and ever."[18] But he found that he couldn't function there as in the United States. The secret police followed him everywhere, inhibiting movements, monitoring conversations, appearing at times even to detect thoughts. His knowledge of Russian only magnified their suspicions.[19]

Berlin was, then, for the first time, tongue-tied. He could understand what people were saying, but didn't dare speak to them for fear of getting them into trouble. Relatives had to whisper what they'd endured over a decade of purges and war. Poets, playwrights, artists, filmmakers, and novelists who should have embodied contemporary Russian culture seemed instead to have emerged from the belly of Jonah's whale: bleached, exhausted, alive but drained of life.[20] Gossip, no longer innocent, was a deadly weapon. Survival itself required apologies.

Silences in Stalin's Russia—predictably for someone so rarely silent—affected Berlin at least as much as cacophonies in America. He'd hardly heard of Anna Akhmatova when he wandered into a Leningrad bookstore one afternoon in November, picked up a volume of her poems, and asked casually if she was still alive. She was, he was told, and lived nearby: would he like to meet her? Of course he would, so a phone call was made, she invited him up, and they talked through the night and the next morning.[21] He'd remember the experience as the most important of his life.[22]

Known in the West as a prerevolutionary poet, Akhmatova hadn't been allowed significant publication since 1925. Her first husband had been executed under Lenin, her second and their son had spent years in the gulag, and she'd survived the Leningrad siege only because Stalin wouldn't let her starve. Back now from the evacuation he'd ordered, she was living alone in the single bare room of a walk-up apartment, with little reason to expect her obscurity ever to end.

Berlin found her defiant, looking and moving "like a tragic queen." She'd met only one other foreigner, she admitted, since the First World War. Berlin, twenty years younger, scrambled to satisfy her curiosity without revealing that he hadn't read her poetry. Each saw the other as from an inaccessible world: he from the Europe from which she'd been cut off; she from the Russia he'd had to leave as a child. What he heard, he recalled years later, "went beyond anything which anyone had ever described to me in spoken words."[23] She, in a poem, wrote him into the future:

> He will not be a beloved husband to me
> But what we accomplish, he and I,
> Will disturb the Twentieth Century.[24]

Machiavelli might have said, of that night, that they were sketching: seeking at least shapes of things they'd have no time to know. Clausewitz would have seen *coups d'oeil*—"inward eyes" grasping truths ordinarily requiring long reflection. But only Tolstoy could have portrayed such a pivoting of lives on a single point: a real and not imaginary hare, at Tarutino.

For Akhmatova, the night ensured another decade of isolation, the unseen presence in the room having been Stalin himself, whose agents kept him well informed. For Berlin, it upended the moral equivalence with which he'd previously viewed the coming Cold War: two great powers doing what great powers had always done. America and Russia differed, he could now see, not just in geographies, histories, cultures, and capabilities, but also, critically, in necessary ecologies. One thrived on cacophony. The other demanded silence.

III.

"What is happening [in the Soviet Union] is . . . unspeakably sordid and detestable," Berlin wrote a friend in November 1946: "[T]he slow humiliation of poets and musicians is more awful in a way than outright shooting."[25] But hadn't Russian artists always suffered under authoritarians? Yes, he'd later concede, but in trying to suppress creativity the tsars had focused it: Russia became, under them, a hothouse for ideas, which "were taken more seriously, and played a greater and more peculiar role [there] than anywhere else."[26] Haunted by the contrast between the history he knew and the present he'd seen, Berlin set out to relate nineteenth-century Russia "to the modern world, [and] to the human condition in general."[27]

The link would be twentieth-century Marxism, as much the offspring of Russian revolutionaries as of Marx himself. Traditional approaches to critical judgment, enlightened or not, had at least evaluated situations on their merits rather than from preconceptions "to which no factual discoveries can ... make any difference." But Marxists claimed "to know in advance whether a man's views are correct ... simply by finding out his social or economic background or condition." They assumed "the irrefutability of [their] own theory."[28] Berlin soon broadened his argument to include fascism, "the culmination and bankruptcy" of the "mystical patriotism" that inflamed Europe's nineteenth-century nationalists. This made the *two* great disruptions of his era—World War II and the Cold War—the results of "totalitarian" determinations to remove contradictions "by means other than thought and argument."[29]

Rationalists had long seen contradictions as carrying within themselves seeds of their own resolution. Conservatives found these in the flow of time, which diminished old controversies by embedding them in new circumstances: Bismarck and Salisbury embodied this tradition. Liberals sought them in structures agreeable to opposing sides: Wilson's "Fourteen Points" attempted that. Both shared the belief—"too obviously to be clearly realized"—that problems could be solved through "the conscious application of truths upon which all men endowed with adequate mental powers could agree."[30]

But what if time flowed too slowly? What if no "truths" existed? What if they did, but were impossible to detect? These were the subversions with which nineteenth-century Russian radicals infected the twentieth century: "[I]f the revolution demanded it," then "everything—democracy, liberty, the rights of the individual—must be sacrificed to it." Marx, Berlin wanted to believe, had been "too European" to go this far. Lenin had no such qualms:

> The masses were too stupid and too blind to be allowed to proceed in the direction of their own choosing. . . . [T]hey could only be saved by being ruthlessly ordered by leaders who had acquired a capacity for knowing how to organize the liberated slaves into a rational planned system.

Hence the "enormities" that, as Berlin put it in his 1953 lecture on Machiavelli, "freeze the blood of ordinary men." And where had the "capacity" come from? From what Marx *had* wholeheartedly contributed: a theory of history that gave those privy to it the self-confidence never to fear the future.[31]

IV.

That, though, is what Berlin would also say, in 1955, of Franklin D. Roosevelt—without the slightest suggestion that the late president had even glanced at the chapter on "Dialectical and Historical Materialism" in Stalin's *History of the All-Union Communist Party (Bolsheviks): Short Course*, published in 1938. FDR wasn't a Bismarckian conservative, or a Wilsonian liberal, or a Marxist-Leninist, or a Nazi. He *was,* however, supremely sure of himself:

> In a despondent world which appeared divided between wicked and fatally efficient fanatics marching to destroy, and bewildered populations on the run, unenthusiastic martyrs in a cause they could not define, he believed in his own ability, so long as he was at the controls, to stem this terrible tide.

That made Roosevelt, for Berlin, "the greatest leader of democracy, the greatest champion of social progress in the twentieth century."[32] So where did *his* self-confidence come from?

Not, I'm sure, from any Polonius-like search for certainty in the shapes of passing clouds. But not from reconciling or eradicating contradictions either: FDR was at once too cynical and too humane to pursue either possibility. Perhaps he was, though, one of those leaders who'd "learnt to live," as Berlin put it, and in the manner of Machiavelli, with "incompatible alternatives in public and private life."[33] "I am a juggler," Roosevelt himself acknowledged in 1942, and "never let my right hand know what my left hand does."[34]

Presidential advisers found this frustrating, even frivolous, and some historians since have agreed.[35] But follow the metaphor more closely: how do you keep one hand from knowing what the other is doing without having a head instruct both? "I may be entirely inconsistent," FDR went on to explain, "*if it will help win the war.*"[36] Consistency in grand strategy, then, was less a matter of logic than of scale: what made no sense to subordinates could make perfect sense to him. For he saw better than anyone relationships of everything to everything else—while sharing what he saw with no one.

Instead he radiated an apparently effortless aplomb, despite spending the longest presidency in American history, and the last third of his life, unable, unassisted, to instruct even his own legs and feet.[37]

It's the late afternoon of March 8, 1933. A limousine pulls up in front of a Georgetown house. The recently inaugurated president of the United States is helped out, wheeled in, and takes the elevator to the library. The recently retired Supreme Court justice Oliver Wendell Holmes, Jr., is in his bedroom, napping off the effects of his ninety-second birthday party earlier that day. But Felix Frankfurter—who hasn't yet met Isaiah Berlin—has arranged a surprise. "Don't be an idiot, boy," Holmes snaps at his clerk, who's awakened him: "He wouldn't call on me." There the president is, though, waiting patiently in the library. So this thrice-wounded veteran of Lincoln's war reassembles himself to greet the Emancipator's latest successor. The chat that follows is pleasantly unmemorable. Not, however, what Holmes says after Roosevelt leaves: "A second-class intellect. *But a first-class temperament!*"[38]

V.

"Any complex activity," Clausewitz writes, "if it is to be carried on with any degree of virtuosity, calls for appropriate gifts of intellect and temperament. If they are outstanding and reveal themselves in exceptional achievements, their possessor is called a 'genius.'"[39] I take this to mean continuing adjustments of "intellect"—which sets courses—to "temperament"—which determines how they're pursued. For just as no politics can be pure, so no "grand strategy" will remain unaffected by the unforeseen.

Why don't you ever see tightrope walkers without long poles? It's because they're stabilizers, as critical to the reaching of destinations as the steps taken toward them. And yet, the poles work by feel, not thought: focusing on them risks falling. Temperament functions similarly, I think, in strategy. It's not a compass—that's intellect. But it is a gyroscope: an inner ear complementing Clausewitz's "inward eye." Like poles on tightropes, temperament makes the difference between slips and safe arrivals.

Xerxes couldn't contain his ambitions while Artabanus couldn't conquer his fears: both yielded, if in different ways, to intemperance. Pericles shifted from tolerance to repression in a single speech, and Athens soon followed. Octavian rose by teaching himself self-control; Antony sank by forgetting it. Augustine and Machiavelli bequeathed the heavy and light hands with which Philip and Elizabeth shaped different new worlds. Napoleon lost his empire by confusing aspirations with capabilities; Lincoln saved his country by not doing so. Wilson the builder disappointed his generation; Roosevelt the juggler surpassed the expectations of his. To paraphrase a Ronald Reagan story about a pony,[40] there's got to be a pattern in here somewhere.

Perhaps it lies in Philip Tetlock's suggestion that we've survived *as a species* by *combining* the habits of Berlin's animals: foxes adapted more easily to rapid changes, but hedgehogs thrived in stable times.[41] Which extends Fitzgerald's "first-rate intelligence" to holding opposites *in behavior* as well as in mind. Which circles back to Tetlock's view of "good judgment" as a "balancing act" that requires "rethinking core assumptions" while "preserving our existing worldview."[42] Or, in simpler terms, but at *all* altitudes, applying common sense.

VI.

This, though, assumes a *morally equivalent* tightrope from which the effects of falling would be as unfortunate on either side. But Berlin by the early 1950s had come to see politics as a polarity, with *inequivalent* concepts of liberty at either end.[43]

One offered freedom *from* the need to make choices by yielding them to some higher authority, whether a collective, a party, a state, an ideology, or even a theory. The other preserved the freedom *to* make such choices. Berlin called the first "positive liberty," but not as a compliment: that liberty, if carried to extremes, led to tyranny—removing contradictions by silencing them. The second, "negative liberty," cultivated contradictions, even cacophonies: without a compass, though, it could produce drift, parochialism, and ultimately anarchy.

Positive liberty, in this book, has been hedgehogs trying to herd foxes: the older Pericles, Julius Caesar, Augustine, Philip II, George III, Napoleon, Wilson, and the twentieth-century totalitarians, all of whom knew with such certainty how the world worked that they preferred flattening topographies to functioning within them. That flattened people, allowing only ranges of "freedoms" extending from—at best—disillusionment or dispossession, to—at worst—slavery or extermination.

Negative liberty has been foxes with compasses: the younger Pericles, Octavian Caesar, Machiavelli, Elizabeth I, the American Founders, Lincoln, Salisbury, and especially Roosevelt, all of whom had the humility to be unsure of what lay ahead, the flexibility to adjust to it, and the ingenuity to accept, perhaps even to leverage, inconsistencies. They respected topographies, crafted choices within them, and evaluated these carefully once made.

Both liberties required crossings, and as on tightropes—or on bridges of boats—no crossing is without risks. But positive liberty claimed to have lessened these, or at least to have postponed them: either way, new worlds on the other side would be promised lands. Negative liberty made no such claims: it acknowledged limits, lowered expectations, and preferred proven means in seeking attainable ends. Positive liberty required no proofs beyond what theory provided, for if ends were compatible, means would automatically converge. Negative liberty expected neither compatibility nor convergence, but valued experience, subjecting theory to its corrections.

That required what Berlin called "pluralism":[44] a recognition, for sure, of persisting evils—man's fallen state, Augustine might have said—but also of the good that can come from balancing them— man's state, Machiavelli might have replied. Provided we don't too much sweat living with the contradictions that, as Berlin did say, have "never given men peace since."[45]

VII.

The date is February 16, 1962. The place is the University of Indonesia in Jogjakarta. Robert F. Kennedy, the United States attorney general, is responding to a student's question about the Mexican War: "Some from Texas might disagree, but I think we were unjustified. I do not think we can be proud of that episode." Many in Texas did disagree, to such an extent that Kennedy had to promise his older brother that he would clear all future observations on that state with the then vice president of the United States.[46] Some months later, as a first-year graduate student at the University of Texas in Austin, I watched a videotaped lecture by the Yale diplomatic historian Samuel Flagg Bemis, a man of clear views on the past's relationship to the present. Unable to resist commenting on Kennedy's claims, Bemis began mildly but concluded memorably: "*You wouldn't want to give it all back, would you?*"

Well, no, if we're really honest with ourselves, most of us wouldn't, even in this more politically correct age. For satisfying the claims of justice in this instance would not only disrupt the present and future, but also the past: wouldn't the Mexicans then have to give it all back to the Spanish, and then the Spanish to the indigenous populations they decimated, and then those peoples to the flora and fauna they displaced after crossing the land bridge from Siberia thousands of years earlier? The argument is absurd, but only because it rejects any coexistence of contradictions in time or space: it thereby confirms Berlin's claim that not all praiseworthy things are simultaneously possible. And that learning to live within that condition—let's call it *history*—requires adaptation to incompatibles.

That's where grand strategy helps. For "in all fair dealings," Burke reminded his parliamentary colleagues in 1775, "the thing bought must bear some proportion to the purchase paid."[47] Proportionality comes from what grand strategy is: the alignment of potentially infinite aspirations with necessarily limited capabilities. And fairness? I'd say from *bending* the alignment *toward* freedom. Or, as Berlin would have put it, toward "negative" liberty.

This is what Clausewitz meant by subordinating "war" to "policy," for what freedom could come from total violence? It's what Augustine sought by seeking to make wars "just." And it's what Sun Tzu, with uncharacteristic gentleness, acknowledged: that "while an angered man may again be happy, and a resentful man again be pleased, a state that has perished cannot be restored, nor can the dead be brought back to life."[48]

The contradiction between the living and the dead is the greatest we'll ever hold, in mind or in spirit, whatever the "present" within which we function. All at either end of that tightrope—well, almost all—deserve respect.

NOTES

PREFACE

1. For Naval War College Strategy and Policy curricula, see www.usnwc.edu /Faculty-and-Departments/Academic-Departments/Strategy-and-Policy -Department. For the Yale course, www.grandstrategy.yale.edu/background; also Linda Kulman, *Teaching Common Sense: The Grand Strategy Program at Yale University* (Westport, Connecticut: Prospecta Press, 2016).

2. Some readers may worry that I've forgotten the Cold War. Not at all—it's just that I've said enough already on that subject. See, most recently, the revised edition of my *Strategies of Containment* (New York: Oxford University Press, 2005), and my article on "Grand Strategies in the Cold War," in Melvyn P. Leffler and Odd Arne Westad, *The Cambridge History of the Cold War* (New York: Cambridge University Press, 2010), vol. 2, pp. 1–21.

3. Special thanks to Anthony Kronman, the former dean of the Yale Law School, for suggesting the relevance of these to grand strategy.

CHAPTER ONE: CROSSING THE HELLESPONT

1. Herodotus, *The History*, Book VII:1–56. I've used David Grene's translation (Chicago: University of Chicago Press, 1987), pp. 466–90. For a recent appreciation of Herodotus, see Robert D. Kaplan, "A Historian for Our Time," *The Atlantic*, January/February 2007.

2. Michael Ignatieff, *Isaiah Berlin: A Life* (New York: Metropolitan Books, 1998), p. 173. See also Ramin Jahanbegloo, *Conversations with Isaiah Berlin*, second edition (London: Halban, 1992), pp. 188–89, and Isaiah Berlin, *Enlightening: Letters*,

1946–1960, edited by Henry Hardy and Jennifer Holmes (London: Chatto and Windus, 2009), p. 31n. The inspiration could also have come from C. M. Bowra, "The Fox and the Hedgehog," *The Classical Quarterly* 34 (January–April 1940), 26–29.

3. Stephen Jay Gould's last book, *The Hedgehog, the Fox, and the Magister's Pox: Mending the Gap Between Science and the Humanities* (Cambridge, Massachusetts: Harvard University Press, 2011), pp. 1–8, has a brief history of the aphorism.

4. Isaiah Berlin, *The Hedgehog and the Fox*, edited by Henry Hardy (Princeton: Princeton University Press, 2013), p. 91. I've also drawn on an essay by a former student, Joseph Carlsmith, "The Bed, the Map, and the Butterfly: Isaiah Berlin's Grand Strategy of Grand Strategy," prepared for the 2011 Yale "Studies in Grand Strategy" seminar.

5. Isaiah Berlin, "The Hedgehog and the Fox: An Essay on Tolstoy's View of History," in his *The Proper Study of Mankind: An Anthology of Essays*, edited by Henry Hardy and Roger Hausheer (New York: Farrar, Straus and Giroux, 1998), pp. 436–37, 498.

6. A. N. Wilson, *Tolstoy: A Biography* (New York: Norton, 1988), pp. 506–17.

7. Berlin, *The Hedgehog and the Fox*, pp. xv–xvi.

8. Herodotus, I:12, p. 38.

9. *Ibid.*, VII:8, 10, pp. 469, 472. See also Tom Holland, *Persian Fire: The First World Empire and the Battle for the West* (New York: Doubleday, 2005), p. 238.

10. Herodotus, VII:8, 22–24, pp. 469, 478–79; Holland, *Persian Fire*, pp. 212–14.

11. For more on the Achilles-Odysseus distinction in strategy, see Lawrence Freedman, *Strategy: A History* (New York: Oxford University Press, 2013), p. 22.

12. Not literally, of course. If born by then, Herodotus would have been a mere tyke.

13. Philip E. Tetlock, *Expert Political Judgment: How Good Is It? How Can We Know?* (Princeton: Princeton University Press, 2005), especially pp. xi, 73–75, 118, 128–29. For a popularization of Tetlock's findings, see Dan Gardner, *Future Babble: Why Expert Predictions Are Next to Worthless, and You Can Do Better* (New York: Dutton, 2011). Tetlock and Gardner have collaborated, in turn, on an update, *Superforecasting: The Art and Science of Prediction* (New York: Crown, 2015).

14. Herodotus, VII:101, 108–26, pp. 502, 505–10.

15. John R. Hale, *Lords of the Sea: The Epic Story of the Athenian Navy and the Birth of Democracy* (New York: Penguin, 2009), pp. 36–39, 55–74; also Barry Strauss, *The Battle of Salamis: The Naval Encounter That Saved Greece—and Western Civilization* (New York: Simon and Schuster, 2005).

16. Aeschylus, *The Persians*, lines 819–20, Seth G. Benardete translation (Chicago: University of Chicago Press, 1956), p. 77. For Themistocles' rumor, see Plutarch, *Lives of the Noble Grecians and Romans*, translated by John Dryden (New York: Modern Library, no date), p. 144.

17. Victor Parker, "Herodotus' Use of Aeschylus' *Persae* as a Source for the Battle of Salamis," *Symbolae Osloenses: Norwegian Journal of Greek and Latin Studies* 82:1, 2–29.

18. Herodotus, VII:8, p. 469.

19. A point linked to more recent examples in Victor Davis Hanson, *The Savior Generals: How Five Great Commanders Saved Wars That Were Lost—from Ancient Greece to Iraq* (New York: Bloomsbury Press, 2013), p. 11.

20. Herodotus, VII:38–39, pp. 483–84.

21. F. Scott Fitzgerald, "The Crack-Up," *Esquire*, February 1936.

22. Jeffrey Meyers, *Scott Fitzgerald: A Biography* (New York: HarperCollins, 1994), pp. 261–65, 332–36.

23. My Yale colleague Charles Hill, often Delphic himself, is fond of quoting the aphorism in seminars without explaining it to puzzled students.

24. This is a simplified summary of three great Berlin essays, "Two Concepts of Liberty" (1958), "The Originality of Machiavelli" (1972), and "The Pursuit of the Ideal" (1988). All are in *The Proper Study of Mankind*, where I've relied particularly on pp. 10–11, 239, 294, and 302. The Halloween kid, however, is my own formulation.

25. Jahanbegloo, *Conversations with Isaiah Berlin*, pp. 188–89. See also Berlin, *The Hedgehog and the Fox*, p. 101, quoting an interview with Michael Ignatieff.

26. Or, as Berlin once put it, on Procrustean beds. Carlsmith develops this point in "The Bed, the Map, and the Butterfly."

27. See Anthony Lane's review, "House Divided," in *The New Yorker*, November 19, 2012.

28. IMDb, *Lincoln* (2012), at www.imdb.com/title/tt0443272/quotes.

29. Tolstoy's tribute concludes the final volume of Michael Burlingame's *Abraham Lincoln: A Life* (Baltimore: Johns Hopkins University Press, 2008), p. 834.

30. I've borrowed elements of this and the previous paragraph from my article "War, Peace, and Everything: Thoughts on Tolstoy," *Cliodynamics: The Journal of Theoretical and Mathematical History* 2 (2011), 40–51.

31. Berlin, "The Hedgehog and the Fox," in *The Proper Study of Mankind*, p. 444.

32. Tetlock, *Expert Political Judgment*, pp. 214–15; Daniel Kahneman, *Thinking, Fast and Slow* (New York: Farrar, Straus and Giroux, 2011), especially pp. 20–21. For Kahneman on Tetlock, see pp. 218–20.

33. Most famously in the 2002 film *Spider-Man*, but the quote has appeared in various forms in the franchise's other movies and comics. Strangely, a close approximation would have shown up in Franklin D. Roosevelt's Jefferson Day dinner address on April 13, 1945, had he lived to deliver it (www.presidency.ucsb.edu /ws/?pid=16602).

34. Homer, *The Iliad*, translated by Robert Fagles (New York: Penguin, 1990), p. 371. Homer, of course, recorded by remembering, since the Greeks of his age had forgotten how to write.

35. I owe this suggestion to my former student Christopher R. Howell, who advances it in "The Story of Grand Strategy: The History of an Idea and the Source of Its Confusion," a 2013 Yale Senior Essay in Humanities, p. 2. See also Freedman, *Strategy*, pp. 3–7.

36. For what he read, see Richard Carwardine, *Lincoln: A Life of Purpose and Power* (New York: Random House, 2006), pp. 4–10; also Fred Kaplan, *Lincoln: The Biography of a Writer* (New York: HarperCollins, 2008). The only other comparably self-educated presidents appear to have been Zachary Taylor and Andrew Johnson.

37. Henry Kissinger, *White House Years* (Boston: Little, Brown, 1979), p. 54.

38. See Michael Billig, *Learn to Write Badly: How to Succeed in the Social Sciences* (New York: Cambridge University Press, 2013). I gave further attention to the relationship between history and theory in *The Landscape of History: How Historians Map the Past* (New York: Oxford University Press, 2002). James C. Scott discusses the distinction between universal and local knowledge in his *Seeing Like a State: How Certain Schemes to Improve the Human Condition Have Failed* (New Haven: Yale University Press, 1998).

39. Niccolò Machiavelli, *The Prince,* translated by Harvey C. Mansfield, second edition (Chicago: University of Chicago Press, 1998), pp. 3–4.

40. The standard edition is Carl von Clausewitz, *On War,* edited and translated by Michael Howard and Peter Paret (Princeton: Princeton University Press, 1976).

41. Donald Rumsfeld, *Known and Unknown: A Memoir* (New York: Penguin, 2011), especially pp. xiii–xiv.

42. For the history of this famous misquotation, see Elizabeth Longford, *Wellington* (London: Abacus, 2001), pp. 16–17.

CHAPTER TWO: LONG WALLS

1. Victor Davis Hanson, *A War Like No Other: How the Athenians and Spartans Fought the Peloponnesian War* (New York: Random House, 2005), p. 66.

2. My description of the Athenian walls comes chiefly from Thucydides, for whom I have used Robert B. Strassler, ed., *The Landmark Thucydides: A Comprehensive Guide to the Peloponnesian War,* a revised version of the Richard Crawley translation (New York: Simon and Schuster, 1996), 1:89–93 [hereafter Thucydides, followed by the book and paragraph numbers standard in all editions]. See also Brent L. Sterling, *Do Good Fences Make Good Neighbors? What History Teaches Us About Strategic Barriers and International Security* (Washington, D.C.: Georgetown University Press, 2009), pp. 15–16; and David L. Berkey, "Why Fortifications Endure: A Case Study of the Walls of Athens During the Classical Period," in Victor Davis Hanson, ed., *Makers of Ancient Strategy: From the Persian Wars to the Fall of Rome* (Princeton: Princeton University Press, 2010), pp. 60–63. Plutarch's comments are in his *Lives of the Noble Grecians and Romans,* translated by John Dryden (New York: Modern Library, no date), pp. 191–93.

3. Victor Davis Hanson, *The Savior Generals: How Five Great Commanders Saved Wars That Were Lost—from Ancient Greece to Iraq* (New York: Bloomsbury Press, 2013), pp. 33–34.

4. Donald Kagan, *Pericles of Athens and the Birth of Democracy* (New York: Free Press, 1991), pp. 4–5.

5. Thucydides, 1:18, p. 14. See also *ibid.,* 1:10, p. 8; and Herodotus, 6:107–8, pp. 450–51.

6. Hanson, *The Savior Generals,* pp. 18–22, 29.

7. An image more often used to describe the positions of France and Great Britain after the battles—both in 1805—of Austerlitz and Trafalgar. For Pericles' characterization of the two strategies, see Thucydides, 1:143, p. 83.

8. Hanson, *The Savior Generals,* pp. 10–12, provides striking quantitative measures of the destruction.

9. Thucydides, 1:21–22. Emphasis added.

10. Kagan, *Pericles,* p. 10. Professor Kagan refers to "Athenians," but I think he won't mind my expanding his scope.

11. Thucydides, 1:89–92, pp. 49–51. See also Plutarch, p. 145.

12. Hanson, *The Savior Generals,* pp. 34–36.

13. The classic life of Pericles is Plutarch's, pp. 182–212, while the best modern biography is Kagan's.

14. Hanson, *The Savior Generals,* p. 18.

15. Hanson, *A War Like No Other,* pp. 38–45. For Pericles' offer, see Thucydides, 2:13, p. 98.

16. Hanson, *A War Like No Other,* pp. 236–39, 246–47; Kagan, *Pericles,* p. 66. See also, for the wider context, John R. Hale, *Lords of the Sea: The Epic Story of the Athenian Navy and the Birth of Democracy* (New York: Penguin, 2009).

17. Plutarch, p. 186.

18. All Pericles quotations in this section are from Thucydides, 2:34–46, pp. 110–18. For the theme of distinctiveness and universality, see Donald Kagan, "Pericles, Thucydides, and the Defense of Empire," in Hanson, *Makers of Ancient Strategy,* p. 31.

19. Kagan, *Pericles,* pp. 49–54, describes how the assembly functioned. See also Cynthia Farrar, "Power to the People," in Kurt A. Raaflaub, Josiah Ober, and Robert W. Wallace, with Paul Cartledge and Cynthia Farrar, *Origins of Democracy in Ancient Greece* (Berkeley: University of California Press, 2007), pp. 184–89.

20. Hanson, *A War Like No Other,* p. 27.

21. For the importance of reassurance as an accompaniment to deterrence, see Michael Howard, *The Causes of Wars,* second edition (Cambridge, Massachusetts: Harvard University Press, 1984), pp. 246–64.

22. Kagan, *Pericles,* pp. 102–5.

23. *Ibid.,* p. 86.

24. Thucydides, 1:24–66, 86–88, pp. 16–37, 48–49. See also J. E. Lendon, *Song of Wrath: The Peloponnesian War Begins* (New York: Basic Books, 2010).

25. The quote is, supposedly, Bismarck's.

26. I base this generalization on Kagan, *Pericles,* p. 192, and Hanson, *A War Like No Other,* pp. 10–12.

27. Thucydides, 1:67–71, pp. 38–41.

28. *Ibid.,* 1:72–79, pp. 41–45.

29. *Ibid.,* 1:79–85, pp. 45–47.

30. *Ibid.,* 1:86–87, p. 48.

31. Kagan, *Pericles,* pp. 206, 214.

32. I've discussed this at greater length in *The Landscape of History: How Historians Map the Past* (New York: Oxford University Press, 2002), pp. 116–18.

33. Thucydides, 1:144, pp. 83–84; Plutarch, p. 199. See also Kagan, *Pericles,* pp. 84, 92, 115–16.

34. Thucydides, 1:77, p. 44.

35. *Ibid.*, 1:140–44, pp. 80–85. I've followed Kagan's analysis of the Megarian decree in his *Pericles,* pp. 206–27.

36. Thucydides, 2:12, p. 97.

37. Plutarch, pp. 194–95; Thucydides, 1:127, p. 70.

38. Kagan, *Pericles,* p. 207.

39. See Shakespeare's *Troilus and Cressida,* act 1, scene 3, lines 112–27.

40. Thucydides, 2:59, p. 123.

41. *Ibid.*, 2:60–64, pp. 123–27.

42. *Ibid.*, 3:82, p. 199.

43. *Ibid.*, 3:2–6, 16–18, 25–26, 35–50, pp. 159–61, 166–67, 171, 175–84. The Mytilenians didn't escape punishment. The Athenians executed the ringleaders of the revolt, pulled down the walls of the city, seized its ships, and expropriated property. This was far less, though, than what Cleon demanded.

44. *Ibid.*, 5:84–116, pp. 350–57.

45. *Ibid.*, 3:82, p. 199.

46. For more on this, see John Lewis Gaddis, "Drawing Lines: The Defensive Perimeter Strategy in East Asia, 1947–1951," in Gaddis, *The Long Peace: Inquiries into the History of the Cold War* (New York: Oxford University Press, 1987), pp. 71–103. Taiwan was not included, because the Chinese Nationalists had fled there. Defending them, the administration feared, would be seen as intervention in the Chinese civil war, which it had hoped to avoid.

47. The casualty figures are from Britannica Online, "Korean War," www.britannica.com.

48. Carl von Clausewitz, *On War,* edited and translated by Michael Howard and Peter Paret (Princeton: Princeton University Press, 1976), p. 471. Emphasis in the original.

49. Plutarch, pp. 204–7; Kagan, *Pericles,* pp. 221–27.

50. Thucydides, 6:6, p. 365.

51. *Ibid.*, 6:9–26, pp. 366–76. There was also a third commander, Lamachus, of whom Thucydides tells us little.

52. *Ibid.*, 7:44, 70–87, pp. 453, 468–78.

53. Hanson, *A War Like No Other,* pp. 205, 217.

54. Henry Kissinger, *White House Years* (Boston: Little, Brown, 1979), p. 1049.

55. See www.archives.gov/research/military/vietnam-war/casualty-statistics.html.

56. For specifics, see Ilya V. Gaiduk, *The Soviet Union and the Vietnam War* (Chicago: Ivan R. Dee, 1996); Qiang Zhai, *China and the Vietnam Wars, 1950–1975* (Chapel Hill: University of North Carolina Press, 2000); and Lien-Hang Nguyen, *Hanoi's Wars: An International History of the War for Peace in Vietnam* (Chapel Hill: University of North Carolina Press, 2012).

57. John Lewis Gaddis, *The Cold War: A New History* (New York: Penguin, 2005), pp. 149–55.

58. Thucydides, 1:140, p. 81; Kennedy remarks to Fort Worth Chamber of Commerce, November 22, 1963, *Public Papers of the Presidents: John F. Kennedy, 1963* (Washington, D.C.: Government Printing Office, 1964), p. 889.

59. To whom I'm grateful for having inspired my *Strategies of Containment: A Critical Appraisal of American National Security Policy During the Cold War,* revised and expanded edition (New York: Oxford University Press, 2005), as well as Yale's long-standing "Studies in Grand Strategy" seminar.

CHAPTER THREE: TEACHERS AND TETHERS

1. Sun Tzu, *The Art of War,* translated by Samuel B. Griffith (New York: Oxford University Press, 1963), pp. 66, 89, 95, 109. I'm indebted to Schuyler Schouten for the marketing analogy.
2. *Hamlet,* act 3, scene 2. Polonius on borrowers and lenders is in act 1, scene 3.
3. *The Art of War,* pp. 63-64, 66, 89, 95, 129. Emphasis added.
4. *Ibid.,* pp. 91-92.
5. I've relied chiefly, for this and the following account of Octavian's upbringing and education, on Anthony Everitt, *Augustus: The Life of Rome's First Emperor* (New York: Random House, 2006), pp. 3-50; and Adrian Goldsworthy, *Augustus: First Emperor of Rome* (New Haven: Yale University Press, 2014), pp. 19-80. Goldsworthy uses Augustus' names as titles for the five sections of his book. The portents are in Suetonius, *The Twelve Caesars,* translated by Robert Graves (New York: Penguin, 2007, first published in 1957), II:94, pp. 94-95.
6. Mary Beard explores the paradox of a republican empire in the first half of her *S.P.Q.R.: A History of Ancient Rome* (New York: Norton, 2015).
7. The most recent account is Barry Strauss, *The Death of Caesar: The Story of History's Most Famous Assassination* (New York: Simon and Schuster, 2015). Plutarch's observation is in his *Lives of the Noble Grecians and Romans,* translated by John Dryden (New York: Modern Library, no date), p. 857.
8. John Williams, *Augustus* (New York: New York Review of Books, 2014; first published in 1971), pp. 21-22. For Caesar's probable intentions for Octavian, see Adrian Goldsworthy, *Caesar: Life of a Colossus* (New Haven: Yale University Press, 2006), pp. 497-98, and Strauss, *The Death of Caesar,* pp. 45-46.
9. At which point, he ceased to use the name Octavian and began to call himself Caesar. To avoid confusion, I've followed the practice of Everitt and most other historians—although not Goldsworthy—and continued to refer to him as Octavian until he himself took the name Augustus.
10. Commentary by Tu Mu, in *The Art of War,* p. 65.
11. The best evidence is Octavian's surprise, apparently genuine, on learning the contents of Caesar's will. Even if Caesar had revealed his intentions, neither he nor Octavian could have anticipated how little time Caesar had left.
12. See Isaiah Berlin's letter to George F. Kennan, February 13, 1951, in Berlin, *Liberty,* edited by Henry Hardy (New York: Oxford University Press, 2007), pp. 341-42.
13. Goldsworthy, *Augustus,* pp. 87-101. For Cicero's shifts, see Anthony Everitt, *Cicero: The Life and Times of Rome's Greatest Politician* (New York: Random House, 2003), pp. 273-96.

14. John Buchan, *Augustus* (Cornwall: Stratus Books, 2003; first published in 1937), p. 32.

15. Goldsworthy, *Augustus*, pp. 105–7.

16. Well described in Plutarch, pp. 1106–7.

17. Everitt, *Augustus*, p. 76. See also, on Octavian's purposefulness, Ronald Syme, *The Roman Revolution* (New York: Oxford University Press, 1939), p. 3.

18. Everitt, *Augustus*, pp. 32, 45, 88–91, 110, 139, 213.

19. Goldsworthy, *Augustus*, pp. 115–25. Antony would later claim that Octavian ran away from the first Mutina battle. [Suetonius, II:10, p. 47.]

20. Syme, *The Roman Revolution*, p. 124.

21. Later immortalized as a cipher by Shakespeare in *Julius Caesar*.

22. The episode anticipates the Treaty of Tilsit, signed by the emperor Napoleon of France and Tsar Alexander I of Russia in the middle of the river Niemen in July 1807, discussed in chapter seven. But they were on a raft, not an island.

23. Everitt, *Cicero*, pp. 313–19. For background on the proscriptions, see Syme, *The Roman Revolution*, pp. 187–201.

24. Goldsworthy, *Augustus*, p. 122.

25. There was a connection. The fortress of Philippi was named for Philip of Macedon, the father of Alexander the Great, who built it in 356 B.C.E. The first *Philippics*, a set of four speeches delivered shortly thereafter by the Greek orator Demosthenes, were directed against Philip. Cicero modeled his fourteen *Philippics* on these.

26. Goldsworthy, *Augustus*, p. 142; Everitt, *Augustus*, pp. 88–94.

27. Appian, *The Civil Wars*, translated by John Carter (New York: Penguin, 1996), V, p. 287. See also Everitt, *Augustus*, pp. 98–99.

28. *Ibid.*, pp. 100–103; also Syme, *The Roman Revolution*, p. 215.

29. Goldsworthy, *Augustus*, pp. 144–47.

30. Suetonius, II:15, p. 49; also Everitt, *Augustus*, pp. 104–5.

31. *Ibid.*, pp. 108–13. Antony also reported to Octavian the disloyalty of the latter's old friend Salvidienus Rufus, who with unclear motives had approached Antony's agents in Gaul. Octavian promptly had him executed. [Appian, *The Civil Wars*, V:65, pp. 312–13.]

32. A point made by Symes, *The Roman Revolution*, p. 114.

33. See, on this point, chapter two.

34. Plutarch, p. 1106.

35. Goldsworthy, *Augustus*, pp. 156–59.

36. The fullest account is in Appian, *The Civil Wars*, V:85–92, pp. 322–26.

37. Everitt, *Augustus*, pp. 129–30.

38. Appian, *The Civil Wars*, V:98–126, pp. 328–42.

39. The Romans' grievance went back to the Parthians' defeat of Marcus Licinius Crassus and his army at the battle of Carrhae in 53, which resulted in the loss of several Roman legions' standards. Julius Caesar had been planning to avenge the humiliation when he was assassinated in 44—this was the mission the young Octavian was training for—and Antony had inherited it after his victory at Philippi two years later.

40. He was also, in the Egyptian manner, his mother's co-monarch Ptolemy XV. Goldsworthy, *Caesar*, pp. 496–97, provides a plausible assessment of the paternity issue.

41. Everitt, *Augustus*, pp. 145–53.

42. Goldsworthy, *Augustus*, pp. 186–88.

43. Plutarch, p. 1142.

44. For an informed suggestion of where the story originated, see Adrian Tronson,
"Vergil, the Augustans, and the Invention of Cleopatra's Suicide—One Asp or
Two?" *Vergilius* 44 (1998), 31–50. I am indebted to Toni Dorfman for this
reference.

45. A point made in Stacy Schiff, *Cleopatra: A Life* (New York: Little, Brown, 2010),
pp. 101, 108, 133.

46. Cassius Dio, *The Roman History: The Reign of Augustus,* translated by Ian Scott-
Kilvert (New York: Penguin, 1987), LI:16, p. 77.

47. For a different view, see Goldsworthy, *Augustus*, p. 207.

48. Robin Lane Fox, *Alexander the Great* (New York: Penguin, 2004; first published in
1973), pp. 369–70, 461–72.

49. *The Art of War,* p. 106. The distinction is most often associated, in the modern
era, with the British strategist B. H. Liddell-Hart, but he has acknowledged Sun
Tzu's anticipation of it. [Foreword, *ibid.,* p. vii.]

50. *The Art of War,* pp. 66–68, 70.

51. For a fictionalization of this principle as applied to writing poems, see Williams,
Augustus, pp. 38–39.

52. *The Georgics of Virgil,* translated by David Ferry (New York: Farrar, Straus and
Giroux, 2005), p. 89.

53. *Ibid.,* p. xix. Wikipedia claims to have counted the hexameters.

54. Buchan, *Augustus*, p. 114. There are more general discussions of Virgil in Everitt,
Augustus, pp. 114–16, and Goldsworthy, *Augustus*, pp. 307–17.

55. Everitt, *Augustus*, pp. 199–211; Goldsworthy, *Augustus*, pp. 217–38.

56. Beard, *S.P.Q.R.*, pp. 354–56, 368–69, 374; also Goldsworthy, *Augustus*, pp.
476–81.

57. *The Aeneid,* translated by Robert Fagles (New York: Viking, 2006), VIII:21–22,
p. 242.

58. *Ibid.,* VI:915, p. 208.

59. Hermann Broch, *The Death of Virgil,* translated by Jean Starr Untermeyer (New
York: Vintage Books, 1995; first published in 1945), pp. 319, 321. My Yale colleague Charles Hill first alerted me to the significance both of the *Georgics* and of
Broch. His commentary on the latter is in Charles Hill, *Grand Strategies: Literature, Statecraft, and World Order* (New Haven: Yale University Press, 2010), pp.
282–85.

60. Beard, *S.P.Q.R.*, pp. 415–16. For two recent accounts of how rules of inheritance
could ruin lives and endanger states, see Geoffrey Parker, *Imprudent King: A New
Life of Philip II* (New Haven: Yale University Press, 2014); and Janice Hadlow, *A
Royal Experiment: The Private Life of King George III* (New York: Henry Holt,
2014).

61. John Williams portrays Julia with particular richness in his novel *Augustus*.

62. Not the one to Mark Antony.

63. Fagles translation, Book VI:993–1021, p. 211. Octavia is said to have fainted when she heard Virgil read these lines.

64. For a graphic illustration of the genealogical complexities Augustus created, see Beard, *S.P.Q.R.*, pp. 382–83.

65. Everitt, *Augustus*, p. 302.

66. Goldsworthy, *Augustus*, p. 453.

67. Cassius Dio, *Augustus*, LVI:30, p. 245; Suetonius, II:99, p. 100.

68. Williams, *Augustus*, p. 228.

69. The term is Greg Woolf's, whose *Rome: An Empire's Story* (New York: Oxford University Press, 2012), provides in its introductory chapters a succinct overview of the Roman legacy.

70. A twist neatly captured in the final line of Williams's *Augustus*, p. 305.

71. See, on this point, Woolf, *Rome*, pp. 216–17; Beard, *S.P.Q.R.*, pp. 412–13.

CHAPTER FOUR: SOULS AND STATES

1. George Kennan, *Tent-Life in Siberia and Adventures Among the Koraks and Other Tribes in Kamtchatka and Northern Asia* (New York: G. P. Putnam and Sons, 1870), pp. 208–12. For more on Kennan, see Frederick F. Travis, *George Kennan and the American-Russian Relationship, 1865–1924* (Athens: Ohio University Press, 1990).

2. See Greg Woolf, *Rome: An Empire's Story* (New York: Oxford University Press, 2012), pp. 113–26; and Mary Beard, *S.P.Q.R.: A History of Ancient Rome* (New York: Norton, 2015), pp. 428–34.

3. The Jews were by no means alone in their monotheism, but its consequences, for them, Christians, and Muslims, shaped subsequent history to a greater extent than in any other faith. For a useful introduction, see Jonathan Kirsch, *God Against the Gods: The History of the War Between Monotheism and Polytheism* (New York: Penguin, 2005).

4. Brilliantly documented in Jack Miles, *God: A Biography* (New York: Knopf, 1995).

5. Edward Gibbon, *The Decline and Fall of the Roman Empire* (New York: Modern Library, 1977), I, pp. 382–83, 386.

6. *Ibid.*, p. 383.

7. Matthew 22:21.

8. St. Augustine, *Confessions*, translated by R. S. Pine-Coffin (New York: Penguin, 1961), pp. 28, 32–33, 39–41. The best biography is still Peter Brown's classic *Augustine of Hippo: A Biography*, revised edition (Berkeley: University of California Press, 2000; first published in 1967).

9. Augustine, *Confessions*, pp. 45–53.

10. For a recent (and controversial) answer, see Robin Lane Fox, *Augustine: Conversions to Confessions* (New York: Basic Books, 2015), especially pp. 522–39.

11. Augustine, *Confessions*, p. 36.

12. Brown, *Augustine of Hippo*, pp. 431–37.

13. *Ibid.*, pp. 131–33.

14. I owe this point to David Brooks, *The Road to Character* (New York: Random House, 2015), p. 212.

15. I've relied chiefly, as a guide, on G. R. Evans's introduction to St. Augustine, *Concerning the City of God Against the Pagans,* translated by Henry Bettenson (New York: Penguin, 2003), pp. ix–lvii, but also on notes prepared by Michael Gaddis, shared with me in a valiant effort to explain *City.*

16. See John Mark Mattox, *Saint Augustine and the Theory of Just War* (New York: Continuum, 2006), pp. 4–6; also David D. Corey and J. Daryl Charles, *The Just War Tradition: An Introduction* (Wilmington, Delaware: ISI Books, 2012), p. 53.

17. *Ibid.,* pp. 56–57.

18. Such is the argument of Douglas Boin's *Coming Out Christian in the Roman World: How the Followers of Jesus Made a Place in Caesar's Empire* (New York: Bloomsbury, 2015), but Gibbon in a backhanded way anticipated it by suggesting complacency, on the part of Rome's inattentive emperors, about Christianity's spread.

19. A kind of order exists even among thugs, as Augustine knew from his adolescent experience, and as viewers of *The Sopranos, The Wire,* and *Breaking Bad* will have reason to understand.

20. With the exception of the emperor Julian's failed attempt to restore the old gods during his brief reign, 361–63.

21. Corey and Charles, *The Just War Tradition,* p. 57.

22. Brown, *Augustine of Hippo,* pp. 218–21. Although Brown later qualified this judgment in the light of new evidence, together with the admission that in the 1960s, when he was writing his first edition, authority figures tended especially to offend younger scholars. [*Ibid.,* p. 446.]

23. See, for examples, Mattox, *Augustine and the Theory of Just War,* pp. 48–49.

24. *Ibid.,* p. 171.

25. As Homer and Virgil, the best ancient guides to the Underworld, make poignantly clear.

26. Corey and Charles survey the process in *The Just War Tradition,* chapters 4 through 9.

27. For an appreciation, see Brown, *Augustine of Hippo,* pp. 491–93.

28. Lane Fox, *Augustine,* pp. 2–3.

29. See James Turner Johnson, *Just War Tradition and the Restraint of War: A Moral and Historical Inquiry* (Princeton: Princeton University Press, 2014; first published in 1981), especially pp. 121–73.

30. I'm extending here, beyond her approval, I fear, a point made by G. R. Evans in her introduction to the *City of God,* p. xlvii.

31. Michael Gaddis, *There Is No Crime for Those Who Have Christ: Religious Violence in the Christian Roman Empire* (Berkeley: University of California Press, 2005), especially pp. 131–50.

32. The unforgettable antihero of Voltaire's *Candide,* who saw everything, even the great Lisbon earthquake of 1755, as for the best. For Augustine's rationalizations, tracked with greater precision than I'm able to do here, see Mattox, *Augustine and the Theory of Just War,* pp. 32–36, 56–59, 94–95, 110–14, 126–31.

33. Sebastian de Grazia, *Machiavelli in Hell* (New York: Random House, 1989), pp. 318–40.

34. *The Discourses on the First Ten Books of Titus Livius*, translated by Leslie J. Walker, S.J., with revisions by Brian Richardson (New York: Penguin, 1970), p. 97. See also De Grazia, *Machiavelli in Hell*, p. 21. The best recent biography is Miles J. Unger, *Machiavelli: A Biography* (New York: Simon and Schuster, 2011).

35. *The Prince*, translated by Harvey C. Mansfield, second edition (Chicago: University of Chicago Press, 1998), p. 103. See also De Grazia, *Machiavelli in Hell*, pp. 58–70.

36. Brown, *Augustine of Hippo*, pp. 400–410, thoroughly explains how.

37. Milan Kundera, *The Unbearable Lightness of Being*, translated by Michael Henry Heim (New York: Harper and Row, 1984).

38. *The Prince*, p. 98. See also Unger, *Machiavelli*, pp. 218–19.

39. Machiavelli in 1504 went so far as to support a scheme, conceived by Leonardo da Vinci, to isolate the rival city of Pisa by diverting the Arno. Fortune defeated the effort, though, through a combination of miscalculated topography, unexpected rainfall, and sabotage by clever Pisans. This was one of several bad breaks that brought an end to Machiavelli's official career. The details are in Unger, *Machiavelli*, pp. 143–46.

40. Machiavelli's careful translator explains the linguistic nonequivalencies in *The Prince*, p. xxv. For a fuller discussion of the term, see Philip Bobbitt, *The Garments of Court and Palace: Machiavelli and the World That He Made* (New York: Grove Press, 2013), pp. 76–77.

41. *The Prince*, p. 22. See also Unger, *Machiavelli*, pp. 33–34.

42. *Ibid.*, p. 273.

43. De Grazia, *Machiavelli in Hell*, p. 64, suggests that Machiavelli read Augustine, but an electronic search turns up no mention of him in *The Prince*, *The Discourses*, or Machiavelli's less well-known *The Art of War*. There's a single glancing reference—not to Augustine but to a monk of his order—in Machiavelli's *History of Florence and Italy*. Nevertheless, there are parallels, perhaps best set forth in Paul R. Wright, "Machiavelli's *City of God*: Civil Humanism and Augustinian Terror," in John Doody, Kevin L. Hughes, and Kim Paffenroth, eds., *Augustine and Politics* (Lanham, Maryland: Lexington Books, 2005), pp. 297–336.

44. *The Prince*, pp. 3–4; Unger, *Machiavelli*, pp. 204–7.

45. Bobbitt, *The Garments of Court and Palace*, p. 5.

46. For the book's reception and reputation, see *ibid.*, pp. 8–16, and Unger, *Machiavelli*, pp. 342–47. Jonathan Haslam tracks Machiavelli's influence on political science in *No Virtue Like Necessity: Realist Thought in International Relations Since Machiavelli* (New Haven: Yale University Press, 2002). The only book that rivals *The Prince* in unsettling my students is the second volume of Robert Caro's Lyndon B. Johnson biography, which argues that LBJ could never have given the 1965 "We Shall Overcome" speech had he not stolen the 1948 Texas Democratic senatorial primary.

47. *The Prince*, pp. 29–33. See also Unger, *Machiavelli*, pp. 129–30, who notes that his subject probably witnessed the spectacle. Remirro's fate curiously parallels that of Pythias' unfortunate son at the hands of Xerxes, as described in Herodotus and cited in chapter one.

48. Quoted in Gaddis, *There Is No Crime for Those Who Have Christ*, p. 138.

49. The phrase became notorious during the Vietnam War after the appearance of a brief news story, "Major Describes Move," in the *New York Times* on February 8, 1968. For the idea as applied to nuclear weapons in the Cold War, see Campbell Craig, *Destroying the Village: Eisenhower and Thermonuclear War* (New York: Columbia University Press, 1998).

50. *The Prince*, pp. 22, 35.

51. The quotes are from Mattox, *Augustine and the Theory of Just War*, p. 60, and *The Prince*, p. 61. They're worth comparing with Sun Tzu, *The Art of War*, translated by Samuel B. Griffith (New York: Oxford University Press, 1963), p. 77: "[T]o win one hundred victories" is not as skillful as "[t]o subdue the enemy without fighting."

52. *The Prince*, p. 61.

53. Harvey C. Mansfield, in his introduction, *ibid.*, p. xi. Italics added.

54. Charles Dickens, *A Tale of Two Cities* (New York: New American Library, 1960), p. 367.

55. *The Prince*, p. 45.

56. *Ibid.*, p. 4.

57. *Ibid.*, p. 20.

58. *Ibid.*, p. 39.

59. *Ibid.*, pp. 38, 40–41, 61, 66–67.

60. Unger, *Machiavelli*, p. 54; Bobbitt, *The Garments of Court and Palace*, p. 80.

61. Unger, *Machiavelli*, pp. 132, 238, 255–56.

62. *Ibid.*, pp. 261–62.

63. The best recent account, unsurprisingly, is Henry Kissinger, *World Order* (New York: Penguin, 2014), pp. 11–95, 283–86.

64. *The Discourses*, p. 275.

65. See, on these points, Unger, *Machiavelli*, pp. 266–68; Kissinger, *World Order*, pp. 256–69; and Bobbitt, *The Garments of State and Palace*, pp. 155–64, who usefully reminds us that Machiavelli assumed the permanence of no international order, and that neither should we.

66. Isaiah Berlin, "The Originality of Machiavelli," in Berlin, *The Proper Study of Mankind: An Anthology of Essays*, edited by Henry Hardy and Roger Hausheer (New York: Farrar, Straus and Giroux, 1998), pp. 269–325.

67. *Ibid.*, p. 279.

68. *The Prince*, pp. 4, 10.

69. Thomas Hobbes, *Leviathan*, edited by C. B. Macpherson (New York: Penguin, 1985; first published in 1651), p. 186.

70. Augustine, *Confessions*, p. 28.

71. Berlin, "The Originality of Machiavelli," pp. 286–91.

72. *Ibid.*, pp. 296–97, 299.

73. *Ibid.*, pp. 312–13.

74. *Ibid.*, p. 310

75. *Ibid.*, pp. 310-11. See also De Grazia, *Machiavelli in Hell*, p. 311; and Gaddis, *There Is No Crime for Those Who Have Christ*, p. 149.

76. Berlin, "The Originality of Machiavelli," p. 311. Italics added. Berlin attributes the insight to Sheldon S. Wolin.

77. "The Pursuit of the Ideal," in Berlin, *The Proper Study of Mankind,* pp. 9–11.

78. Berlin, "The Originality of Machiavelli," pp. 324–25.

CHAPTER FIVE: PRINCES AS PIVOTS

1. I've used Dictionary.com.

2. As argued, most famously, by Thomas Hobbes in *Leviathan,* first published in 1651.

3. Virginia Woolf, *Orlando: A Biography* (New York: Harcourt Brace, 1956; first published in 1928), p. 22.

4. Quoted in Geoffrey Parker, *Imprudent King: A New Life of Philip II* (New Haven: Yale University Press, 2014), p. 363.

5. See Anne Somerset, *Elizabeth I* (New York: Random House, 2003; first published in 1991), p. 572.

6. Parker, *Imprudent King,* p. 366.

7. For a classic account, see Garrett Mattingly, *The Armada* (New York: Houghton Mifflin, 1959), pp. 11–12. Machiavelli was himself an occasional poet and a playwright. See Sebastian de Grazia, *Machiavelli in Hell* (New York: Random House, 1989), pp. 360–66.

8. *Elizabeth I: Collected Works,* edited by Leah S. Marcus, Janet Mueller, and Mary Beth Rose (Chicago: University of Chicago Press, 2000), p. 54.

9. Parker, *Imprudent King,* p. 29; Miles J. Unger, *Machiavelli: A Biography* (New York: Simon and Schuster, 2011), pp. 343–44; and, for Elizabeth's linguistic proficiency, Somerset, *Elizabeth I,* pp. 11–12.

10. Robert Hutchinson, *The Spanish Armada* (New York: St. Martin's, 2013), p. xix. Henry VIII died in 1547, to be succeeded by his nine-year-old son, Edward VI, who in turn died in 1553.

11. Alison Weir, *The Life of Elizabeth I* (New York: Random House, 2008; first published in 1998), p. 11; A. N. Wilson, *The Elizabethans* (New York: Farrar, Straus and Giroux, 2011), pp. 7–14, 32–33.

12. The imperial title and its central European possessions went to Charles's brother Ferdinand, thereby splitting the Hapsburg empire into Austrian and Spanish branches, an early acknowledgment of what Paul Kennedy has called "imperial overstretch." See his *The Rise and Fall of the Great Powers: Economic Change and Military Conflict from 1500 to 2000* (New York: Random House, 1987), pp. 48–49.

13. Parker, *Imprudent King,* pp. 4–5, 23.

14. *Ibid.,* p. 276. See also Parker's second set of plates.

15. Geoffrey Parker, *The Grand Strategy of Philip II* (New Haven: Yale University Press, 1998), p. 72, contrasts Elizabeth's attitude toward delegation with that of Philip.

16. Mattingly, *The Armada,* p. 24.

17. Parker, *Imprudent King,* pp. xv, 61–64, 85 103–6; also Parker, *The Grand Strategy of Philip II,* pp. 47–75; and Robert Goodwin, *Spain: The Center of the World, 1519–1682* (New York: Bloomsbury, 2015), pp. 129–41.

18. Parker, *Imprudent King,* pp. 43–49, 51–58. For an assessment of England's strengths and weaknesses at the time of Elizabeth's accession, see Kennedy, *The Rise and Fall of the Great Powers,* pp. 60–61.

19. Somerset, *Elizabeth I,* pp. 42–43.

20. *Ibid.*, pp. 311–12.

21. *Ibid.*, pp. 48–51.

22. *Ibid.*, p. 56.

23. Popes and Holy Roman emperors were elected, but even there blood ties were influential.

24. Weir, *The Life of Elizabeth I*, p. 25; Somerset, *Elizabeth I*, pp. 91–92.

25. *Ibid.*, pp. 50–51.

26. Parker, *Imprudent King*, pp. 121–25.

27. For a list, see Arthur Salusbury MacNalty, *Elizabeth Tudor: The Lonely Queen* (London: Johnson Publications, 1954), p. 260.

28. Weir, *The Life of Elizabeth I*, pp. 47–48.

29. Mattingly, *The Armada*, p. 24.

30. Parker, *The Grand Strategy of Philip II*, p. 151; Parker, *Imprudent King*, p. 58.

31. *Ibid.*, p. 364. The Hapsburgs also, through their intermarriages, debilitatingly depleted their gene pool. See *ibid.*, pp. 180–81.

32. *Ibid.*, p. 2.

33. For a sympathetic assessment, see Hugh Thomas, *World Without End: Spain, Philip II, and the First Global Empire* (New York: Random House, 2014), pp. 285–99.

34. Mauricio Drelichman and Hans-Joachim Voth, *Lending to the Borrower from Hell: Debt, Taxes, and Default in the Age of Philip II* (Princeton: Princeton University Press, 2014). For the more conventional argument on Philip's finances, see Kennedy, *The Rise and Fall of the Great Powers*, pp. 46–47.

35. Parker, *Imprudent King*, pp. 126, 129, 256–57.

36. Thomas, *World Without End*, p. 17.

37. Weir, *The Life of Elizabeth I*, pp. 11, 26. See also Somerset, *Elizabeth I*, pp. 58–59.

38. I have based this paragraph on Weir, *The Life of Elizabeth I*, pp. 17–18, and on Mattingly, *The Armada*, p. 23. The "heart and stomach" quotation is in Elizabeth I's *Collected Works*, p. 326.

39. James Anthony Froude, *History of England from the Fall of Wolsey to the Defeat of the Spanish Armada* (London: Longmans, Green, 1870), XII, p. 558. See also J. B. Black, *The Reign of Elizabeth, 1558–1603* (Oxford: Oxford University Press, 1959), p. 23.

40. Weir, *The Life of Elizabeth I*, p. 30. Somerset, *Elizabeth I*, pp. 72–88, provides a thorough analysis of Elizabeth's religious policies.

41. Somerset, *Elizabeth I*, pp. 280–82; Kennedy, *The Rise and Fall of the Great Powers*, pp. 60–61. For a thorough discussion of Elizabethan finance, see William Robert Smith, *The Constitution and Finance of the English, Scottish and Irish Joint-Stock Companies to 1720* (Cambridge: Cambridge University Press, 1911), pp. 493–99.

42. Somerset, *Elizabeth I*, pp. 70–71.

43. For a rousing account, see A. N. Wilson's chapter on Sir Francis Drake in *The Elizabethans*, pp. 173–84.

44. Thought, by a few fools even now, to have written the plays of William Shakespeare.

45. Weir, *The Life of Elizabeth I*, p. 257. The story first appeared in John Aubrey, *Brief Lives*, compiled between 1669 and 1696 (Oxford: Clarendon Press, 1898), p. 305.

46. Niccolò Machiavelli, *The Prince,* translated by Harvey C. Mansfield, second edition (Chicago: University of Chicago Press, 1998), p. 69. For Machiavelli's views on women, see *ibid.,* p. 101; but also De Grazia, *Machiavelli in Hell,* pp. 229–32.

47. Parker, *Imprudent King,* p. 295.

48. *Antony and Cleopatra,* act 2, scene 2.

49. De Grazia, *Machiavelli in Hell,* pp. 102–3.

50. N. A. M. Rodger, *The Safeguard of the Sea: A Naval History of Britain, 660–1649* (New York: HarperCollins, 1998), pp. 238–48.

51. I've followed, in these paragraphs, Parker, *The Grand Strategy of Philip II,* pp. 153–57.

52. *Ibid.,* pp. 158–59. See also Christopher Tyerman, *God's War: A New History of the Crusades* (Cambridge, Massachusetts: Harvard University Press, 2006), pp. 902–3; and, on the evolution of Augustinian doctrine, James Turner Johnson, *Just War Tradition and the Restraint of War: A Moral and Historical Inquiry* (Princeton: Princeton University Press, 1981), pp. 167–69.

53. Parker, *The Grand Strategy of Philip II,* pp. 157–62.

54. Somerset, *Elizabeth I,* p. 246.

55. *Ibid.,* pp. 237–38.

56. *Ibid.,* pp. 249–62; Parker, *The Grand Strategy of Philip II,* pp. 160–63.

57. Examples also include Julius Caesar, Caesar Augustus, Napoleon, the Duke of Wellington, Lincoln, and, as it happens, Philip II. See Parker, *Imprudent King,* pp. 293–94.

58. Somerset, *Elizabeth I,* pp. 405–8; Parker, *Imprudent King,* pp. 206–7. The quotation is from Stephen Alford, *The Watchers: A Secret History of the Reign of Elizabeth I* (New York: Bloomsbury, 2012), p. xvii. See also John Cooper, *The Queen's Agent: Sir Francis Walsingham and the Rise of Espionage in Elizabethan England* (New York: Pegasus, 2012).

59. John Guy, *Elizabeth: The Forgotten Years* (New York: Viking, 2016), particularly emphasizes this point.

60. Lisa Hilton, *Elizabeth: Renaissance Prince* (New York: Houghton Mifflin Harcourt, 2015), p. 224.

61. Mattingly, *The Armada,* pp. 75–76. See also Felipe Fernández-Armesto, *Pathfinders: A Global History of Exploration* (New York: Norton, 2006), pp. 129–38.

62. Rodger, *The Safeguard of the Sea,* pp. 243–46.

63. *Ibid.,* pp. 248–50.

64. Somerset, *Elizabeth I,* pp. 405–11.

65. *Ibid.,* pp. 47–48, 389–93, 396–405.

66. *Ibid.,* pp. 424–42.

67. Parker, *The Grand Strategy of Philip II,* pp. 163–69, 179. The quotation is on p. 166.

68. *Ibid.,* pp. 179–80; Parker, *Imprudent King,* pp. 281, 305–7. For Philip's non-reaction to Mary's death, see Mattingly, *The Armada,* pp. 69–81.

69. Parker, *Imprudent King,* pp. 307–19.

70. Hutchinson, *The Spanish Armada,* p. 52.

71. This, and the dates that follow, are New Style, the calendar employed in Europe at the time. The English calendar ran ten days behind in Elizabeth's time.

72. Hutchinson, *The Spanish Armada,* p. 202; Parker, *The Grand Strategy of Philip II,* pp. 269–70.

73. Philip sent two smaller armadas against England in 1596 and 1597, but storms forced both back before they'd even entered from the Channel.

74. Parker, *The Grand Strategy of Philip II,* pp. 270–71. See also Parker, *Imprudent King,* pp. 324, 367–68.

75. *Ibid.,* p. 369.

76. Parker, *The Grand Strategy of Philip II,* p. 283. See also Barbara Farnham, ed., *Avoiding Losses/Taking Risks: Prospect Theory and International Conflict* (Ann Arbor: University of Michigan Press, 1995).

77. Parker, *The Grand Strategy of Philip II,* pp. 275–76.

78. *Ibid.,* p. 276, and *Imprudent King,* p. 369.

79. Speech of November 30, 1601, in Elizabeth I's *Collected Works,* p. 339.

80. Wilson, *The Elizabethans,* p. 371.

81. *Ibid.,* pp. 366–68. The definition comes, again, from Dictionary.com.

82. Robert B. Strassler, ed., *The Landmark Thucydides: A Comprehensive Guide to the Peloponnesian War,* a revised version of the Richard Crawley translation (New York: Simon and Schuster, 1996), 3:82.

83. Keith Roberts, *Pavane* (Baltimore: Old Earth Books, 2011; first published in 1968), pp. 11–12. Geoffrey Parker precedes me in using this passage to conclude his counterfactual account of the Armada's "success" in "The Repulse of the English Fireships," in Robert Cowley, ed., *What If? The World's Foremost Military Historians Imagine What Might Have Been* (New York: Berkley Books, 1999), pp. 149–50.

84. Roberts, *Pavane,* p. 147.

85. *Ibid.,* pp. 151, 238–39.

86. I'm indebted to my colleague Paul Kennedy for pointing this out.

CHAPTER SIX: NEW WORLDS

1. Keith Roberts, *Pavane* (Baltimore: Old Earth Books, 2011; first published in 1968), p. 11.

2. I echo here the title of Michel Faber's novel on faith and extraterrestrial exploration, *The Book of Strange New Things* (New York: Hogarth, 2014). Felipe Fernández-Armesto's *Pathfinders: A Global History of Exploration* (New York: Norton, 2006) places the terrestrial process in a broad comparative context.

3. Jay Sexton, *The Monroe Doctrine: Empire and Nation in Nineteenth-Century America* (New York: Hill and Wang, 2011), pp. 3–8.

4. Geoffrey Parker, "The Repulse of the English Fireships," in Robert Cowley, ed., *What If? The World's Foremost Military Historians Imagine What Might Have Been* (New York: Berkley Books, 1999), pp. 141–42.

5. J. Hamel, *Early English Voyages to Northern Russia* (London: Richard Bentley, 1857), p. 5.

6. Fernández-Armesto, *Pathfinders,* pp. 218–22. See also, for Elizabeth's curiosity, A. N. Wilson, *The Elizabethans* (New York: Farrar, Straus and Giroux, 2011), pp.

183–84; and, for cooling, Geoffrey Parker, *Global Crisis: War, Climate Change, and Catastrophe in the Seventeenth Century* (New Haven: Yale University Press, 2013).

7. J. H. Elliott, *Empires of the Atlantic World: Britain and Spain in America, 1492–1830* (New Haven: Yale University Press, 2006), pp. 23–28.

8. *Ibid.*, p. 177.

9. In this way resembling monoculture in forestry. See James C. Scott, *Seeing Like a State: How Certain Schemes to Improve the Human Condition Have Failed* (New Haven: Yale University Press, 1998), pp. 11–22.

10. Elliott, *Empires of the Atlantic World*, p. 134. See also Nick Bunker, *An Empire on the Edge: How Britain Came to Fight America* (New York: Knopf, 2014), pp. 13–14.

11. I've adapted this paragraph from *The Landscape of History*, p. 87, which in turn draws on M. Mitchell Waldrop, *Complexity: The Emerging Science at the Edge of Order and Chaos* (New York: Viking, 1992), pp. 292–94.

12. Anne Somerset, *Elizabeth I* (New York: Random House, 1991), pp. 188–91.

13. See Robert Tombs, *The English and Their History* (New York: Knopf, 2015), pp. 224–45.

14. Elliott, *Empires of the Atlantic World*, p. 177. See also Tim Harris, *Restoration: Charles II and His Kingdoms, 1660–1685* (New York: Allen Lane, 2005), especially pp. 46–47.

15. The phrase is Daniel Defoe's, quoted in Tombs, *The English and Their History*, p. 252.

16. Elliott, *Empires of the Atlantic World*, pp. 150–52; also Steve Pincus, *1688: The First Modern Revolution* (New Haven: Yale University Press, 2009), pp. 316–22, 475.

17. John Locke, *Second Treatise of Government*, 1690, section 149.

18. Tombs, *The English and Their History*, p. 263.

19. "Speech on Conciliation with America," in *The Writings and Speeches of Edmund Burke*, III, edited by W. M. Elofson (Oxford: Clarendon Press, 1996), pp. 118, 124. David Bromwich provides context and analysis in *The Intellectual Life of Edmund Burke: From the Sublime and Beautiful to American Independence* (Cambridge, Massachusetts: Harvard University Press, 2014), pp. 228–61.

20. Gabriel Johnson to Lord Wilmington, February 10, 1737, quoted in James A. Henretta, *"Salutary Neglect": Colonial Administration Under the Duke of Newcastle* (Princeton: Princeton University Press, 1972), p. 324.

21. "Observations Concerning the Increase of Mankind," 1751, published in 1755, *The Papers of Benjamin Franklin*, Digital Edition, IV, 225–34. See also Dennis Hodgson, "Benjamin Franklin on Population: From Policy to Theory," *Population and Development Review* 17 (December 1991), 639–61.

22. The details are in Ron Chernow, *Washington: A Life* (New York: Penguin, 2010), pp. 78–116.

23. Bunker, *An Empire on the Edge*, pp. 17–18; Tombs, *The English and Their History*, p. 348. See also Colin G. Calloway, *The Scratch of a Pen: 1763 and the Transformation of North America* (New York: Oxford University Press, 2006), pp. 11–12.

24. A point made by Bromwich, *The Intellectual Life of Edmund Burke*, pp. 190–91.

25. Speech to Parliament, May 13, 1767, in *Burke Writings and Speeches*, II, edited by Paul Langford (Oxford: Clarendon Press, 1981), p. 59.
26. Speech to Parliament, April 19, 1769, in *ibid.*, p. 231.
27. Speech to Parliament, March 22, 1775, in *ibid.*, III, pp. 157, 165.
28. Bromwich, *The Intellectual Life of Edmund Burke*, p. 193.
29. See chapter two.
30. Thomas Paine, *Common Sense* (Wisehouse Classics, 2015), p. 21. See also Trevor Colbourn, *The Lamp of Experience: Whig History and the Intellectual Origins of the American Revolution* (Indianapolis: Liberty Fund, 1998; originally published in 1965), pp. 26, 237–43; and Bernard Bailyn, "1776: A Year of Challenge—a World Transformed," *The Journal of Law and Economics* 19 (October 1976), especially pp. 437–41.
31. Paine, *Common Sense*, pp. 13–14, 23.
32. *Ibid.*, pp. 19, 23–24.
33. *Ibid.*, pp. 25–26.
34. For Paine's impact, see Joseph J. Ellis, *American Creation: Triumphs and Tragedies at the Founding of the Republic* (New York: Random House, 2007), pp. 41–44; John Ferling, *Whirlwind: The American Revolution and the War That Won It* (New York: Bloomsbury, 2015), pp. 141–43; and the chapter on Paine in Sophia Rosenfeld, *Common Sense: A Political History* (Cambridge, Massachusetts: Harvard University Press, 2011).
35. National Archives and Records Administration transcription of the Declaration of Independence, available at: www.archives.gov/exhibits/charters. Emphases added.
36. Joseph J. Ellis, *American Sphinx: The Character of Thomas Jefferson* (New York: Random House, 1996), pp. 11, 27–28.
37. The phrase "clearer than truth" is Dean Acheson's, from his *Present at the Creation: My Years in the State Department* (New York: Norton, 1969), p. 375.
38. Ferling, *Whirlwind*, p. 164.
39. Paine, *Common Sense*, p. 39.
40. John Adams to Abigail Adams, July 3, 1776, Adams Family Papers: An Electronic Archive, Massachusetts Historical Society: www.masshist.org/digitaladams/. Adams mistakenly believed that the celebrations would commemorate the signing on July 2, not the approval by the Continental Congress on July 4.
41. Paine, *Common Sense*, p. 21; Benjamin Franklin to Joseph Priestley, October 3, 1775, *The Papers of Benjamin Franklin*, Digital Edition, XXII, 217–18. See also Hodgson, "Benjamin Franklin on Population," pp. 653–54.
42. George Washington to John Adams, September 25, 1798, quoted in Chernow, *Washington*, p. 208. See also Ellis, *American Creation*, pp. 4–5.
43. Eliga H. Gould, *Among the Powers of the Earth: The American Revolution and the Making of a New World Empire* (Cambridge, Massachusetts: Harvard University Press, 2012), pp. 10, 142.
44. Quoted in *ibid.*, p. 127. See also Ferling, *Whirlwind*, pp. 235–38, 320–21.
45. George C. Herring, *From Colony to Superpower: U.S. Foreign Relations Since 1776* (New York: Oxford University Press, 2008), pp. 26–34.

46. See Gordon S. Wood, *The Creation of the American Republic, 1776-1787* (Chapel Hill: University of North Carolina Press, 1998; first published in 1969), p. ix.

47. Here I respectfully dissent from Ellis, *American Creation*, p. 18, who dissents from himself, I think, on p. 9.

48. Wood points out the parallel in *Empire of Liberty: A History of the Early Republic, 1787-1815* (New York: Oxford University Press, 2006), p. 54.

49. Wood, *The Creation of the American Republic*, p. 16.

50. Quoted in *ibid.*, p. 395. I have followed, in these paragraphs, Wood's analysis in his chapter ten, but see also his summary in *Empire of Liberty*, pp. 14-20.

51. Quoted in Gould, *Among the Powers of the Earth*, p. 128.

52. Travel times from the Mississippi to the East Coast could, in this pre-railroad era, approach those across the Atlantic before there were steamships.

53. *Thoughts upon the Political Situation of the United States of America in Which That of Massachusetts Is More Particularly Considered*, attributed to Jonathan Jackson (Worcester, Massachusetts, 1788), pp. 45-46, quoted in Gould, *Among the Powers of the Earth*, p. 133.

54. For the pyramid, see David O. Stewart, *Madison's Gift: Five Partnerships That Built America* (New York: Simon and Schuster, 2015), pp. 18-25.

55. Chernow, *Washington*, pp. 313, 356, 518, 607-10. British repression after the Boston "tea party," an earlier Massachusetts tax protest, had pushed Washington into rebellion [*ibid.*, pp. 198-201] but Shays' Rebellion put the shoe on the other foot.

56. Washington in this sense, but few others, anticipated Woody Allen.

57. See www.comparativeconstitutionsproject.org/chronology/, based in turn on Zachary Elkins, Tom Ginsburg, and James Melton, *The Endurance of National Constitutions* (New York: Cambridge University Press, 2009).

58. The Constitution, without amendments, comes to about 4,500 words. *The Federalist* contains some 170,000.

59. Chernow, *Hamilton*, pp. 261-69.

60. James Boswell, *Life of Johnson*, edited by R. W. Chapman (New York: Oxford University Press, 1998; first published in 1791), p. 849.

61. "We must, indeed, all hang together, or most assuredly we shall all hang separately." [Quoted, without a source, in Jared Sparks, *The Works of Benjamin Franklin* (Boston: Hilliard Gray, 1840), I, p. 408.]

62. *The Federalist*, Modern Library College Edition (New York: Random House, no date), *#1*, pp. 3-4. Emphases added.

63. See Lynne Cheney, *James Madison: A Life Reconsidered* (New York: Penguin, 2014), pp. 2-8.

64. *Federalist #10*, pp. 53-58. Emphases in the original.

65. There are only three direct references to Machiavelli in the online edition of Madison's papers, none substantive. The link is: www.founders.archives.gov/about/Madison.

66. *The Discourses on the First Ten Books of Titus Livius*, translated by Leslie J. Walker, S.J., with revisions by Brian Richardson (New York: Penguin, 1970), p. 275; also chapter four. For a thorough recent discussion, see Alissa M. Ardito, *Machiavelli*

and the Modern State: The Prince, the Discourses on Livy, *and the Extended Territorial Republic* (New York: Cambridge University Press, 2015).

67. *Federalist #10,* pp. 60–61. For Burke's "inconveniences," see his speech to Parliament of March 22, 1775, discussed above.

68. For a similar argument about the Constitution, see Daniel M. Braun, "Constitutional Fracticality: Structure and Coherence in the Nation's Supreme Law," *Saint Louis University Law Journal* 32 (2013), 389–410, although the Roman analogy is my own.

69. Akhil Reed Amar succinctly explains why in *America's Constitution: A Biography* (New York: Random House, 2005), pp. 19–21.

70. In its most recent official edition of the Constitution, the Government Printing Office, normally scrupulous in its neutrality, calls the exclusion a "strained attempt" that "scarcely hid the regional divisions that would remain unresolved under the terms of union agreed to in 1787." ["Historical Note," *The Constitution of the United States of America, as Amended* (Washington, D.C.: Government Printing Office, 2007), p. vi.] Madison may have influenced the editors, but he isn't referenced.

71. *Federalist #42, #54,* pp. 272–73, 358.

72. The choice is succinctly stated in Ellis, *American Creation,* pp. 18–19.

73. Hamilton's argument is in *Federalist #11,* p. 65, which, interestingly, immediately follows Madison's better-known *#10.* For Hamilton on slavery, see Chernow, *Hamilton,* pp. 210–16.

74. Ellis, *American Sphinx,* pp. 154–55.

75. Thomas Jefferson to John B. Colvin, September 20, 1810, in the Founders Online edition of the Jefferson papers at: founders.archives.gov. The territory acquired ran from the Mississippi to Texas in the south, and to the intersection of the Rocky Mountains and the 49th parallel in the north.

76. John Quincy Adams to Abigail Adams, June 30, 1811, quoted in Samuel Flagg Bemis, *John Quincy Adams and the Foundations of American Foreign Policy* (New York: Knopf, 1949), p. 182.

77. Elliott chronicles the process in his *Empires of the Atlantic World,* pp. 369–402.

78. John Quincy Adams to George W. Erving, U.S. minister in Madrid, November 28, 1818, quoted in Bemis, *John Quincy Adams,* p. 327. See also Charles N. Edel, *Nation Builder: John Quincy Adams and the Grand Strategy of the Republic* (Cambridge, Massachusetts: Harvard University Press, 2014), pp. 138–54.

79. Thoroughly covered in William Earl Weeks, *John Quincy Adams and American Global Empire* (Lexington: University Press of Kentucky, 1992), with full attention to how negotiation of the "Transcontinental Treaty" intersected with the earlier Florida controversy.

80. Monroe's message was the equivalent of what would later become the presidential State of the Union address, but in the nineteenth century they weren't given in person.

81. Sexton, *The Monroe Doctrine,* pp. 49–50.

82. *Federalist #11,* p. 65.

83. The quotations are from Adams's diary, March 3 and November 29, 1820, quoted in Edel, *Nation Builder,* pp. 157–59. Edel analyzes Adams's dilemma in terms of Isaiah Berlin's irreconcilable incompatibilities, discussed in chapter four.

84. Charles H. Sherrill, "The Monroe Doctrine and the Canning Myth," *The Annals of the American Academy of Political and Social Science* 94 (July 1914), 96–97. See also Wendy Hinde, *George Canning* (Oxford: Basil Blackwell, 1989), pp. 345–74, 422.

85. The quotation is from the typescript notes for the speech, in the Churchill Archive, CHAR 9/140A/9-28, at: www.churchillarchive.com. For background, see John Lukacs, *Five Days in London: May 1940* (New Haven: Yale University Press, 1999).

86. "Reply of a South American to a Gentleman of This Island [Jamaica]," September 6, 1815, in *Selected Writings of Bolívar,* translated by Lewis Bertrand (New York: Colonial Press, 1951), I, p. 118.

87. Bolívar's argument here anticipates Jared Diamond, who has argued that it is far easier to organize regions spread across latitude than longitude. See his *Guns, Germs, and Steel: The Fates of Human Societies* (New York: Norton, 1999), pp. 176–91.

88. Bolívar, "Reply," pp. 109, 118. The Greeks, of course, didn't build a single state either, but maybe Bolívar, like Keats placing "stout Cortez" on a peak in Darien, merits a certain poetic license. Panama seems to bring out the need for one.

89. Bolívar, "Reply," p. 111.

90. *Ibid.,* p. 122.

91. Sexton, *The Monroe Doctrine,* provides the context at pp. 36–46.

92. Available online at: www.millercenter.org/president/jqadams/speeches/speech-3484.

CHAPTER SEVEN: THE GRANDEST STRATEGISTS

1. Leo Tolstoy, *War and Peace,* translated by Richard Pevear and Larissa Volokhonsky (New York: Knopf, 2007), p. 774. For more on this passage, see W. B. Gallie, *Philosophers of Peace and War: Kant, Clausewitz, Marx, Engels and Tolstoy* (New York: Cambridge University Press, 1978), pp. 117–19; and Lawrence Freedman, *Strategy: A History* (New York: Oxford University Press, 2013), pp. 98–99. I've adapted portions of this chapter from my article "War, Peace, and Everything: Thoughts on Tolstoy," *Cliodynamics: The Journal of Theoretical and Mathematical History* 2 (2011), 40–51.

2. Donald Stoker, *Clausewitz: His Life and Work* (New York: Oxford University Press, 2014), pp. 94–128.

3. Alan Forrest and Andreas Herberg-Rothe assess the likelihood in their respective contributions to Rick McPeak and Donna Tussing Orwin, eds., *Tolstoy on War: Narrative Art and Historical Truth in "War and Peace"* (Ithaca: Cornell University Press, 2012), pp. 115, 143–44.

4. Michael Howard, "The Influence of Clausewitz," in Carl von Clausewitz, *On War,* edited and translated by Michael Howard and Peter Paret (Princeton: Princeton University Press, 1976), pp. 32–41; also Christopher Bassford, *Clausewitz in English: The Reception of Clausewitz in Britain and America, 1815–1945* (New York: Oxford University Press, 1994).

5. Clausewitz, *On War,* p. 113. Emphasis added.

6. Tolstoy, *War and Peace,* pp. 799–801.

7. Clausewitz, *On War,* p. 467.

8. *Ibid.,* p. 370.

9. Mikhail Kizilov, "The Tsar in the Queen's Room: The Visit of Russian Emperor Alexander I to Oxford in 1814," no date, available at: www.academia.com.

10. Clausewitz, *On War,* p. 605.

11. "A Few Words Apropos of the Book *War and Peace,*" in Tolstoy, *War and Peace,* p. 1217.

12. "The Hedgehog and the Fox," in Isaiah Berlin, *The Proper Study of Mankind: An Anthology of Essays,* edited by Henry Hardy and Roger Hausheer (New York: Farrar, Straus and Giroux, 1997), p. 458.

13. Clausewitz employs a wrestling analogy as early as the second paragraph of *On War,* p. 75.

14. Tolstoy, *War and Peace,* p. 1200.

15. Clausewitz, *On War,* p. 151. Emphasis added.

16. "Author's Preface to an Unpublished Manuscript on the Theory of War," in *ibid.,* p. 61.

17. Peter Paret, *Clausewitz and the State: The Man, His Theories, and His Times* (Princeton: Princeton University Press, 1985: first published by Oxford University Press in 1976), pp. 169–79.

18. Michael Howard, *Clausewitz: A Very Short Introduction* (New York: Oxford University Press, 2002), p. 41. Sir Michael doubts (p. 21) that Clausewitz, even if blessed with longevity, would have employed it to achieve brevity.

19. Tolstoy, *War and Peace,* p. 1181.

20. Dictionary.com.

21. Andrew Roberts, *Napoleon: A Life* (New York: Viking, 2014), pp. 577–80, 634–35.

22. Clausewitz, *On War,* pp. 75–76. The first italics are in the original; the remaining ones are mine.

23. I'm following here—although oversimplifying—Gallie, *Philosophers of Peace and War,* p. 52; also Howard, *Clausewitz,* pp. 13–14, and Peter Paret, "The Genesis of *On War,*" in Clausewitz, *On War,* pp. 2–3, 15–16.

24. Clausewitz, *On War,* p. 523.

25. Howard, *Clausewitz,* pp. 4, 18–19. For the Americans' role, see R. R. Palmer's classic *The Age of Democratic Revolution: A Political History of Europe and America, 1760–1800* (Princeton: Princeton University Press, 2014; first published in two volumes in 1959 and 1964).

26. These English equivalents for Clausewitz's term *Politik* draw on Bassford, *Clausewitz in English,* p. 22.

27. Thereby anticipating fears of all-out thermonuclear war during the Cold War, one of several reasons for the post–World War II revival of interest in Clausewitz. An influential example is Bernard Brodie, *War and Politics* (New York: Macmillan, 1973).

28. Clausewitz, *On War,* p. 87.

29. Roberts, *Napoleon,* pp. 555–79, provides a thorough account.

30. The exception was the Peninsular Campaign in Spain and Portugal.
31. Quoted in Roberts, *Napoleon*, p. 595.
32. For Kutuzov's abandonment of Moscow, see Dominic Lieven, *Russia Against Napoleon: The True Story of the Campaigns of* War and Peace (New York: Viking, 2010), pp. 209–14.
33. Clausewitz, *On War*, p. 97.
34. *Ibid.*, p. 161. For the role of emotion in Clausewitz's thinking, see Jon Tetsuro Sumida, "The Relationship of History and Theory in *On War*: The Clausewitzian Ideal and Its Implications," *Journal of Military History* 65 (April 2001), 337–38.
35. Tolstoy, *War and Peace*, pp. 993, 1000–1001.
36. Roberts, *Napoleon*, pp. 612–34; also Lieven, *Russia Against Napoleon*, pp. 252–57.
37. John Quincy Adams to John Adams, August 16, 1812, and to Abigail Adams, December 31, 1812, quoted in Samuel Flagg Bemis, *John Quincy Adams and the Foundations of American Foreign Policy* (New York: Knopf, 1949), pp. 177–78.
38. Clausewitz, *On War*, pp. 100, 112.
39. Sumida, "The Relationship of History and Theory in *On War*," pp. 345–48.
40. Clausewitz, *On War*, pp. 102, 109. Which is similar, I think, to what Malcolm Gladwell describes in *Blink: The Power of Thinking Without Thinking* (New York: Little, Brown, 2005).
41. See chapter four.
42. *Ibid.*, pp. 104, 119. For Tolstoy on travelers, inns, and plans gone awry, see *War and Peace*, pp. 347–49.
43. Paret, *Clausewitz and the State*, pp. 197–99, provides a thorough discussion.
44. Roberts, *Napoleon*, p. 596.
45. "Preface to an Unpublished Manuscript," in Clausewitz, *On War*, p. 61.
46. See, for elaborations, Hew Strachan, *Carl von Clausewitz's* On War: *A Biography* (London: Atlantic Books, 2007), p. 153; Howard, *Clausewitz*, p. 25; and Fred R. Shapiro, *The Yale Book of Quotations* (New Haven: Yale University Press, 2006), for admirably comprehensive derivations of the last two principles.
47. Clausewitz, *On War*, p. 120.
48. *Ibid.*, p. 103.
49. *Ibid.*, p. 112.
50. Tolstoy, *War and Peace*, pp. 618–27.
51. *Ibid.*, pp. 738–45.
52. See chapter three.
53. "Preface to an Unpublished Manuscript," in Clausewitz, *On War*, p. 61.
54. *Ibid.*, pp. 122, 141, 374.
55. *Ibid.*, p. 142.
56. *Ibid.*, pp. 168–69. Emphases in the original.
57. Quoted in Stoker, *Clausewitz*, p. 109.
58. Tolstoy, *War and Peace*, p. 640.
59. Pierre and Natasha do this at the end of *War and Peace*, pp. 1174–77.
60. Clausewitz, *On War*, pp. 85–86.

61. *Ibid.*, p. 89.

62. See Alan Beyerchen, "Clausewitz, Nonlinearity, and the Unpredictability of War," *International Security* 17 (Winter 1992–93), especially pp. 61–72.

63. Clausewitz, *On War*, pp. 107, 135.

64. *Ibid.*, p. 595.

65. See chapter four.

66. Tolstoy, *War and Peace*, p. 1203.

67. For more on this, see chapter six.

68. Tolstoy, *War and Peace*, pp. 1212–13.

69. A. N. Wilson, *Tolstoy* (New York: Norton, 1988), pp. 297–301.

70. A point well made in Paret, *Clausewitz and the State*, p. 338.

71. See Paul Bracken, "Net Assessment: A Practical Guide," *Parameters* (Spring 2006), 90–100.

72. Clausewitz, *On War*, p. 158.

73. Never better explained than in John Keegan, *The Face of Battle: A Study of Agincourt, Waterloo, and the Somme* (New York: Penguin, 1983).

74. Lieven, *Russia Against Napoleon*, p. 259.

75. *The Federalist*, Modern Library College Edition (New York: Random House, no date), *#28*, p. 171.

76. Clausewitz, *On War*, p. 523.

CHAPTER EIGHT: THE GREATEST PRESIDENT

1. Adams was there as United States minister from 1809 to 1814, but he'd also spent 1781–82 as a teenage French translator for Francis Dana, who'd unsuccessfully sought diplomatic recognition from Catherine II. James Traub, *John Quincy Adams: Militant Spirit* (New York: Basic Books, 2016), pp. 28–30, 160–82, provides the best recent account.

2. John Quincy Adams diary, May 8, 1824, Massachusetts Historical Society online edition, at: www.masshist.org/jqadiaries. See also Charles Edel, *Nation Builder: John Quincy Adams and the Grand Strategy of the Republic* (Cambridge, Massachusetts: Harvard University Press, 2014), pp. 194–96. The Adams diaries, some fourteen thousand pages in fifty-one volumes, extend, with gaps, from 1779 to 1848. For a new abridgement, see *John Quincy Adams: Diaries,* edited by David Waldstreicher, two volumes (New York: Library of America, 2017).

3. See Samuel Flagg Bemis, *John Quincy Adams and the Foundations of American Foreign Policy* (New York: Knopf, 1949), especially pp. 566–72.

4. Washington, Jefferson, Madison, and Monroe had all come from Virginia.

5. Adams diary, May 8, 1824.

6. For his annihilation of the British at the battle of New Orleans, fought in January 1815, after Adams and his fellow peace negotiators had concluded the Treaty of Ghent on December 24, 1814, but before word of it had crossed the Atlantic.

7. Sean Wilentz, *The Rise of American Democracy: Jefferson to Lincoln* (New York: Norton, 2005), p. 255. See also Edel, *Nation Builder,* p. 192.

8. The Adams message, dated December 6, 1825, is available online from the University of Virginia's Miller Center of Public Affairs at: www. millercenter.org/the -presidency/presidential-speeches/december-6-1825-message-regarding-congress -american-nations. For its reception, see Traub, *John Quincy Adams,* pp. 322–27; also Fred Kaplan, *John Quincy Adams: American Visionary* (New York: Harper Collins, 2014), pp. 404–5.

9. These explanations appear, respectively, in Edel, *Nation Builder,* p. 188; Traub, *John Quincy Adams,* p. 294; Walter Russell Mead, *Special Providence: American Foreign Policy and How It Changed the World* (New York: Knopf, 2001), pp. 218–63; and Robert Kagan, *Dangerous Nation: America's Place in the World from Its Earliest Days to the Dawn of the Twentieth Century* (New York: Knopf, 2006), pp. 265–300. For Adams on the Missouri Compromise, see chapter six.

10. *The Congressional Globe* for February 21, 1848, records two votes on the resolution, with Adams and Lincoln both against in each instance. Just after the second, the *Globe* notes a hasty adjournment after "the venerable John Quincy Adams . . . was observed to be sinking from his seat in what appeared to be the agonies of death." See also Traub, *John Quincy Adams,* pp. 525–28.

11. Michael Burlingame, *Abraham Lincoln: A Life* [2 vols.], vol. 1 (Baltimore: Johns Hopkins University Press, 2008), pp. 4, 26–27, 43–44, 172. Mark Twain's novel wouldn't appear in the United States until 1885.

12. Burlingame, *Lincoln I,* pp. 1, 41–42. See also Richard Carwardine, *Lincoln: A Life of Purpose and Power* (New York: Random House, 2006), pp. 50–51.

13. Burlingame, *Lincoln I,* pp. 53–56. See also Doris Kearns Goodwin, *Team of Rivals: The Political Genius of Abraham Lincoln* (New York: Simon and Schuster, 2005), p. 50.

14. Carwardine, *Lincoln,* pp. 39–40.

15. Fred Kaplan, *Lincoln: The Biography of a Writer* (New York: HarperCollins, 2008), especially pp. 30–59.

16. Burlingame, *Lincoln I,* pp. 51, 66–71, 75–81. Lincoln's military service took place, he'd have said ingloriously, as a volunteer in the Black Hawk War of 1832. The New Salem general store he co-owned briefly went bankrupt, and he appears to have spent more time as the town's postmaster telling stories than putting up mail. Rail-splitting, I've had to explain to my students, involved the construction of wooden fences, not railroads.

17. *Ibid.,* pp. 71–75, 81–85.

18. A process described carefully in Wilentz, *The Rise of American Democracy,* pp. 482–518.

19. Although their successful candidate, William Henry Harrison, died shortly after taking office in 1841, leaving the vice president John Tyler, a closeted southern Democrat, to succeed him.

20. Burlingame, *Lincoln I,* pp. 264–70.

21. *Ibid.,* pp. 296–310.

22. Lincoln speech at Peoria, Illinois, October 16, 1854, in *Abraham Lincoln Speeches and Writings, 1832–1858* (New York: Library of America, 1989), pp.

337–38 [hereafter *Lincoln Speeches and Writings I*]. All capitalizations and emphases from this source are in the original.

23. The compromise of 1820 admitted Missouri to the Union as a slave state, but left territories to the north and west of it, as far as the Rocky Mountains, free. In the 1850 compromise that followed the Mexican War, California became a free state, with slavery to be allowed in the New Mexico and Utah territories if their citizens supported it.

24. Lincoln to George Robertson, August 15, 1855, in *Lincoln Speeches and Writings I*, p. 359. For the increasing profitability of slavery, see Sven Beckert, *Empire of Cotton: A Global History* (New York: Knopf, 2014), pp. 105–20.

25. Lewis E. Lehrman, *Lincoln at Peoria: The Turning Point* (Mechanicsburg, Pennsylvania: Stackpole Books, 2008), pp. 71–99, provides a careful assessment of Douglas and his motives. See also Burlingame, *Lincoln I*, pp. 370–74.

26. Quoted in *ibid.*, p. 374.

27. *Lincoln Speeches and Writings I*, p. 315. Lincoln spoke at Springfield on October 4 and in Peoria on October 16, 1854, with Douglas present on both occasions. Only the Peoria version of the speech was published, however. Lehrman, *Lincoln at Peoria*, provides the best account of the speech's origins, content, and implications.

28. Burlingame describes the circuit in *Lincoln I*, pp. 322–32.

29. *Ibid.*, p. 418.

30. *Ibid.*, pp. 333–34. For Adams on Euclid, see his diary, March 26, 1786.

31. *Lincoln Speeches and Writings I*, p. 303.

32. *Ibid.*, pp. 322, 328–33.

33. Lehrman, *Lincoln at Peoria*, p. 107, calls this a "hijacking," although a "sincere and shrewd" one.

34. *Lincoln Speeches and Writings I*, pp. 308–9, 316–17, 320–21, 323, 337, 340.

35. Goodwin makes a similar point in *Team of Rivals*, p. 103.

36. *Lincoln Speeches and Writings I*, p. 426. See also Wilentz, *The Rise of American Democracy*, pp. 677–715.

37. For *Dred Scott v. Sandford*, see Don E. Fehrenbacher, *The Dred Scott Case: Its Significance in American Law and Politics* (New York: Oxford University Press, 1978).

38. *Lincoln Speeches and Writings I*, p. 426.

39. Douglas had included the most inflammatory provision of the Kansas-Nebraska Act, the explicit repeal of the Missouri Compromise, only at the last minute because southern congressmen made it the price of their support. See Wilentz, *The Rise of American Democracy*, p. 672.

40. The quotation is from Jesus, at Mark 3:25.

41. *Lincoln Speeches and Writings I*, p. 426.

42. The voluminous transcripts are in *ibid.*, pp. 495–822.

43. *Ibid.*, pp. 769, 814.

44. Senators would not be popularly elected until after the ratification of the Seventeenth Amendment, in 1913.

45. I'm appropriating here J. H. Hexter's taxonomy in his *On Historians* (Cambridge, Massachusetts: Harvard University Press, 1979), pp. 241–43. Burlingame, *Lincoln I*, pp. 598–99, explains the origins of Lincoln's nickname.

46. With a few exceptions, summarized in Carwardine, *Lincoln*, pp. 93–94.

47. Their portraits, as they appeared in *Harper's*, are in Goodwin, *Team of Rivals*, pp. 1–2.

48. Lincoln to Samuel Galloway, March 24, 1860, in *Abraham Lincoln Speeches and Writings, 1859-1865* (New York: Library of America, 1989), p. 152 [hereafter *Lincoln Speeches and Writings II*].

49. See *ibid.*, pp. 29–101, 111–50.

50. He'd have had in mind the "corrupt bargain" charges that ruined John Quincy Adams's presidency.

51. Kevin Peraino, *Lincoln in the World: The Making of a Statesman and the Dawn of American Power* (New York: Crown, 2013), pp. 7–8.

52. Burlingame, *Lincoln I*, pp. 627–83, provides a full account.

53. Quoted in Goodwin, *Team of Rivals*, p. 319. See also Burlingame, *Lincoln I*, p. 720.

54. Lincoln to William Seward, February 1, 1861, in *Lincoln Speeches and Writings II*, p. 197. For Lincoln's consideration of compromises, see Burlingame, *Lincoln I*, pp. 745–53.

55. Parmenas Taylor Turnley, *Reminiscences, From the Cradle to Three-Score and Ten* (Chicago: Donohue and Henneberry, 1892), p. 264. I owe this quotation to Burlingame, who cites it incorrectly in *Lincoln I*, p. 903.

56. Thus echoing the Athenians at Sparta.

57. *Lincoln Speeches and Writings II*, pp. 215–24.

58. James M. McPherson, *Tried by War: Abraham Lincoln as Commander in Chief* (New York: Penguin, 2008), pp. 20–21.

59. Carwardine, *Lincoln*, pp. 24–26.

60. Russell F. Weigley, *The American Way of War: A History of United States Military Strategy and Policy* (New York: Macmillan, 1973), pp. 97–127.

61. Henry Halleck to Lincoln, January 6, 1862, quoted in McPherson, *Tried by War*, p. 70. See also Weigley, *The American Way of War*, p. 83; and Mark Greenbaum, "Lincoln's Do-Nothing Generals," *New York Times*, November 27, 2011.

62. Lincoln to Halleck and Don C. Buell, January 13, 1862, in *Lincoln Speeches and Writings II*, p. 302.

63. See Weigley, *The American Way of War*, p. 95; and McPherson, *Tried by War*, pp. 70–71.

64. Weigley, *The American Way of War*, pp. 77–91; Peter Paret, *Clausewitz and the State: The Man, His Theories, and His Times* (Princeton: Princeton University Press, 1985; first published by Oxford University Press in 1976), pp. 152–53; Christopher Bassford, *Clausewitz in English: The Reception of Clausewitz in Britain and America, 1815-1945* (New York: Oxford University Press, 1994), pp. 56–59. Francis Lieber, a Prussian émigré whose writings on the laws of war influenced Lincoln, was a careful student of Clausewitz, whom he read in the original German. See John Fabian Witt, *Lincoln's Code: The Laws of War in American History* (New York: Free Press, 2012), pp. 185–86.

65. McPherson lists the failed generals in *Tried by War*, p. 8.

66. *Ibid.*, p. 142; also James M. McPherson, *Abraham Lincoln and the Second American Revolution* (New York: Oxford University Press, 1991), pp. 68–72.

67. Carl von Clausewitz, *On War,* edited and translated by Michael Howard and Peter Paret (Princeton: Princeton University Press, 1976), p. 75.

68. Quoted in Burlingame, *Lincoln II,* p. 154; also Lincoln to Orville H. Browning, September 22, 1861, in *Lincoln Speeches and Writings II,* p. 269.

69. Allen C. Guelzo, *Lincoln's Emancipation Proclamation: The End of Slavery in America* (New York: Simon and Schuster, 2004), pp. 31-33, 46-59.

70. Lincoln to Albert G. Hodges, April 4, 1864, in *Lincoln Speeches and Writings II,* p. 585.

71. Clausewitz, *On War,* p. 87. See also McPherson, *Tried by War,* pp. 5-6.

72. Guelzo, *Lincoln's Emancipation Proclamation,* pp. 3-4; McPherson, *Lincoln and the Second American Revolution,* p. 91. Clausewitz states his paradox in *On War,* p. 119.

73. McPherson, *Tried by War,* p. 52.

74. Quoted in *ibid.,* p. 66.

75. McPherson, *Lincoln and the Second American Revolution,* pp. 85-86.

76. Guelzo, *Lincoln's Emancipation Proclamation,* pp. 83-90; McPherson, *Tried by War,* pp. 158-59.

77. Lincoln to Greeley, August 22, 1862, in *Lincoln Speeches and Writings II,* p. 358; Carwardine, *Lincoln,* p. 209.

78. Charles Francis Adams, *John Quincy Adams and Emancipation Under Martial Law (1819-1842),* in Adams and Worthington Chauncey Ford, *John Quincy Adams* (Cambridge, Massachusetts: John Wilson and Son, 1902), pp. 7-79. See also Guelzo, *Lincoln's Emancipation Proclamation,* pp. 123-27; and Witt, *Lincoln's Code,* pp. 204-5.

79. Preliminary Emancipation Proclamation, September 22, 1862, in *Lincoln Speeches and Writings II,* p. 368.

80. Guelzo, *Lincoln's Emancipation Proclamation,* p. 173.

81. Annual Message to Congress, December 1, 1862, in *Lincoln Speeches and Writings II,* pp. 393-415.

82. Eulogy on Henry Clay, July 6, 1852, in *Lincoln Speeches and Writings I,* p. 264.

83. See, for example, *ibid.,* pp. 315, 340.

84. Special Message to Congress, July 4, 1861, *Lincoln Speeches and Writings II,* p. 259.

85. Quoted in Burlingame, *Lincoln II,* p. 167.

86. *Lincoln Speeches and Writings II,* pp. 409-11.

87. See note 8, above.

88. Edel, *Nation Builder,* p. 298; Kagan, *Dangerous Nation,* pp. 258-64, 269; McPherson, *Lincoln and the Second American Revolution,* pp. 39-40.

89. Peraino, *Lincoln in the World,* pp. 183, 187.

90. Beckert, *Empire of Cotton,* pp. 242-65; Witt, *Lincoln's Code,* pp. 142-57.

91. Quoted in Burlingame, *Lincoln II,* pp. 119, 167.

92. Peraino, *Lincoln in the World,* pp. 66-69; also Walter Stahr, *Seward: Lincoln's Indispensable Man* (New York: Simon and Schuster, 2012), pp. 269-73.

93. Lincoln to Seward, April 1, 1861 (apparently not sent), in *Lincoln Speeches and Writings II,* p. 228.

94. Witt, *Lincoln's Code,* pp. 164–69. See also Burlingame, *Lincoln II,* pp. 221–29; and Peraino, *Lincoln in the World,* pp. 123–62.

95. For a good account of this neglected episode, see *ibid.,* pp. 224–95. Maximilian went to Mexico anyway, despite Union victories and Napoleon's withdrawal of support. He wound up before a firing squad there in 1867.

96. Richard Overy, *Why the Allies Won* (London: Pimlico, 1995), pp. 282–313, stresses the importance of moral high ground in a more recent major war.

97. Peraino, *Lincoln in the World,* pp. 207–15; Guelzo, *Lincoln's Emancipation Proclamation,* pp. 253–54. For an older but comprehensive assessment, see D. P. Crook, *The North, the South, and the Powers, 1861–1865* (New York: Wiley, 1974), pp. 236–55.

98. Beckert, *Empire of Cotton,* pp. 265–67. See also McPherson, *Lincoln and the Second American Revolution,* pp. vii–viii, 6–7.

99. *Ibid.,* pp. 17–18.

100. Memorandum on Probable Failure of Re-election, August 23, 1864, in *Lincoln Speeches and Writings II,* p. 624. For more on the "blind memorandum," which Lincoln made his cabinet sign but only later allowed them to read, see Burlingame, *Lincoln II,* pp. 674–76.

101. McPherson, *Tried by War,* pp. 231–44.

102. Quoted in Burlingame, *Lincoln II,* p. 729.

103. Address of the International Working Men's Association to Abraham Lincoln, President of the United States of America, written by Marx in late November 1864, and presented to Ambassador Charles Francis Adams, January 28, 1865, available at: www.marxists.org/archive/marx/iwma/documents/1864/lincoln-letter.htm.

104. Quoted in Edel, *Nation Builder,* pp. 157–59. For the context, see chapter six.

105. J. David Hacker, "Recounting the Dead," *New York Times,* September 20, 2011. The regimental figures are from www.civilwararchive.com/regim.htm, and the service estimates from www.civilwar.org/education/history/faq. The best overall account is Drew Gilpin Faust, *This Republic of Suffering: Death and the American Civil War* (New York: Knopf, 2008).

106. See note 55, above.

107. McPherson, *Lincoln and the Second American Revolution,* pp. 23–25, 41–42.

108. Weigley, *The American Way of War,* pp. xxi–xxiii; also Paul Kennedy, *The Rise and Fall of the Great Powers: Economic Change and Military Conflict from 1500 to 2000* (New York: Random House, 1987), pp. 178–82.

109. Gettysburg Address, *Lincoln Speeches and Writings II,* November 19, 1863; *ibid.,* p. 536; Edel, *Nation Builder,* stresses this line of inheritance at pp. 297–99.

110. Burlingame, *Lincoln I,* p. xii. Burlingame's "conclusion" comes at the beginning of his 1976-page two-volume biography.

111. I'm expanding, here, on an argument made in McPherson, *Lincoln and the Second American Revolution,* pp. 93–95.

112. It's revealing, in this respect, to compare *Federalist #10* with the constitutional doctrines of the mature John C. Calhoun, who saw costs in all compromises. See Merrill D. Peterson, *The Great Triumvirate: Webster, Clay, and Calhoun* (New York: Oxford University Press, 1987), pp. 409–13.

113. See Carwardine, *Lincoln,* pp. 221–35.

114. *Ibid.,* p. 228.

115. Guelzo, *Lincoln's Emancipation Proclamation,* pp. 171–72.

116. "Meditation on the Divine Will," September 1862, in *Lincoln Speeches and Writings II,* p. 359.

117. *Ibid.,* p. 687.

118. Lee surrendered, at Appomattox, on April 9, 1865.

119. See Rosamund Bartlett, *Tolstoy: A Russian Life* (Boston: Houghton Mifflin Harcourt, 2011), pp. 251–93.

120. Lincoln to Albert G. Hodges, April 4, 1864, in *Lincoln Speeches and Writings II,* p. 586.

CHAPTER NINE: LAST BEST HOPE

1. Andrew Roberts, *Salisbury: Victorian Titan* (London: Phoenix, 2000), pp. 46–50, 170. I prefer the term "Great War" for the years before anyone knew to call it "World War I."

2. Walter Stahr, *Seward: Lincoln's Indispensable Man* (New York: Simon and Schuster, 2012), pp. 482–504. For the larger pattern of decentralization, see John A. Thompson, *A Sense of Power: The Roots of America's Global Role* (Ithaca: Cornell University Press, 2015), pp. 38–39.

3. Robert Kagan, *Dangerous Nation: America's Place in the World from Its Earliest Days to the Dawn of the Twentieth Century* (New York: Knopf, 2006), p. 302; also C. Vann Woodward, "The Age of Reinterpretation," *American Historical Review* 66 (October 1960), 2–8.

4. Roberts, *Salisbury,* pp. 105–6, 436–37, 490.

5. Olney's July 20 note is in U.S. Department of State, *Papers Relating to the Foreign Affairs of the United States, 1895,* vol. I, pp. 542–63. Jay Sexton, *The Monroe Doctrine: Empire and Nation in Nineteenth-Century America* (New York: Hill and Wang, 2011), pp. 201–8, provides context.

6. The classic account is Henry Kissinger, "The White Revolutionary: Reflections on Bismarck," *Daedalus* 97 (Summer 1968), 888–924. See also Jonathan Steinberg, *Bismarck: A Life* (New York: Oxford University Press, 2011), pp. 441–50.

7. Quoted in Paul Kennedy, *The Rise of the Anglo-German Antagonism, 1860–1914* (London: Allen and Unwin, 1980), p. 220.

8. Roberts, *Salisbury,* pp. 619–26; Kennedy, *The Rise of the Anglo-German Antagonism,* pp. 464–65. See also Paul Kennedy, *The Rise and Fall of the Great Powers: Economic Change and Military Conflict from 1500 to 2000* (New York: Random House, 1987), p. 201.

9. Quoted in Roberts, *Salisbury,* p. 610.

10. For comprehensive accounts, see Bradford Perkins, *The Great Rapprochement: England and the United States, 1895–1914* (New York: Atheneum, 1968); Stephen R. Rock, *Why Peace Breaks Out: Great Power Rapprochement in Historical Perspective* (Chapel Hill: University of North Carolina Press, 1989), pp. 24–63; and Charles A. Kupchan, *How Enemies Become Friends: The Sources of Stable Peace* (Princeton: Princeton University Press, 2010), pp. 73–111.

11. See Roberts, *Salisbury,* p. 633. For an alternative view, see Michael Howard, *The Continental Commitment: The Dilemma of British Defence Policy in the Era of the Two World Wars* (London: Ashfield Press, 1989; first published in 1972), pp. 29–30.

12. The phrase is from Georgi Arbatov, as quoted in Jean Davidson, "UCI Scientists Told Moscow's Aim Is to Deprive U.S. of Foe," *Los Angeles Times,* December 12, 1988.

13. Roberts, *Salisbury,* pp. 51–52.

14. See chapter six.

15. Quoted in Roberts, *Salisbury,* p. 662.

16. *Ibid.,* p. 512.

17. H. J. Mackinder, "The Geographical Pivot of History," *The Geographical Journal* 23 (April 1904), 421–44. See also Brian W. Blouet, *Halford Mackinder: A Biography* (College Station: Texas A&M University Press, 1987); and, for the railroad revolution, Christian Wolmar, *Blood, Iron, and Gold: How the Railroads Transformed the World* (New York: Public Affairs, 2010).

18. Mackinder, "The Geographical Pivot of History," p. 437.

19. Blouet, *Mackinder,* pp. 118–20.

20. For background on the Crowe memorandum, which remained unpublished until 1928, see K. M. Wilson, "Sir Eyre Crowe on the Origin of the Crowe Memorandum of 1 January 1907," *Historical Research* 56 (November 1983), 238–41; also Zara S. Steiner, *The Foreign Office and Foreign Policy, 1898–1914* (Cambridge: Cambridge University Press, 1969), pp. 108–18; and, for Crowe's continuing influence, Jeffrey Stephen Dunn, *The Crowe Memorandum: Sir Eyre Crowe and Foreign Office Perceptions of Germany, 1918–1925* (Newcastle upon Tyne: Cambridge Scholars Publishing, 2013). I've discussed the "long telegram" in *George F. Kennan: An American Life* (New York: Penguin, 2011), pp. 215–22.

21. Memorandum on the Present State of British Relations with France and Germany, January 1, 1907, in *British Documents on the Origins of the War, 1898–1914,* III, pp. 397–420, available at: www.dbpo.chadwyck.com/marketing/index.jsp. All quotations below are from this version.

22. See chapter two.

23. For a 1951 version of this argument, see my *George F. Kennan,* p. 415.

24. Steinberg, *Bismarck,* pp. 180–81.

25. For Bismarck's colonial policy, see Kennedy, *The Rise of the Anglo-German Antagonism,* pp. 167–83.

26. Emphasis added.

27. The classic account remains Barbara Tuchman, *The Guns of August* (New York: Macmillan, 1962). But see also Christopher Clark, *The Sleepwalkers: How Europe Went to War in 1914* (New York: HarperCollins, 2013); Margaret MacMillan, *The War That Ended Peace: The Road to 1914* (New York: Random House, 2013); and Sean McMeekin, *July 1914: Countdown to War* (New York: Basic Books, 2013).

28. Wikipedia thoroughly assesses the complicated statistics.

29. Henry Kissinger, *Diplomacy* (New York: Simon and Schuster, 1994), p. 200.

30. Howard, *The Continental Commitment,* pp. 30–31.

31. Total British army deaths, including those from the dominions and the colonies, exceeded 900,000 (www.1914-1918.net/faq.htm). The maximum estimate for Civil War deaths is now 750,000, as discussed in chapter eight.

32. Sir John Robert Seeley, *The Expansion of England: Two Courses of Lectures* (New York: Cosimo Classics, 2005; first published in 1891), p. 8.

33. Mackinder himself developed this idea in a book, *Democratic Ideals and Reality: A Study in the Politics of Reconstruction* (New York: Henry Holt, 1919), which never gained the influence of his article. See also Blouet, *Mackinder,* pp. 164–65.

34. Roberts, *Salisbury,* pp. 812–14.

35. See Christopher Howard, "Splendid Isolation," *History* 47, 159 (1962), 32–41.

36. Kennedy, *The Rise and Fall of the Great Powers,* p. 248. The comparisons in this paragraph are from pp. 200–202; but see also Robert J. Gordon, *The Rise and Fall of American Growth: The U.S. Standard of Living Since the Civil War* (Princeton: Princeton University Press, 2016), pp. 27–318.

37. Kennedy, *The Rise and Fall of the Great Powers,* p. 248.

38. See Walter Lippmann, *U.S. Foreign Policy: Shield of the Republic* (Boston: Little, Brown, 1943), especially pp. 11–26.

39. I owe this point to Michael Howard, in *The Continental Commitment,* p. 9. See also Thompson, *A Sense of Power,* pp. 41–43.

40. Quoted in John Milton Cooper, *Woodrow Wilson: A Biography* (New York: Random House, 2009), p. 263.

41. Charles E. Neu, *Colonel House: A Biography of Woodrow Wilson's Silent Partner* (New York: Oxford University Press, 2015), pp. 23, 142. House wasn't a real colonel, but had been awarded that title by Texas governor James Stephen Hogg in 1893, presumably for political services rendered.

42. David Milne, *Worldmaking: The Art and Science of American Diplomacy* (New York: Farrar, Straus and Giroux, 2015), pp. 95–96.

43. Neu, *Colonel House,* p. 142; also Cooper, *Woodrow Wilson,* pp. 263–66.

44. See Katherine C. Epstein, *Torpedo: Inventing the Military-Industrial Complex in the United States and Great Britain* (Cambridge, Massachusetts: Harvard University Press, 2014).

45. Cooper, *Woodrow Wilson,* pp. 285–89; also Erik Larson, *Dead Wake: The Last Crossing of the* Lusitania (New York: Broadway Books, 2015).

46. Neu, *Colonel House,* p. 270.

47. Thomas Boghardt, *The Zimmermann Telegram: Intelligence, Diplomacy, and America's Entry into World War I* (Annapolis: Naval Institute Press, 2012).

48. Cooper, *Woodrow Wilson,* p. 387; also David Runciman, *The Confidence Trap: A History of Democracy in Crisis from World War I to the Present* (Princeton: Princeton University Press, 2013), pp. 39–40.

49. Cooper, *Woodrow Wilson,* p. 380.

50. *Ibid.,* pp. 341–42, 462–66; also A. Scott Berg, *Wilson* (New York: G. P. Putnam's Sons, 2013), pp. 515–23.

51. Neu, *Colonel House,* p. 384; Cooper, *Woodrow Wilson,* p. 421.

52. Paul Cambon, quoted in Berg, *Wilson,* p. 534. See also Cooper, *Woodrow Wilson,* p. 419, and, for an overall assessment, Gaddis Smith, *Woodrow Wilson's Fourteen*

Points After 75 Years (New York: Carnegie Council for Ethics in International Affairs, 1993).

53. Here, and in the following paragraph, I've used the text of the "Fourteen Points" speech, available at: www.avalon.law.yale.edu/20th_century/wilson14.asp.

54. A recent comprehensive account is Sean McMeekin, *The Russian Revolution: A New History* (New York: Basic Books, 2017). See also Arno J. Mayer's earlier but influential *Wilson vs. Lenin: The Political Origins of the New Diplomacy, 1917–1918* (Cleveland: World Publishing, 1964; first published under the subtitle by the Yale University Press in 1959).

55. The best accounts are still George F. Kennan's two Princeton University Press volumes: *Soviet-American Relations, 1917–1920: Russia Leaves the War* (1956) and *The Decision to Intervene* (1958).

56. I've discussed this paradox in *Russia, the Soviet Union, and the United States: An Interpretive History*, second edition (New York: McGraw Hill, 1990), pp. 71–72. For a reassessment of the German victory in the east and its aftermath, see Adam Tooze, *The Deluge: The Great War, America and the Remaking of the Global Order* (New York: Penguin, 2014), pp. 108–70.

57. Runciman, *The Confidence Trap*, pp. 74–75, makes a similar argument.

58. See Jonathan D. Spence, *God's Chinese Son: The Taiping Heavenly Kingdom of Hong Xiuquan* (New York: Norton, 1996).

59. A point made by Kennan in *The Decline of Bismarck's European Order*, pp. 3–7.

60. See chapter two.

61. Shrewdly assessed in Thompson, *A Sense of Power*, pp. 76–79.

62. In the sense of the support for war on which each belligerent relied, not the more rigorous definitions devised by "democratic peace" theorists in their efforts to convince themselves that democracies don't fight one another. Bruce Russett summarizes these in *Grasping the Democratic Peace: Principles for a Post–Cold War World* (Princeton: Princeton University Press, 1993), pp. 73–83.

63. See note 53, above.

64. Paul Kennedy, *The Parliament of Man: The Past, Present, and Future of the United Nations* (New York: Random House, 2006), pp. 3–8.

65. Keith Robbins, *Sir Edward Grey: A Biography of Lord Grey of Fallodon* (London: Cassell, 1971), pp. 156–57, 319–20; also Howard, *The Continental Commitment*, pp. 51–52; and Neu, *Colonel House*, pp. 214–15.

66. Kissinger, *Diplomacy*, p. 223.

67. See chapter six.

68. Kissinger, *Diplomacy*, pp. 78–102; also Erez Manela, *The Wilsonian Moment: Self-Determination and the International Origins of Anticolonial Nationalism* (New York: Oxford University Press, 2007).

69. See Berg, *Wilson*, p. 585.

70. Robert B. Strassler, ed., *The Landmark Thucydides: A Comprehensive Guide to the Peloponnesian War*, a revised version of the Richard Crawley translation (New York: Simon and Schuster, 1996), 4:65.

71. *Ibid.*, 5:89.

72. See Robert V. Daniels, *The Rise and Fall of Communism in Russia* (New Haven: Yale University Press, 2007), pp. 32, 48.

73. Lenin's speech of November 27, 1920, in Jane Degras, ed., *Soviet Documents on Foreign Policy* (New York: Oxford University Press, 1951), I, p. 221.

74. Quoted in Catherine Merridale, *Lenin on the Train* (New York: Metropolitan Books, 2017), p. 195.

75. See chapter one.

76. Quoted in Stephen Kotkin, *Stalin: The Paradoxes of Power, 1878–1928* (New York: Penguin, 2014), p. 612. See also, for this and the following paragraph, Gaddis, *Russia, the Soviet Union, and the United States,* pp. 98–116.

77. Robert Gellately, *Lenin, Stalin, and Hitler: The Age of Social Catastrophe* (New York: Knopf, 2007), pp. 163–65.

78. Thompson, *A Sense of Power,* pp. 110–11, 127–31. Lenin's concept of dictatorship as vanguard dates back to his 1902 pamphlet "What Is to Be Done?" available at: www.marxists.org/archive/lenin/works/1901/witbd/index.htm.

79. Tooze, *The Deluge,* pp. 515–16.

80. Adam Tooze, *The Wages of Destruction: The Making and Breaking of the Nazi Economy* (New York: Penguin, 2007), especially pp. xxiv–xxvi and 7–12; also Timothy D. Snyder, *Black Earth: The Holocaust as History and Warning* (New York: Tim Duggan, 2015), pp. 11–28.

81. Tooze, *Wages of Destruction,* pp. 12–33.

82. Stalin's report is available at: www.marxists.org/reference/archive/stalin/works/1933/01/07.htm.

83. Isaiah Berlin, *Personal Impressions,* edited by Henry Hardy, third edition (Princeton: Princeton University Press, 2014), pp. 37–39, 41. Berlin's essay on Roosevelt first appeared as "Roosevelt Through European Eyes," *The Atlantic* 196 (July 1955), 67–71.

84. Conrad Black, *Franklin Delano Roosevelt: Champion of Freedom* (New York: Public Affairs, 2003), pp. 126–27, 254–55; Alonzo L. Hamby, *For the Survival of Democracy: Franklin Roosevelt and the World Crisis of the 1930s* (New York: Free Press, 2004), pp. 129–35.

85. Gaddis, *Russia, the Soviet Union, and the United States,* pp. 118–21; also Thomas R. Maddux, *Years of Estrangement: American Relations with the Soviet Union, 1933–1941* (Tallahassee: University Presses of Florida, 1980), pp. 11–26; Mary E. Glantz, *FDR and the Soviet Union: The President's Battles over Foreign Policy* (Lawrence: University Press of Kansas, 2005), pp. 15–23.

86. Black, *Roosevelt,* pp. 21, 60, 65–66. See also Alonzo L. Hamby, *Man of Destiny: FDR and the Making of the American Century* (New York: Basic Books, 2015), pp. 54–55; and www.fdrlibrary.tumblr.com/post/ 94080352024/day-77-fdr-visits-the -panama-canal.

87. Robert Dallek, *Franklin D. Roosevelt and American Foreign Policy, 1932–1945* (New York: Oxford University Press, 1979), pp. 75–76. See also David Kaiser, *No End Save Victory: How FDR Led the Nation into War* (New York: Basic Books, 2014), pp. 22–23.

88. Germany had finally been admitted to the League in 1926. Japan was a founding member.

89. Dallek, *Franklin D. Roosevelt and American Foreign Policy*, pp. 75, 175–76.

90. Maddux, *Years of Estrangement*, pp. 85–88.

91. See chapter eight.

92. The secretary of the navy, Josephus Daniels, willingly relinquished that responsibility. See Hamby, *Man of Destiny*, pp. 73–81.

93. David M. Kennedy, *Freedom from Fear: The American People in Depression and War, 1929–1945* (New York: Oxford University Press, 1999), pp. 56–57, 106–7, 120–24.

94. Samuel I. Rosenman, *Working with Roosevelt* (New York: Harper, 1952), p. 167.

95. Dallek, *Franklin D. Roosevelt and American Foreign* Policy, pp. 101–68; Thompson, *A Sense of Power*, pp. 145–50; and, on the last point, Gaddis, *George F. Kennan*, pp. 101–8.

96. Maddux, *Years of Estrangement*, pp. 90–91; Glantz, *FDR and the Soviet Union*, pp. 33–35, 43–52. See also Elizabeth Kimball MacLean, *Joseph E. Davies: Envoy to the Soviets* (Westport, Connecticut: Praeger, 1992), pp. 24–26, 45; and David Mayers, *The Ambassadors and America's Soviet Policy* (New York: Oxford University Press, 1995), pp. 118–19.

97. MacLean, *Joseph E. Davies*, p. 67; Charles E. Bohlen, *Witness to History, 1929–1969* (New York: Norton, 1973), pp. 67–87.

98. Speech to the American Youth Congress, February 10, 1940, available at: www .fdrlibrary. marist.edu/_resources/images/msf/msf01314.

99. Adolf Berle, quoted in Dallek, *Franklin D. Roosevelt and American Foreign Policy*, p. 215.

100. Glantz, *FDR and the Soviet Union*, pp. 54–57.

101. Robert E. Sherwood, *Roosevelt and Hopkins: An Intimate History*, revised edition (New York: Grosset and Dunlap, 1950), pp. 233–34. The Lincoln quote comes from an 1879 article by Noah Brooks, "Lincoln's Imagination," republished in Harold K. Bush, *Lincoln in His Own Time: A Biographical Chronicle of His Life* (Iowa City: University of Iowa Press, 2011), p. 176. See also Henry Wadsworth Longfellow Dana, "Sail On, O Ship of State!," *Colby Library Quarterly* 2 (February 1950), 1–6.

102. Susan Dunn, *1940: FDR, Willkie, Lindbergh, Hitler—the Election amid the Storm* (New Haven: Yale University Press, 2013), pp. 278–79. Dunn's book ably covers the events I've summarized in the preceding paragraph.

103. Churchill's February 9, 1941, radio address is available at: www.youtube.com /watch?v=rJuRv2ixGaM.

104. I've chiefly followed, in these three paragraphs, Maddux, *Years of Estrangement*, pp. 128–55. But see also Glantz, *FDR and the Soviet Union*, pp. 71, 77–87; MacLean, *Joseph E. Davies*, pp. 76–77; and my own *Russia, the Soviet Union, and the United States*, pp. 145–47.

105. Winston S. Churchill, *The Second World War: The Grand Alliance* (New York: Bantam Books, 1962; first published in 1950), pp. 511–12.

106. I've estimated American combat deaths at 400,000, and equivalents for all participants in World War II at 23 million. These figures exclude civilian casual-

ties from both totals. For details, see: www.en.wikipedia.org/wiki/World_War_II_casualties.

107. Thompson, *A Sense of Power*, p. 230.

108. Hal Brands and Patrick Porter, "Why Grand Strategy Still Matters in a World of Chaos," *The National Interest*, December 10, 2015, available at: www.nationalinterest.org/feature/why-grand-strategy-still-matters-world-chaos-14568.

109. Berlin, *Personal Impressions*, pp. 39–44, 48–49.

110. I owe this story to Robert Kaplan, whose 2015 road trip and subsequent book, *Earning the Rockies: How Geography Shapes America's Role in the World* (New York: Random House, 2017), was inspired by it. DeVoto's account is in his "Letter from Santa Fe," *Harper's Magazine* 181 (July 1940), 333–36. See also Arthur M. Schlesinger, Jr., *A Life in the 20th Century: Innocent Beginnings, 1917–1950* (Boston: Houghton Mifflin, 2000), pp. 168–71, 232–35.

111. John J. O'Neill, "Enter Atomic Power," *Harper's Magazine* 181 (June 1940), 1–10.

112. Radio address, "On National Defense," May 26, 1940, at: www.docs.fdrlibrary.marist.edu/052640.

CHAPTER TEN: ISAIAH

1. Berlin to Stephen Spender, February 26, 1936, in Henry Hardy, ed., *Isaiah Berlin: Letters, 1928–1946* (New York: Cambridge University Press, 2004), p. 152 [hereafter *Berlin Letters, 1928–1946*]. Berlin admired E. M. Forster and Virginia Woolf, but claimed to find them intimidating. [*Ibid.*, pp. 70–71, 166.]

2. Berlin to Marion Frankfurter, June 23, 1940, in *ibid.*, p. 306. See also Michael Ignatieff, *Isaiah Berlin: A Life* (New York: Henry Holt, 1998), p. 10.

3. *Ibid.*, p. 82.

4. The most recent biographies are Andrew Lownie, *Stalin's Englishman: Guy Burgess, the Cold War, and the Cambridge Spy Ring* (New York: St. Martin's, 2015); and Stewart Purvis and Jeff Hulbert, *Guy Burgess: The Spy Who Knew Everyone* (London: Biteback, 2016).

5. Editorial note, *Berlin Letters, 1928–1946*, p. 319; also Ignatieff, *Isaiah Berlin*, pp. 97–99.

6. Berlin to Mary Fisher, July 30, 1940, in *Berlin Letters, 1928–1946*, p. 322. See also p. 319.

7. Ignatieff, *Isaiah Berlin*, p. 98.

8. Christopher Nolan's 2017 film *Dunkirk* movingly evokes Churchill's speech.

9. John Wheeler-Bennett, *Special Relationships: America in Peace and War* (London: Macmillan, 1975), pp. 87–88.

10. Berlin explains the format in his introduction to H. G. Nicholas, ed., *Washington Despatches, 1941–1945: Weekly Political Reports from the British Embassy* (Chicago: University of Chicago Press, 1981), pp. vii–xiv.

11. Summaries for January 12, February 4, March 20, August 16, 1942, *ibid.*, pp. 12, 18, 26, 71; also Berlin's introduction, pp. x–xi.

12. Summaries for May 14, November 21, 1942, March 14, 1943, *ibid.*, pp. 38-39, 116, 160.

13. Summaries for February 28, April 3, October 22, 1943, *ibid.*, pp. 157, 172, 263.

14. Summaries for December 29, 1943, January 17, 18, 1944, *ibid.*, pp. 288, 307, 309.

15. Summaries for February 28, April 25, 1943, January 18, February 20, December 24, 1944, *ibid.*, pp. 155-56, 184, 309, 319, 485-86.

16. Ignatieff, *Isaiah Berlin*, p. 126. Berlin's own account is in *Berlin Letters, 1928-1946*, pp. 478-80.

17. Isaiah Berlin to Marie and Mendel Berlin, August 16, 1943, in *ibid.*, p. 456; Berlin to Katharine Graham, January 1949, in Isaiah Berlin, *Enlightening: Letters, 1946-1960*, edited by Henry Hardy and Jennifer Holmes (London: Chatto and Windus, 2009), p. 73.

18. Berlin to Stuart Hampshire, June 6, 1945, in *Berlin Letters, 1928-1946*, p. 569.

19. Ignatieff, *Isaiah Berlin*, pp. 138-39.

20. *Ibid.*, p. 137.

21. Except for being raucously summoned by an inebriated Randolph Churchill, son of the (now) former prime minister, to translate instructions to his hotel's staff on how to ice down caviar. Few unforgettable moments are unattended by others better forgotten.

22. Ignatieff, *Isaiah Berlin*, p. 168. I've followed Ignatieff's account at pp. 148-69; but also Berlin's reminiscences, composed in 1980, which appear in his *The Proper Study of Mankind: An Anthology of Essays*, edited by Henry Hardy and Roger Hausheer (New York: Farrar, Straus and Giroux, 1998), pp. 525-52.

23. *Ibid.*, pp. 541, 543, 547.

24. *The Complete Poems of Anna Akhmatova*, translated by Judith Hemschemeyer (Boston: Zephyr Press, 1997), p. 547.

25. Berlin to Philip Graham, November 14, 1946, in Berlin, *Enlightening*, p. 21.

26. Isaiah Berlin, "Russian Intellectual History," written in 1966 and reprinted in *The Power of Ideas*, edited by Henry Hardy (Princeton: Princeton University Press, 2000), p. 84.

27. *Berlin Letters, 1928-1946*, pp. 488-89. See also Ignatieff, *Isaiah Berlin*, p. 131.

28. Berlin to Alan Dudley, March 17, 1948, in Berlin, *Enlightening*, pp. 46-47.

29. Isaiah Berlin, "Political Ideas in the Twentieth Century," *Foreign Affairs* 28 (April 1950), 356-79.

30. *Ibid.*, pp. 362-63.

31. *Ibid.*, pp. 364-66; also Berlin, "The Originality of Machiavelli," in Berlin, *The Proper Study of Mankind*, p. 310.

32. Isaiah Berlin, *Personal Impressions*, edited by Henry Hardy (Princeton: Princeton University Press, 2014), pp. 41-42, 46. See also Noel Annan's introduction to Berlin, *The Proper Study of Mankind*, p. xxxv; and, for the *Short Course*, Stephen Kotkin, *Stalin: Waiting for Hitler, 1929-1941* (New York: Penguin Press, 2017), pp. 569-79.

33. Berlin, "The Originality of Machiavelli," in Berlin, *The Proper Study of Mankind*, pp. 324-25. It's "no accident," as the Marxists used to like to say, that one of the best early studies of Roosevelt's leadership is James MacGregor Burns, *Roosevelt:*

The Lion and the Fox (New York: Harcourt, Brace, and World, 1956), a title inspired by Machiavelli.

34. Quoted in Warren F. Kimball, *The Juggler: Franklin Roosevelt as Wartime Statesman* (Princeton: Princeton University Press, 1991), p. 7.

35. *Ibid.*, pp. 8–19. See also Wilson D. Miscamble, C.S.C., *From Roosevelt to Truman: Potsdam, Hiroshima, and the Cold War* (New York: Cambridge University Press, 2007), especially pp. 79–86.

36. Kimball, *The Juggler*, p. 7. Emphasis added.

37. Geoffrey C. Ward, *A First-Class Temperament: The Emergence of Franklin D. Roosevelt, 1905–1928* (New York: Vintage Books, 1989), chapters 13–16.

38. *Ibid.*, pp. xiii–xv.

39. Carl von Clausewitz, *On War*, edited and translated by Michael Howard and Peter Paret (Princeton: Princeton University Press, 1976), p. 100.

40. In one of several versions, a small boy finds a large pile of manure under a Christmas tree. Undaunted, he shouts excitedly that "there's got to be a pony in here somewhere," and starts digging. For the provenance, see www.quoteinvestigator.com/2013/12/13/pony-somewhere/.

41. Philip E. Tetlock, *Expert Political Judgment: How Good Is It? How Can We Know?* (Princeton: Princeton University Press, 2005), pp. 214–15; further discussed in chapter one.

42. Tetlock, *Expert Political Judgment*, p. 215. The citation of Fitzgerald is on p. 67.

43. Isaiah Berlin, "Two Concepts of Liberty," in Berlin, *The Proper Study of Mankind*, pp. 191–242.

44. I'm following here Noel Annan's explanation of Berlin's "pluralism" in his foreword to *ibid.*, pp. xii–xiii, although the tightrope metaphor is my own.

45. Berlin, "The Originality of Machiavelli," in *ibid.*, p. 324.

46. "Robert F. Kennedy Shocks Texans by Questioning Mexican War," *New York Times*, February 17, 1962; "Robert Kennedy Bows in 'War' with Texas," *New York Times*, March 5, 1962. See also Arthur M. Schlesinger, Jr., *Robert F. Kennedy and His Times* (Boston: Houghton Mifflin, 1978), p. 568.

47. See chapter six.

48. Sun Tzu, *The Art of War*, translated by Samuel B. Griffith (New York: Oxford University Press, 1963), pp. 142–43.

INDEX

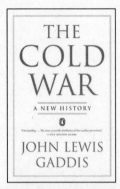

THE COLD WAR

A New History

The "dean of Cold War historians" (*The New York Times*) presents the definitive account of the global confrontation that dominated the last half of the twentieth century. Brilliant, accessible, almost Shakespearean in its drama, *The Cold War* stands as a triumphant summation of the era that, more than any other, shaped our own.

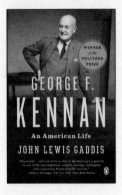

GEORGE F. KENNAN

An American Life

Winner of the Pulitzer Prize in Biography

In the late 1940s, George F. Kennan—then a bright but relatively obscure American diplomat—wrote the documents that laid out the United States' strategy for containing the Soviet Union—a strategy which Kennan himself questioned in later years. Based on exclusive access to Kennan and his archives, this landmark history illuminates a life that both mirrored and shaped the century it spanned.

PENGUIN BOOKS